ANIMATING
REAL-TIME GAME
CHARACTERS

ANIMATING REAL-TIME GAME CHARACTERS

PAUL STEED

CHARLES RIVER MEDIA, INC.

Hingham, Massachusetts

Publisher: Jenifer Niles
Production: Publishers' Design and Production Services, Inc.
Cover Design: The Printed Image
Cover Images: Paul Steed

CHARLES RIVER MEDIA, INC.
20 Downer Avenue, Suite 3
Hingham, Massachusetts 02043
781-740-0400
781-740-8816 (FAX)
info@charlesriver.com
www.charlesriver.com

This book is printed on acid-free paper.

Paul Steed. Animating Real-Time Game Characters.
ISBN: 1-58450-270-3

All *Dotty Bad* characters © 2002 WildTangent. All rights reserved.

Library of Congress Cataloging-in-Publication Data

Steed, Paul.
    Animating real-time game characters / Paul Steed.
        p.   cm.
    ISBN 1-58450-270-3 (paperback with CD-ROM : alk. paper)
    1. Computer animation.   2. Computer games—Design.   3. Video game
characters.   4. Real-time programming.   I. Title.
    TR897.7 .S72 2003
    794.8'15—dc21
                        2002014664

Printed in the United States of America
02 7 6 5 4 3 2   First Edition

This book is for my wife, my son, and my daughter. Marion, Trent, and Brianna make every challenge an achievement and every accomplishment a victory.

CONTENTS

Preface		xiii
Acknowledgments		xv
Foreword		xvii
About the Author		xix

CHAPTER 1   **BUILT TO MOVE**   **1**

Design	2
Aesthetic Considerations	2
Technical Considerations	4
Understanding Reference	4
Modeling: Form	8
Using Reference	8
Basic Modeling Tips	13
Modeling Techniques	15
Starting With Primitives	15
Extruding Shapes Or Faces	16
Using Booleans	16
High Resolution Mesh Template	17
Patch Modeling With Surface Tools	20
Surface Issues	21
Optimization	29
Modeling: Function	31
Model Breakdown	31
Animation Accommodation	32
Neck and Head	33
Shoulders	34
Waist	35
Hips and Rear	35
Elbows and Knees	37
Hands and Fingers	37

Wrists and Ankles	38
Fitting the Biped	38
Texture: Maps	39
UVW Coverage	39
Quality of the Texture	46
Summary	48

CHAPTER 2   RIGGING YOUR CHARACTERS WITH BIPED   51

Setting up a Typical Biped	52
Steps to Setting up a Biped Rig	52
Loading Your Character's Mesh	53
Creating Your Biped	55
Adjusting the Structure of Your Biped	58
Adjusting the Biped's Body and Head	59
Adjusting the Biped's Arms and Legs	61
Saving the Biped's Pose	67
Rigging a Four-legged Character	68
Adjusting the Structure	68
Adjusting the Body, Head, and Tail	70
Adjusting the Legs and Arms	72
Other Types of Character Rigs	73
A Dog	73
A Dolphin	74
A Goat-Girl?	75
Facial Rigs	76
Face Rig Level 1	78
Face Rig Level 2	79
Face Rig Level 3	80
A Higher-Resolution Character Rig	81
Ta Da Vinci or Not Ta Da Vinci?	81
A Face Rig for a Higher-Resolution Mesh	83
Adding Bones and Using Different Controllers	84
Summary	89

**CHAPTER 3   WEIGHTING A CHARACTER USING MANUAL
VERTEX ASSIGNMENT   91**

A Typical Game Character	92
Steps to Applying Physique	92
Applying and Initializing Physique	93

Assigning Vertices to a Link   95
Typing in Weighting Values   99
Removing Vertices from Links   105
Adjusting the Elbow Area   107
Working on the Hand and Fingers   113
Saving Your Weighting Values   116
Assigning the Neck, Shoulders, and Torso   117
Weighting the Other Leg   120
Loading a .Bip File into Biped   123
Tackling the Hips   125
Adjusting the Gun Arm   128
Summary   133

CHAPTER 4   WEIGHTING A CHARACTER USING ENVELOPES   137

Conquering Envelopes   138
Steps to Applying Physique   138
Turning Off Unnecessary Envelopes   139
Adjusting the Radial Scale of the Envelopes   144
Adjusting the Parent/Child Overlap of the Envelopes   147
Copying and Pasting to Symmetrical Limbs   150
Removing Any Vertices from Links   153
Weighting the Waist, Hips, and Legs   153
Resorting to Type-in Weights   156
Assigning the Breast Vertices   158
Adjusting the Head and Face   163
Summary   168

CHAPTER 5   THINGS TO CONSIDER BEFORE YOU ANIMATE   171

Know Your Character   172
Appearance Dictates Identity   173
Uniqueness Required   174
The Animation Set   175
Genre   175
Environment   177
Size Still Matters   177
Game Controls   179
Game Technology   180
Keyframe or Motion Capture?   181
Keyframing Defined   182

When to Keyframe   183
When to Use Mocap   183
Tips on the Mocap Process   184
Implementing the Character   186
Perpetual Windup Toy   187
Fitting the Technology   188
Summary   189

CHAPTER 6   KEYFRAME ANIMATION: PART I   191

First Things First   192
Footsteps versus Freeform   192
Think Animation Folder   192
Preparing the Biped   193
Keyframe Animation Basics   196
Frame Zero   196
The Track View   197
Configuring Time   200
Copying Keyframes   201
Animation Space Buffer   202
Track View and Active Animation Range   204
Posing the COM and Limbs   204
Locking Down the Feet and Hands   205
Refining the Idle Pose   207
Tension, Continuity, and Bias   209
Ease To and Ease From   212
Keyframes and the Time Slider Bar   216
Keyboard Shortcut Override Toggle   217
Secondary Motion   219
Animating the Tail   220
Using Layers   224
Using Time Tags   229
Summary   231

CHAPTER 7   KEYFRAME ANIMATION: PART II   233

Betty's Animations   234
One Chick, One Gun   234
Special Moves   235
Idles   235
It's All in the Pose   236
Anchor Keys   238

Doubling Keys   240
Secondary Motion   243
Join To Previous IK Key   246
The Third Idle   248
Shooting   250
The Firing Pose   250
Adding Recoil   254
The Other Two Idle Attacks   255
Aiming Mechanism   257
Jumps   259
Standing and Running Jumps   259
Implementing the Real-Time Jump   261
See Betty Jump   262
See Betty Jump . . .Again   267
Turnaround Jumper   268
Jumping while Shooting   273
Using Snapshot for Reference Objects   274
Hitting the Ground Shooting   277
Animation Ideology   280
Swimming   281
Treading Water   281
Creating a Smooth Loop   284
Swimming Forward   286
Summary   292

CHAPTER 8   **USING MOTION CAPTURE**   **295**
Motion Capture Files   296
CSM Format   296
BVH Format   296
Converting CSM and BVH Files   297
Using Key Reduction   299
Deciding Which Mocap Files to Use   305
A Bad Run Animation   305
A Good Run Animation   307
Creating a Looping Run   308
Determining the Loop Length   308
Grabbing the Best Loop Segment   310
Comparing the Loop Segments   314
Doubling the loop   316
Refining the Loop with Layers   317
Creating a Death Animation   325

Using the Motion Flow Editor to Rotate the Biped   325
Adding Secondary Motion with Layers   331
Deleting Frames to Increase Impact Effect   336
Repurposing a Mocap File   337
Copying Posture   338
Loading the Getting-Hit Animation   340
Paste Pose/Posture/Track   341
Moving the COM   341
Creating the Firing Motion   343
Moving the Recoil Closer   344
Aligning the Right Foot by Moving the COM   344
Adjusting the Upper Body   348
Making Adjustments with the Set Multiple Keys Function   351
Summary   354

CHAPTER 9   **PUTTING IT ALL TOGETHER**   **357**

Motion Flow Mode   358
Preparing an Animation for Motion Flow   358
Creating the Motion Flow Script   361
Adjusting Transition Length between Motion Clips   366
Rotating Motion Clips   366
The Export Process   372
Installing the WildTangent 3DS Max 4 Exporters   373
Creating and Exporting an Actor   374
Exporting an Actor with Animations   376
Final Thoughts   379

APPENDIX   **ABOUT THE CD-ROM**   **381**

Recommended System Requirements   381
Chapter Directories   381
Demo Files   382
Mocap Files   382

INDEX   **383**

PREFACE

G reetings! Thanks for buying or considering this book. Investing your money in books like this is not an easy decision. There are many to choose from and many to consider.

My intent in writing *Animating Real-Time Game Characters* has been to share my work methods, thoughts, and ideas about animating real-time characters in 3ds max 4™ and character studio 3®. Any factor that affects the animation process using these two tools has been covered. Design, modeling, texturing, rigging, weighting, keyframing, motion capture, and exporting to a game engine are all in here. Written for the relatively new or intermediate user of 3ds max, the book isn't just a rehash of the manuals and tutorials that came with your software, it's a companion to them. Make sure that you know your way around 3ds max 4 at a basic level and that you have at least gone through the animation tutorials in order to understand the terminology that will be used. Since I usually wait at least a year after the latest version of 3ds max comes out until I begin using it, the information presented doesn't include or apply to 3ds max 5. However, with the exception of a couple of key features, I'm confident that many of the tips and tricks covered will work for 3ds max 3 and 3ds max 5 as well.

To illustrate ideas, tips, tricks, and techniques, I've used several characters from games or projects I've completed over the last year and a half, but most often I've used a character called Betty Bad from the self-titled game that was released January 2002 by WildTangent. This is primarily to show you the thought and work that goes into an *implemented* game character. By doing so, I've hopefully given you a snapshot of what I do every day and have been doing every day for the past nine years: character animation. It's not just my job, it's my hobby, passion, and the thing I love to discuss with others.

However, making sure that this book is useful has been the most important consideration and goal. Like most of you, I have many other books on computer graphics and on 3ds max in particular. Unfortunately,

xiii

only a few of them have that worn, coffee-stained look indicating that they have been used frequently. This attrition isn't the fault of the authors of those books I only glance through—rather, it's *my* fault because I'm very picky, and I often look for something that just isn't there. I'm very hard to satisfy in my quest for an easier, better way to do something. That's one of the main reasons I've written this book—there isn't one out there like it, and in writing it, I'm confident I've reduced the learning curve for you and shed some light on most of the relevant aspects of character animation. My unique background and experience give me a ground-level perspective when discussing the topics covered. I work with the tools *every day*.

You've picked this book because you want to learn something useful, something that will help you animate that gorgeous player model so you can get it into *Quake III Arena™* or *Unreal Tournament™*. You want to get just enough insight into character animation so you can meet your deadline of creating 36 enemies by March of next year. You don't want anything but a little nudge, a little assistance.

Well, hopefully that's what I've accomplished—I hope to have given you something that does help and does provide a glimpse into the trenches of making and animating real-time characters for games. So please, don't treat this book like a reverent tome of arcane knowledge. I want you to fold corners, break the spine, and inflict a little tear here and there, staining it with everything from Starbucks coffee to tomato sauce or French-fry grease. That way, I know I've accomplished my goal in writing it.

> Good luck, and never stop striving to improve.
> Paul Steed
> Sammamish, WA

ACKNOWLEDGMENTS

Writing a book is a stressful and difficult task that rarely involves sleep or fun, but which inevitably becomes a source of pride and inspiration. I'd like to thank the following people for helping me get through it once again: First and foremost, thanks to Jenifer Niles and her crew at Charles River Media for their patience and perseverance in dealing with a cantankerous author; thanks also to Peter Lewis, who, after editing my first book, still wanted to be my second set of eyes on this one; comic book legend Jim Lee, founder of Wildstorm Productions, for being a constant source of inspiration and a role model for a successful artist; Joe Madureira for his loan of Red Monika and his art over the years; Shalom Mann at Sony Pictures Digital Entertainment for giving me the chance to work on cool projects that made it possible for me to take the time to write this book; and to WildTangent for letting me use and abuse my little tough-girl, Betty. Finally, I'd like to once again thank id Software for the experience, recognition, and opportunities that I now enjoy.

FOREWORD

Many of you reading this Foreword may be wondering why a comic book artist such as myself would be writing this—an introduction to a book on computer 3D modeling! Well, to be honest, there is a bona fide professional angle here, so bear with me. As a video game "enthusiast," let me be the first to admit that there are a ton of gamers (read *addicts*) working in the comic book business and *they* have been following with great interest the incredible technological advances the video game industry has made in recent years. And, yes, that's how I justify (read rationalize) playing hours of computer games. Research, ya know!

All the advances in the industry have come about because of faster CPUs and because of video graphics cards that are drastically more powerful than ever before. More significantly, 3D modeling programs have become both more intuitive and user-friendly in design and more affordable in cost, so everyone now has access to the very same tools with which to create mindblowingly realistic imagery. But, unfortunately, having the right tools does not an artist make.

That's why I marvel at guys like Paul Steed—guys who can turn thought into image into 3D model. A sculptor in virtual space, Paul not only knows how his 2D images will translate into 3D models, but more important, he knows how to explain this process in words that a layman can understand. He cuts through all the terminology and lingo that often hinder the learning process and gets down to the nitty-gritty of how to *create*—and with style.

Back in the days when I was obsessed with learning my craft but had not yet broken into the comic book business, I often went to the library and checked out every book on drawing and storytelling that I could. The one book that made it all "click" for me was by an artist named George Bridgeman, whose book on life drawing showed me how to see the human form in ways I did not understand before. It was not a slavish approach to learning anatomy by memorizing all the names and locations of the muscles in the human body, but a blueprint to understanding how the human figure is constructed in basic three-dimensional shapes; it explained how to maximize the dynamics and power of one's 2D figure drawings by manipulating the relationships between these shapes in 3D in your mind.

Paul's books take these same lessons to the next level, teaching us how to make the leap from 2D to 3D, with impressive results. By taking the very same tricks and principles of exaggeration we use in comic book art and applying them to computer 3D modeling and animation, Paul makes what seems like "real life" bigger and better than the ordinary, infusing his figures with rippling power and striking sensuality. Bigger shoulders, bigger guns, bigger, um, everything!

But it is finding the line between exaggeration and distortion that differentiates the visceral and the sublime from the grotesque. Paul is one of the modern-day wizards who possess both the talent and the knowledge to show us the differences between the two. So now, we *all* have no more excuses. No more procrastination. No more "researching" *Quake III Arena*.

Sit down already and *create*! We now have the blueprint for how to do it, thanks to the efforts of Paul Steed.

Jim Lee
La Jolla, CA

ABOUT THE AUTHOR

For the past 11 years, Paul Steed has been making computer games for companies like Origin Systems and id Software. Author of *Modeling A Character In Max*, Steed is best known for his work on the best-selling *Wing Commander* and *Quake* series. Currently, he runs his own contracting firm making real-time games and demos for companies like Sony Pictures Digital and WildTangent, that can be downloaded over the Internet. He is a regular speaker at the Game Developers Conference in San Jose, CA and serves as an Advisory Board member for *Game Developer* magazine. Paul Steed lives and works in the Seattle area and can be reached at *st33d@nak3d.com*.

BUILT TO MOVE

A great real-time game character can be measured by the success of five elements: the character's *design*, the *model* built on that design, the *texture map* applied to that model, the *animations* that bring the textured model to life, and the *sounds* that complete the package. Making sure your character is *built to move* means that the design is achievable, the model supports proper form and function, and the texture map is of the highest quality.

DESIGN

The design is the starting point for constructing the character, and it needs to be fleshed out clearly on paper, in clay, or in Photoshop™ well beforehand. Modeling from a vision in one's head is a fortunate and useful skill, but having some sort of physical reference will always ensure the character stays true to its design. The rendering of the character has to impart a solid sense of its *identity*, whether it is a loose sketch or tight diagram. At the same time, a great sketch that looks fantastic and imparts a unique and interesting identity also has to be *doable*. It has to work within the given restrictions of the game technology being used, and it has to fit stylistically in the game world into which it's going to be dropped. Therefore, there are three primary things to keep in mind when you design your character: *aesthetic considerations*, *technical considerations*, and *reference*.

Aesthetic Considerations

An *aesthetic consideration* refers to your sense of the appearance or beauty of something and is basically just another term for what you determine to be "cool." Age, taste, education, favorite movies, favorite games, and favorite artists factor into the equation. *Anime* and *Manga* are particularly good sources of creative inspiration for real-time characters, especially the work of traditional modeler and awesome character designer, Yasushi Nirasawa. Some other memorable fantasy and sci-fi artists to check out are Oscar Chichoni, Brom, Simon Bisley, Luis Royo, *WarHammer*™ artist Kevin Walker, and *Mutant Chronicle*™ painting studs Alessandro Horley and Paul Bonner. They all have a dynamic art style and a great sense of weight with their characters.

While everyone has their own definition of what pleases their eye, there are some common factors that can apply to and/or guide the aesthetics of game character design. First, the design should be unique yet adhere to whatever written description has been attached to it. Even if intentionally derivative ("Make the character like the character from

Game X . . ."), it can still be cool and have an identity of its own—if enough time and thought are put into it. Uniqueness applies to not only a comparison of characters done before, but also of other characters within the same game. Using different color combinations is an easy way to distinguish characters, but one of the most effective ways to keep your characters distinctly recognizable is the *silhouette* principle. Figure 1.1 illustrates the design differences between a few of the enemies from *Betty Bad*™.

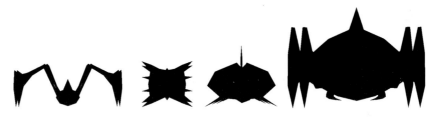

FIGURE 1.1   Visualizing a character in silhouette helps achieve uniqueness and should always be a part of the design process.

A trick used to group a *set* of unique characters is to develop rules and characteristics for the character(s) being designed. In *Betty Bad*, for example, the alien bad guys vary in size and configuration, but always have the common design element of a glowing dot for an eye or orifice. Most of the time the dot is red, but occasionally it appears in other colors. Figure 1.2 shows just a few of the plethora of characters that renowned painter and production designer-for-hire, Richard Hescox (*www.richardhescox.com*), came up with during the development of *Betty Bad* that have this common design thread.

Another important consideration is whether a character's design successfully fits whatever genre the game is being placed under, whether

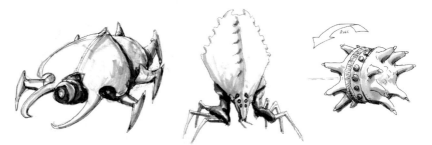

FIGURE 1.2   Some character designs need to differ while maintaining common design elements.

that is sci-fi, fantasy, or Western. Finally, the polygon count of a character impacts its design, although this is also an important *technical* consideration. Because of real-time characters' polygonal nature, highly organic or sinewy shapes and flowing cloth or hair elements are very difficult to pull off convincingly in a character that is built with less than 1,000 triangles.

Technical Considerations

As mentioned earlier, a polygon count restriction is a technical consideration that has a definite impact on the design. However, the number of polygons varies per platform and *application* of the real-time character. The difference that 1,000, 2,000, and 5,000 triangles make in a character's design is huge, but ultimately a good artist will accomplish plenty with whatever budget is handed to them. Games played on the new consoles like Xbox™ and PlayStation 2™ are seeing characters that have up to (and sometimes more than) 5,000 polygons. However, main characters seen in PC-based real-time games played over the Internet need to be anywhere from 500 to 2,000 triangles. In addition to the lower polygon limit, many games use what's known as *level of detail* (LOD) to give the game engine fewer polygons to render at a given distance. This means the character is created in versions with a high, medium, and low LOD. Figure 1.3 illustrates the typical difference between three successive levels of detail.

Another technical consideration that impacts design is how the character is implemented in the game engine itself. Some games use vertex deformation for their animation system, which means that each frame of animation is a keyframe for the vertices in the mesh of the character to deform to or *interpolate* to. This effectively ties the animations more closely to the frame rate set by the artist in whatever animation tool was used (such as 3ds max). Other systems use a skeletal animation system, as in *Half Life*™ and *Betty Bad*, where the animations rely on an underlying bone structure and on time instead of frames to play back animations. Any of these systems could also rely on an actual structural limitation where the head would have to be a separate object from the torso, which in turn would have to be separate from the legs. This sort of breakup of the character prevents any sort of uni-bodied or *contiguous* mesh approach.

Understanding Reference

Now that you are armed with all the data you need for creating a character, it's time to generate some reference to build it. There are two ap-

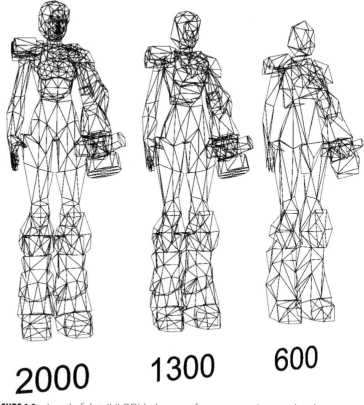

2000   1300   600

FIGURE 1.3   Level of detail (LOD) helps puts fewer constraints on the character design by giving the game engine fewer polygons to render at various distances.

proaches to reference: loose and tight. The choice of approach relates more to pose and finality than anything else, and each method is really a personal preference of the modeler. *Betty Bad* was created using the loose approach (Figure 1.4).

"A tough, sexy heroine with an attitude and maybe a gun integrated into her combat armor with a look that's reminiscent of the ABC Warrior seen in the *British 2000 A.D.* comics and the *Judge Dredd* movie."

The level of reference in that description was enough to build the *Betty Bad* character. If the artist building the model has the freedom to design it, this sort of loose reference works fine. If, however, the character being built has to conform to a *known* character, then a different sort of reference is needed. To attain the requisite level of accuracy when called for, it's best to think of your reference as more of a *diagram* than a drawing. While the action-pose approach works for most modelers, it always runs the risk of

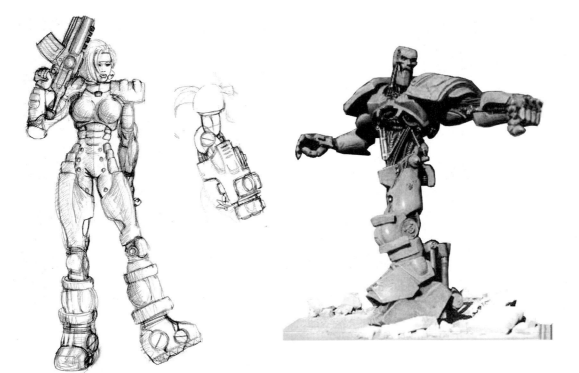

FIGURE 1.4   The loose approach was chosen for creating *Betty Bad.*

something being lost or modified from the designer's original vision when it's used as a basis for building the mesh. For example, look at several panels that feature a character called *Red Monika* (Figure 1.5).

She's the extremely buxom *femme fatale* from the Image Comics book by Joe Madueira called *Battle Chasers*. Building a character model for this design requires a tighter reference approach than a very stylized comic book illustration. A character *diagram* needs to be created (Figure 1.6).

The bottom line when it comes to reference is that you should go with what feels most comfortable to you. If scribblings on a napkin work for you, and the modeler is okay with it, then go for it. If, however, extreme accuracy is required, then go with a more schematic or diagrammed approach. It will ensure that the modeler nails the design exactly true to the character.

FIGURE 1.5   These drawings of Red Monika are nice to look at, but not very good references from which to build a model.

FIGURE 1.6   This shows a tighter, more diagrammatic approach to reference—and the result.

MODELING: FORM

Great character animation relies on the foundation of a well-built model that adheres to and successfully translates a well thought-out design into 3D. The most important aspect of a model in this regard is its *form*. Suggesting mass and identity, form is defined by the proper distribution of vertices, edges, and faces. A great real-time character model uses all geometry succinctly and efficiently—every vertex counts. However, the first step in attaining the proper form is to make use of that reference you spent so much time creating.

Using Reference

There are several ways to utilize reference images in 3ds max. You can bring one into the background view, map it onto a plane in the scene, or you can even bring it up via the Asset Browser in the Utilities command panel (Figure 1.7).

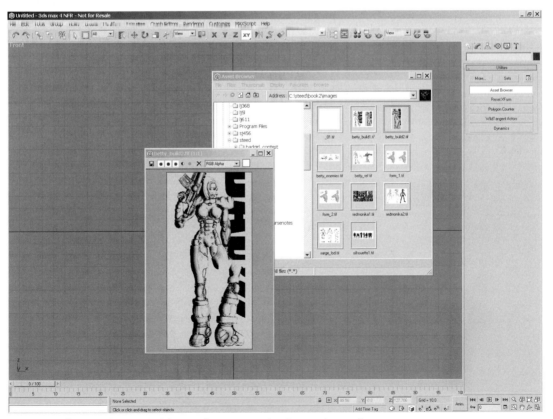

FIGURE 1.7 The Asset Browser in 3ds max allows you to view images in any directory.

Seeing your reference in via the Asset Browser works well because it gives you the ability to see both the mesh and the image it's based on as you build; however, the best way to use your reference images is to make them into a *3D outline*. To do this, bring the image into 3ds max as a background image. Then, using the Line tool, trace the image, creating a 3D version of the reference drawing or picture. Note that you first need to prepare your drawing before bringing it into 3ds max by darkening and re-sizing it in Photoshop or your 2D program of choice (Figure 1.8).

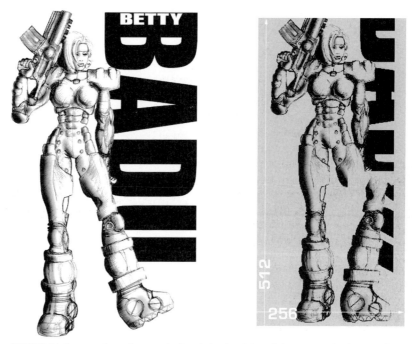

FIGURE 1.8   Prepare the reference before bringing it into 3ds max as a background image.

You can see in Figure 1.8 that the original sketch of Betty has been darkened, her leg has been repositioned to make it more useful to the modeler, and the image has been re-sized to have a "power of two" aspect ratio (in this case, 512 × 256). These extra steps ensure the best image fidelity when brought into the 3ds max background using a machine with hardware acceleration.

Bring the image into the background by going to the Views pull-down menu and clicking on Viewport Background (or just hit Alt-B). Load your reference in by clicking on the Files button at the top of the Viewport Background menu and finding the appropriate image file. Once the file is loaded, make sure the Match Bitmap, Display Background, and Lock Zoom/Pan boxes are all checked (Figure 1.9).

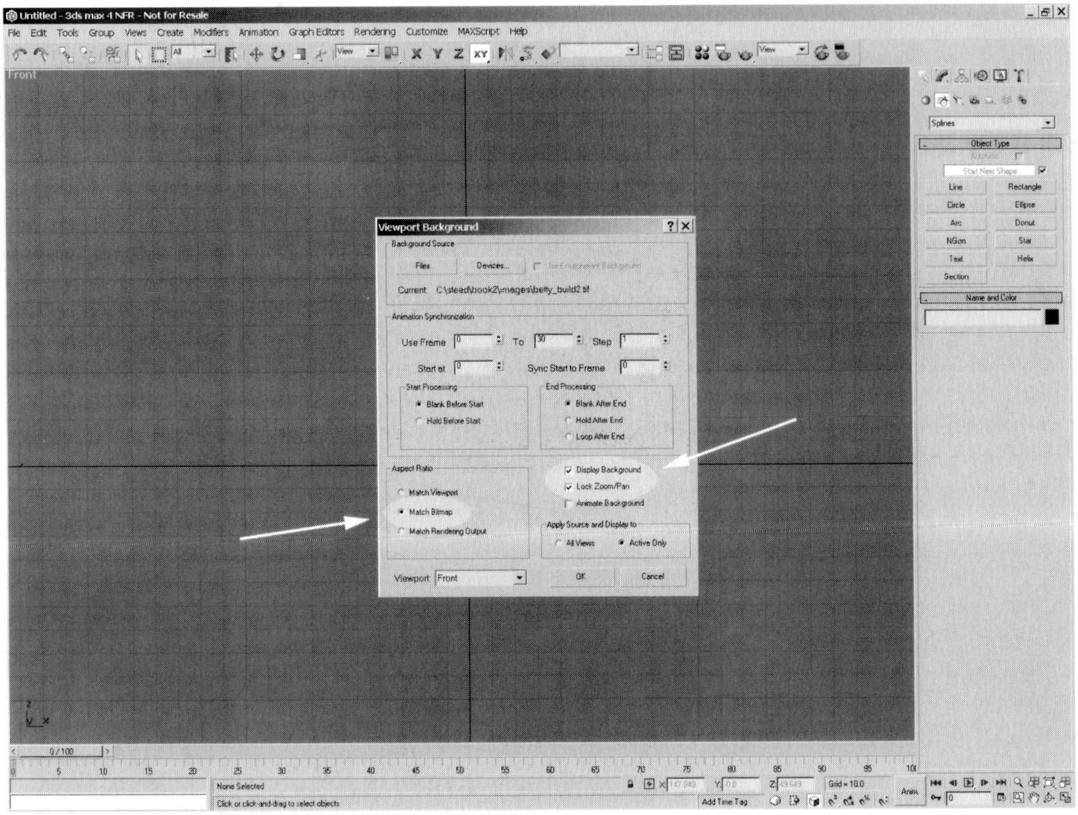

FIGURE 1.9   Bringing an image into the viewport background in 3ds max is very easy.

Click OK, and the image should appear in the viewport background at the correct aspect ratio and at a fixed size relative to the viewport navigation controls. If your construction grid is visible in the viewport, you may want to turn it off so you can see your image better; you can do this by hitting the G key.

If for some reason the image does not appear when you try to bring it into the viewport background, go back up to the Viewport menu and click on Update Background Image or hit Alt-Shift-Ctrl-B (Figure 1.10).

Once the background image has been successfully brought into 3ds max, trace it using the line tool under the Create | Shapes panel. Make

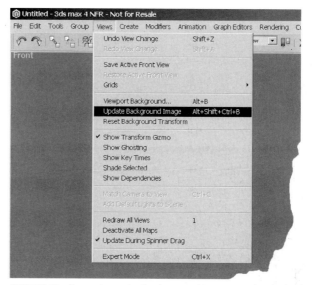

FIGURE 1.10   Sometimes the background image needs a little jumpstart to show up.

sure the Start New Shape box is *unchecked,* so you don't end up with a bunch of separate lines (Figure 1.11).

FIGURE 1.11   Uncheck the Start New Shape box to avoid the step of attaching the lines together later.

Don't worry about the complexity of the line as you create it, since it will only be used as reference.

Hitting the I key centers the view on wherever the cursor happens to be. In the case of tracing an outline, it allows you to create continuous lines without having to right-click and pan over to the area you're trying to get to.

Once the image has been traced, turn off the background image, re-name the line to "Guide," and use the outline shape to help create your model in whatever view you desire (Figure 1.12).

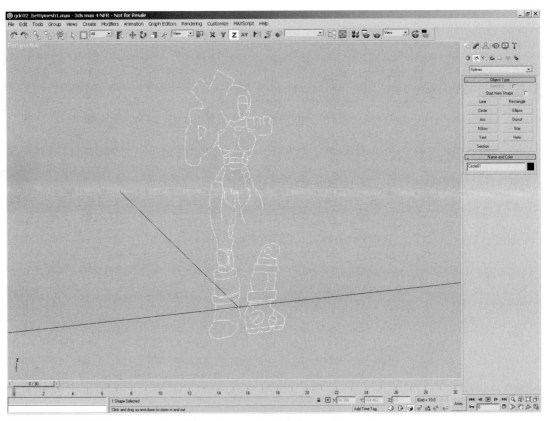

FIGURE 1.12 A 3D line representation of the reference sketch helps you in any view.

 Modeling in one viewport by toggling the W key is the best way to stay up-close and personal with your work. You can even get rid of parts of the menus to give you more room by hitting the 3 key. If you're really the daring type, hit Ctrl-X to make all but the very top menu bar disappear.

Bringing reference images into 3ds max is easy once you have them saved on your computer's hard drive. However, unless you've created them in a paint or graphics program like Photoshop, you need to use a decent flatbed scanner to bring in a digital copy (scanners continue to come down in price, and buying one is an investment that will pay off over the years). Using your reference, however you bring it into 3ds max, will always result in a more solid and accurate representation of your design. It's the first step in attaining and maintaining *form*. Once you have your reference finalized, you can move on to *modeling*.

Basic Modeling Tips

The following are some general modeling tips that apply to almost any modeling program:

Build a character one part at a time. Concentrate on one particular area and make it look like you want it to *before* moving on to the next area. Model the head until you are happy with it, and move on to the torso. Don't be afraid to even build a body part and save your work as a completely separate file. You can always merge it into your main character model file any time you want. This approach works for elements of individual parts as well. Build a perfect nose, or a perfect eye, or a perfect ear, or the perfect boot. Make your own body shop if you feel like it!

Cannibalize when you can. Why always model a character from scratch? It's important to be able to build an original character model from start to finish at least once or twice to go through that pain and reward, but try to avoid reinventing the wheel. In fact, always keep future characters in mind as you build *any* model. When you reach the point in the model's development at which it's complete yet generic enough to use in the future, save that file separately for reference and move on. Having this "stable" of body parts and whole characters to draw upon saves you work, and more important, it saves you *time*.

Work in one window. Use up as much screen space as you can when modeling. Having multiple windows or views open is necessary sometimes, but don't lean in and squint at your work. Bouncing back and forth between views should be as easy as hitting the F (front), L (left), R (right), or T (top) keys as needed.

Build in halves. If the geometry of your design is at all symmetrical, build a bisecting line into it as you work. This enables you to build it in halves: build one half, then copy, flip, and join the copy to the original first half. In addition to saving time and effort during the building process, this technique also saves time and effort in the texturing process as well (more on texturing later). By creating a reference when mirroring a copy of the geometry you're working on, you can effectively build both halves at the same time using a *reference* of the half. A reference is just what it sounds like. It's a copy, but whatever you do to the original half is reflected on the copy. This gives you a better picture of how a symmetrical mesh is coming along as you build it (Figure 1.13).

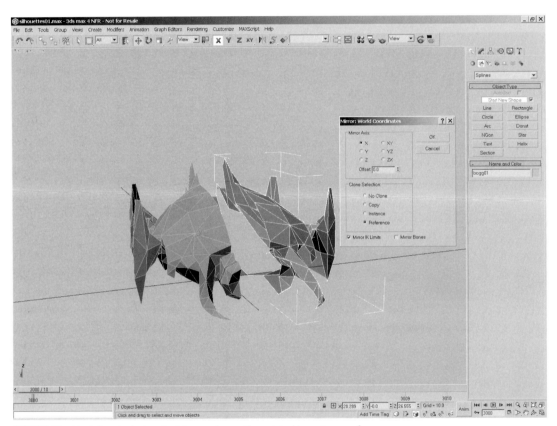

FIGURE 1.13   Modeling by halves in 3ds max is greatly assisted by using a reference.

Make every vertex count. Always keep this thought in the back of your mind when modeling. More about this is covered in the Optimization section later in this chapter, but it's a very important thing to remember and think about.

Make the modeling program your own. This relates to any sort of customization you apply to your modeling package and to your use of any hotkeys that speed up your work. Make the tool work for you instead of the other way around. The more comfortable you are in your modeling environment, the better your work will be, and the *faster* it will get done.

Stick with what works. While it's occasionally useful to experiment with alternate ways to do things in a program like 3ds max, don't be afraid to stick with what works for you. Modeling and animation is as much affected by the modeler's personality and his comfort with a technique as by any other factor. Everyone has their own methods and their own reasons for using those methods. Never feel guilty for only scratching the surface of a modeling program. The end result is all that's important: a great model.

Modeling Techniques

In 3ds max (as in other modeling packages), there are always multiple ways to accomplish the same goal. When it comes to modeling real-time game characters, *polygon modeling* is usually the best approach. *Patch modeling* is particularly useful when creating organic or soft-surface geometry like hair, cloth, or an undulating surface like water. Other modeling methods, such as non-uniform rational B-splines (NURBs) and sub-divided surfaces, are valid and valuable tools but are more appropriate for *rendered* characters than real-time characters. Modeling at the base level and sub-object level by manipulating vertices, edges, and faces is the absolute best way to maintain control of the overall face count and, more important, the *form* of your character model.

Some of the more common polygon modeling methods include starting with primitives, extruding shapes or faces, using Booleans, and even using a higher resolution model as a template upon which to build a lower resolution model.

Starting With Primitives

This method is an approach to modeling that employs a "just give me enough real estate to work with" mentality. All modeling packages have a great quantity of primitives that you can create and shape as you want, such as boxes, cylinders, and spheres. One of the best examples of this modeling technique is the use of a cylinder in combination with your reference guideline to build a leg (Figure 1.14). First, the cylinder needs enough sides and segments (A) to go up each row of vertices (segments); they are roughly scaled and rotated to fit the guide (B). After adjusting the shape in the front view to fit that guide perspective, the leg geometry is adjusted further with edge divides, and with turns and vertices moved. The shape is thus optimized and completed (C).

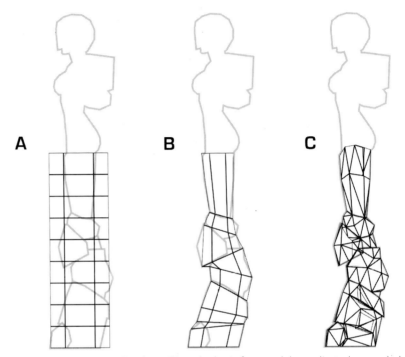

FIGURE 1.14   Primitives can be shaped into the basic form and then adjusted as needed.

Extruding Shapes Or Faces

Using extrusions are another common method for modeling your character. Figure 1.15 shows how extruding a shape *and* extruding faces are the quickest ways to build a shoulder pad for Betty Bad. The pad is started by creating an outline of a shape that approximates a cross section (A). Then an Extrude modifier with three segments is applied to it, and the shape is extruded outward to give it depth (B). Next, an Edit Mesh modifier is applied to align the vertices and select the faces at the top of the shoulder (C). The selected faces are then extruded upward to match the desired shape via the sub-object Extrude button (D). Finally the shape is adjusted, optimized, and slid into place (E).

Using Booleans

The use of Booleans is another useful way to model. The technique involves joining, subtracting, or taking the result of the intersection of two

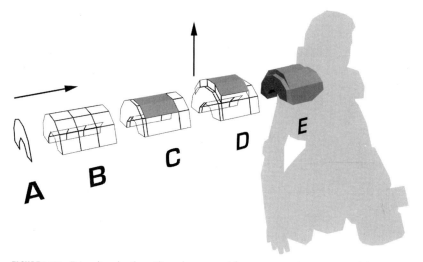

FIGURE 1.15 Extruding both outline shapes and faces are great ways to model.

objects in order to arrive at the desired shape. It is a useful method for situations such as merging limbs with a torso or joining legs to a pelvis. The only drawback to using Booleans is that they create excess geometry that has to be cleaned up. For example, look at Figure 1.16. Once Betty's hips and legs are built and completely closed (A), they're positioned so they intersect one another (B). After they're joined together using a "union" Boolean, there's an unnecessary geometry created (C). Cleaning up the geometry, adjusting the shape, then mirroring the proper faces gives Betty her legs (D).

Whenever performing Booleans, make sure all your geometry is closed beforehand. Use the Cap Holes modifier or manually build faces to close any openings. If you don't close these open areas, the Boolean may not work, or the results may not be quite what you expected.

High Resolution Mesh Template

If you have access to higher resolution models, you might try using one as a *template*. They're much too high in polygon count to use in a real-time character situation, and the work it would take to optimize them is too crazy to even consider. But what if you could trace a low-poly mesh on top of the high-resolution model, as if you were tracing a photograph onto onionskin? This really just takes the concept of using reference to its logical conclusion. That is, if you had the ability to take a person or action

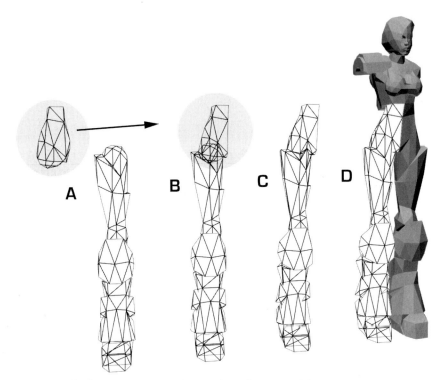

FIGURE 1.16   Booleans are messy to clean up but a fast way to join geometry.

figure/maquette and shove it into your 3ds max scene to use as a guide to build a model, you would. Think about it—it would be the perfect reference!

ON THE CD

Of course, building a mesh in this way requires a high-res mesh. Go to the Chapter1 directory on the CD-ROM that comes with this book, and load Boot.max to see the process firsthand (Figure 1.17).

The trick to modeling, as illustrated by our boot sample, is to first isolate the proper vertices integral to the boot's shape. A good rule of thumb to remember is that the number of vertices that make up a mesh are approximately *half* the number of faces. Once you have a target range of how many faces you want to spend on the new lower resolution model, just keep the isolated vertices down to half that number (1,000 faces = 500 vertices).

On the Sub-Object panel there is a counter for selected sub-objects such as vertices, edges, and faces (Figure 1.18).

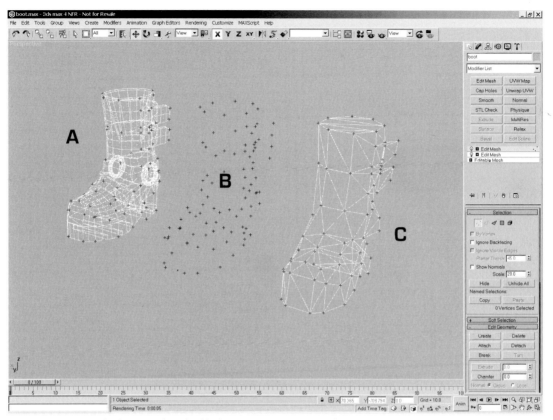

FIGURE 1.17   Using a high-res mesh to build a lower-res mesh is a very fast way to model.

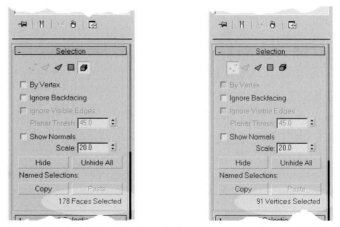

FIGURE 1.18   The Sub-Object panel gives you a convenient count of any selected sub-objects.

Using a high-res mesh to build a low-res mesh can be considered an optimization technique, technically, but really involves more building than reducing.

Patch Modeling With Surface Tools

Another approach worth mentioning (although it's not really a polygonal modeling method) is the use of Surface tools. This is a spline-based, patch modeling technique in 3ds max, which is ideal for making hair and other organic geometry because the mesh is created using adjustable *splines*. **ON THE CD** Load Hair.max from the Chapter1 directory on the book's CD-ROM (Figure 1.19).

FIGURE 1.19 Surface Tools is a great way to make organic geometry like hair.

The Surface modifier allows you to turn a spline cage or referenced spline cage into a parametric mesh. In the Hair.max file, move the vertices of the splines on the right and watch how the geometry of the mesh to the left is affected. This use of a referenced object is key to the utility of Surface.

When working with spline cages, turn the Weld threshold down to 0 instead of the default 1; this prevents you from receiving the annoying "Weld Coincident End-points?" message that pops up if you move any segments or splines (Figure 1.20).

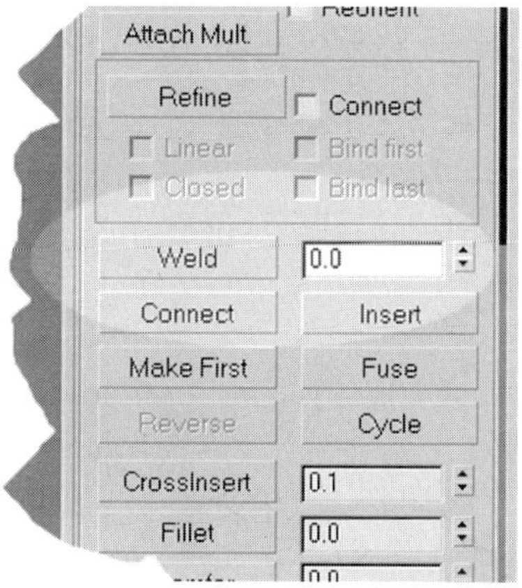

FIGURE 1.20   Lower the Weld threshold to avoid an annoying message prompt.

The 3ds max software comes with an excellent tutorial that shows the application of the Surface modifier. Experiment with this powerful modeling tool and you'll quickly find yourself using splines to make hair, or even a character. The ability to dial in different resolutions may even result in the target triangle count you need for your character.

Surface Issues

After a model is built, and even during the building phase, it's a good idea to examine the surface, or faces, of the mesh for flaws that can be fixed. Paying attention to issues relating to the surface of a mesh helps attain the goal of good form. The first issue to address is bad edges. If there's a "dent" in the mesh where there shouldn't be, turn the edges necessary to complete the illusion of mass. Otherwise, the surface will have a slight (or severe) imperfection.

It's easier to identify bad concave edges if you view your model in a flat-shaded *instead of* smooth-shaded *viewing mode. Just right-click on the name of the viewport in the upper left-hand corner, and select Facets (Figure 1.21).*

ON THE CD   Load Edge.max from the Chapter1 directory on this book's CD-ROM (Figure 1.22).

FIGURE 1.21 Right-click on the viewport name to change the shading mode in 3ds max.

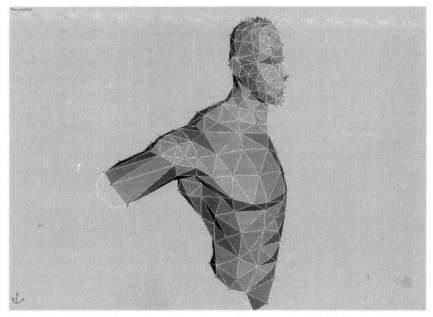

FIGURE 1.22 Turning edges is an important part of keeping a model's surface integrity.

Go to a flat-shaded viewing mode and examine the Edge.max model in a Perspective viewport. Toggle the Edit Mesh modifier (renamed to "edge turn") on and off to see the difference the turned edges make.

Turning them results in a surface that looks smoother and more uniform, which achieves a more effective sense of solidity.

 The default 3ds max lighting works fine when seeking out surface imperfections in your mesh. Just use Arc Rotate (Ctrl-R) to catch highlights and shadows, rotating your view around the mesh to see any edges that need turning.

 Applying a Smooth modifier to a model is the quickest way to remove its smoothing groups and give it a faceted look as well. That way, even if you're in a smooth-shaded viewing mode, the model will always look flat-shaded (Figure 1.23).

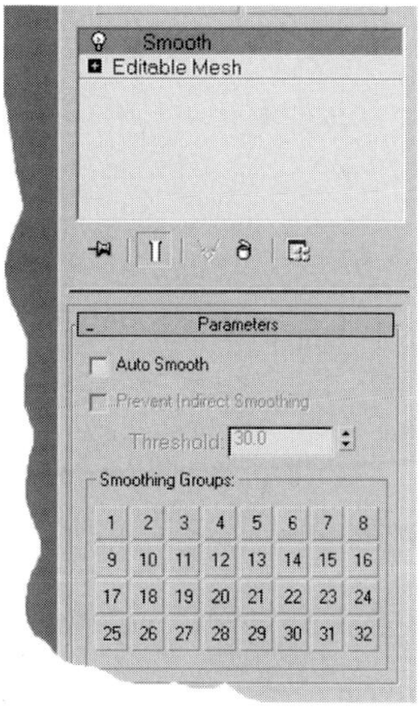

FIGURE 1.23 Applying a Smooth modifier to a mesh results in stripping its smoothing groups (at first).

ON THE CD Speaking of smoothing groups, most real-time game engines have no way of recognizing different smoothing groups in a mesh unless the vertices that make up a triangle are detached. This is an unfortunate yet easily remedied shortcoming of the technology. Load Betty01.max from the Chapter1 directory on this book's CD-ROM (Figure 1.24).

In Betty01.max, select the mesh, toggle the Edit Mesh modifier on and off to see the effects that merging the geometry at the rear has in regards to the smoothing, and then delete the modifier. Betty's mesh avoids problems with *over*-smoothing by having geometry that intersects each other and forms a crease where the faces meet, creating a more realistic look without the vertices being merged together. This technique works particularly well for cleavage on female characters.

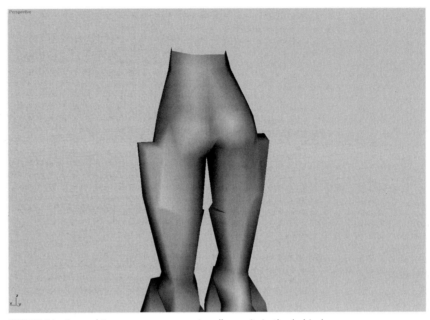

FIGURE 1.24   Smoothing groups are occasionally a pain in the *behind*.

ON THE CD

A more popular way to overcome the automatic assigning of one smoothing group to all the faces of a mesh by a game engine is to manually detach the faces and reattach them only at certain points. This gives a selective smoothing group effect that works within the constraints imposed by the real-time game engine. Load Betty02.max from the Chapter1 directory on the book's CD-ROM (Figure 1.25).

Fix Betty's face in Betty02.max by detaching and re-attaching certain polygons. Switch to wireframe viewing mode, then select and apply Detach to Element to the faces shown in Figure 1.26.

Hitting the F2 key will make selected faces appear solid and more visible. Hit F2 again to go back to normal selection mode.

By default, the command panel on the right is a single column in which you can pan up and down. Another way to display it, however, is to make it into two columns. Do this by putting your cursor over the right edge of the viewport window (the left edge of the panel) until you see the horizontal window re-size arrow. Then click on the edge and drag left (Figure 1.27).

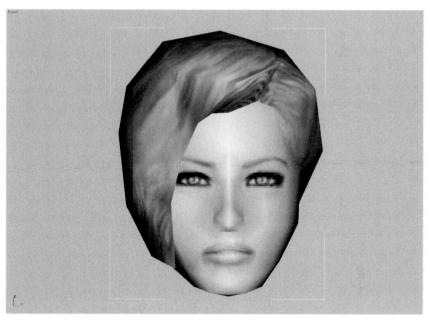

FIGURE 1.25   One smoothing group applied to Betty's face doesn't look too hot.

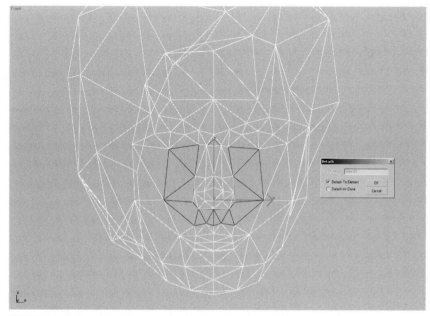

FIGURE 1.26   Select these faces on the head to detach and then re-attach.

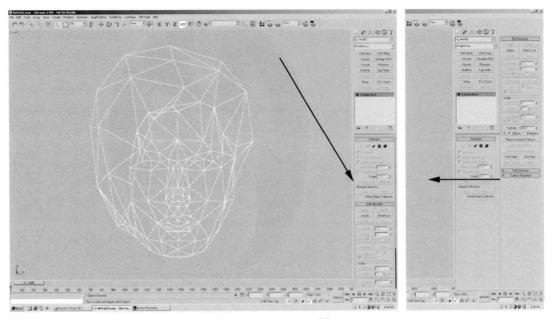

FIGURE 1.27   Resizing the menu makes the sub-menus more accessible.

This effectively opens up the menu so you won't have to continually scroll up and down to find the right sub-menu. Next, select the vertices at the perimeter of the group of faces you just detached; leave the Weld Selected value set at the default 0.1, and weld the selected vertices by clicking on the Selected button (Figure 1.28).

Rotate your view so you can look through the back of the head geometry. Note that the faces around the nose are made apparent by the lines where no lines should be visible (Figure 1.29). This indicates detached faces and/or vertices.

Lines can be seen through objects only when Backface Cull is selected in the object's Properties menu.

Next, you're going to select the triangles of the upper lip and Detach them to Element. Making the upper lip a detached element eliminates the strange-looking uni-smoothing effect, making the surface around the mouth look more realistic (Figure 1.30).

Now turn the smooth-shading mode back on and you should see that the surface of the face looks a lot cleaner and the features are more distinguishable (Figure 1.31).

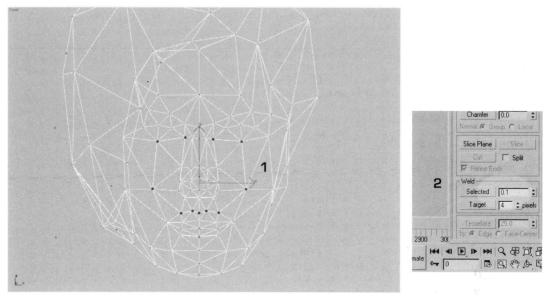

FIGURE 1.28   Select and weld these vertices only.

FIGURE 1.29   Lines seen through the back side of a mesh indicate that the vertices are detached.

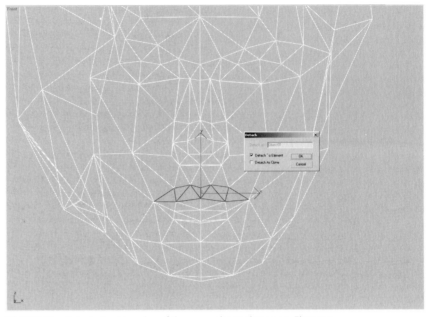

FIGURE 1.30   Detach the triangles of the upper lip to their own Element.

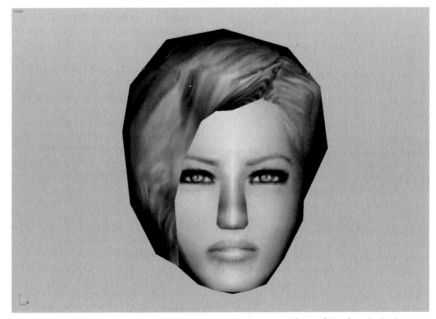

FIGURE 1.31   With the smoothing broken up manually, the surface of the face looks better.

Again, the reason for this "detach and reattach" process is because most real-time engines ignore the smoothing groups you assign in 3ds max and apply their own form of smoothing as they draw your character's mesh while rendering. This is the only way to simulate multiple smoothing groups. Constantly policing edges and smoothing groups this way is mandatory if you want to attain the best surface form for your character's mesh.

Optimization

While fixing smoothing anomalies and correcting dents or divots by turning wayward edges is a one way to keep things tight, another aspect of form is making sure the model is optimized and efficient. "Efficient" means *making every vertex count*—a vertex only exists to support the shape of the design. Real-time characters are always built and animated under a polygon budget constraint, so extra vertices that just *exist* and don't carry their share of the load translate into unnecessary triangles that could push you over your limit.

Use the Polygon Counter found in the Utilities panel in 3ds max to keep track of your polygon count. It allows you to enter a target limit for the number of faces in your character and uses an easy coloring scheme to tell you when you're approaching your target face count. (Figure 1.32).

ON THE CD

Load Vertex.max from the Chapter1 directory on the book's CD-ROM and toggle the "vertex weld" Edit Mesh modifier on and off to see the effects of just a few vertex welds used to manually optimize the mesh (Figure 1.33).

Since the pectoral region of a male character deforms very little, if at all, it's a prime candidate for optimization and can be made with a relatively simpler geometry compared to the triangle-demanding deltoid/shoulder area. In 3ds max, you can quickly weld two vertices by selecting them and raising the Weld threshold to an excessively high number (such as 10 or even 100, depending on your character's scale) before clicking the Weld Selected button. Target Weld is another way to merge a vertex to any of its neighbors.

Although there *is* an Optimize modifier (and the very useful Multi-Res Mesh modifier) to take care of basic optimizing situations, it's better in most cases to optimize manually. It's a little slower than simply pressing a button, but it gives you ultimate control over the (sometimes) painful reduction process.

FIGURE 1.32   The Polygon Counter tool can help you stay within your face count budget.

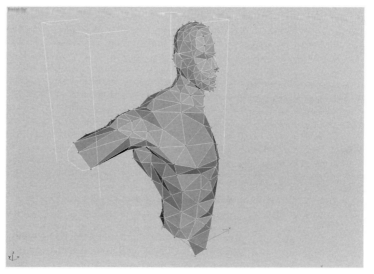

FIGURE 1.33   Optimizing a mesh ensures the target face count is maintained.

The Multi-Res Mesh (MRM) modifier is a great "quick-and-dirty" reduction tool because it gives you the power to keep UVW mapping coordinates (UVW will be explained later in the chapter) and specific vertices while optimizing the rest of the mesh. It's especially good at making LODs quickly!

Regardless of how you get rid of unnecessary vertices, you can never be too critical when eradicating them. Even if the face-count budget is high, don't let yourself be sloppy. Hunting down and eliminating stray vertices that don't contribute to shape definition will keep the model at its most efficient, giving other areas of the game (such as weapons, effects, environment) even more triangles to use. This keeps the quality level and speed of the game as high as possible.

MODELING: FUNCTION

If the aspects of form dictate the shape of the real-time character, function applies to the shape as it *deforms* during animation. Function is a very important area to consider when building your character model. After all, real-time game characters aren't statues frozen for all time, unmoving as they're admired for their artistry—they have to animate convincingly like living creatures. They need to twist, stretch, bend, and generally deform properly as they go through their motions, and all with a limited number of polygons. To be properly functional, the character mesh needs to be broken down both to allow access to vertices during the weighting process and to conform to any technological constraints imposed by the game engine. Most important, however, the mesh needs to accommodate animation geometrically and be correctly aligned to a Biped in character studio™ during the rigging and weighting phase.

Model Breakdown

In a real-time game environment, it's a good general rule to make the characters as consolidated a mesh as is possible, allowing the game engine to process fewer pieces. This means the character model is comprised of the fewest number of separate *objects*.

ON THE CD

Load Betty03.max from the Chapter1 directory on the book's CD-ROM. Notice the breakdown of the mesh. The left arm and torso (including the right shoulder) are one object (A); the head, right arm, and left leg are one object (B); the hips, abs, and right leg are one object (C); finally, the gun tip (D) is one object (Figure 1.34).

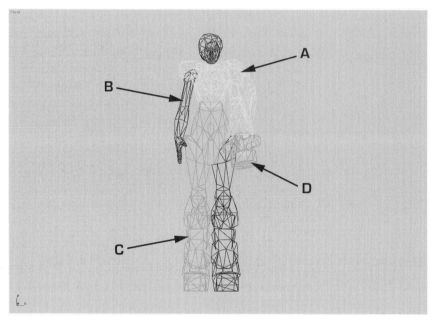

FIGURE 1.34   A mesh needs to be comprised of the least number of objects as possible.

Betty's mesh is broken up the way it is for two reasons: game design and ease of access during weighting. Originally, the end of Betty's gun was supposed to switch between two tip designs, based on which configuration or energy type she chose. Although the idea was scrapped, the element stayed separate (just in case). The rest of the objects are separate solely for ease of access during the weighting process. There's no point in struggling with locating and isolating vertices that are painfully close to each other if it can be helped. The choice between making your job easier and taking the risk of a performance hit due to the multiple objects is a calculated decision that comes from experience more than anything else.

 To change the color of a mesh, simply click on the small colored box to the upper right (Figure 1.35).

Animation Accommodation

Gross functionality of a character's mesh depends on its structure; however, in order for a character to support or *accommodate* animation properly, it must have enough vertices and faces in key areas to avoid unsightly crimping or collapsing. This section covers the various areas of a model that need special attention when your character will be animated.

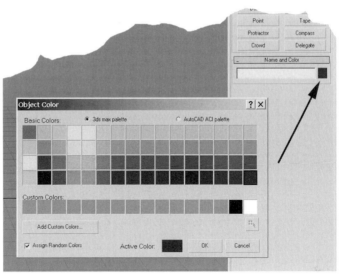

FIGURE 1.35   It is easy to change the mesh color of an object.

Neck and Head

Accommodating the neck and the head is straightforward enough. The head is always attached to the Biped head *completely* and, unless the character talks, is a single mass that swivels on the neck joint. The neck generally doesn't have to deform too much with the head atop it, but sometimes the uppermost vertices can deform slightly as the head turns. You don't have to put a lot of work into this unless the character has a long flexible neck (Figure 1.36).

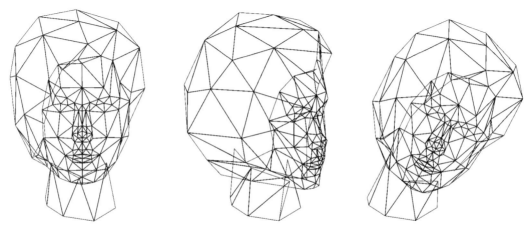

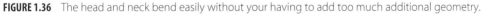

FIGURE 1.36   The head and neck bend easily without your having to add too much additional geometry.

Shoulders

The shoulder of an animated character is perhaps the most difficult area to work with. Unfortunately, it's a very complex mechanism that is hard to approximate with much success in a game character, even in a higher-poly character. If possible, take the easy way out and make the arms detached, using an "action figure" approach, and just stick the arm and shoulder to the torso. Hiding the arms underneath armor is another way to avoid the amount of effort it takes to deform a shoulder area properly (Figure 1.37).

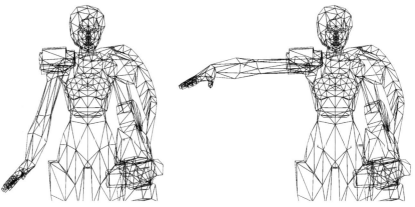

FIGURE 1.37   Take the easy way out and hide shoulders under shoulder pads.

In a higher polygon count character (4,000 to 6,000 triangles), it's possible to create an accordion/fan arrangement of faces so the shoulder deforms well in both the front view (Figure 1.38) . . .

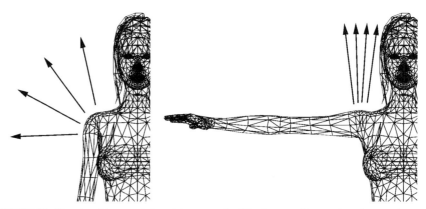

FIGURE 1.38   The shoulder needs to retain as much of its shape as it can when the arm is both up and down.

. . .and the top view (Figure 1.39).

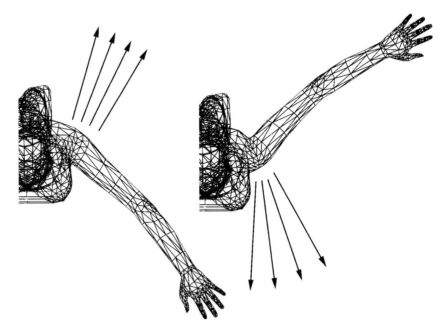

FIGURE 1.39   Side to side movement needs to be accommodated as well.

Shoulders not only require a lot of experimentation to get them right, but they're different from character to character. The key to successful shoulder geometry is to retain as much of its shape in as many positions as possible, while making sure it looks right from the *most commonly seen* poses.

Waist

The waist is easy enough to animate. Just make sure you have included enough triangles and that they're positioned properly to support twisting and bending the trunk (Figure 1.40).

Hips and Rear

The hips and rear areas are sometimes just as problematic as the shoulder area and need to support a full range of motion for the legs. The main area you need to worry about is the rear area; make sure that as the upper leg moves forward and backward, the shape of the gluteus maximus stays solid (Figure 1.41).

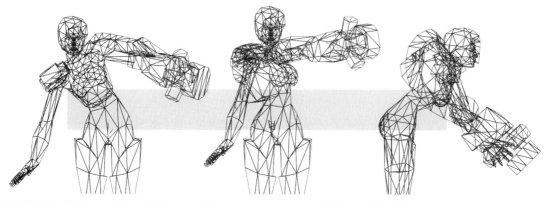

FIGURE 1.40   Make sure the waist has enough geometry to support twisting and bending.

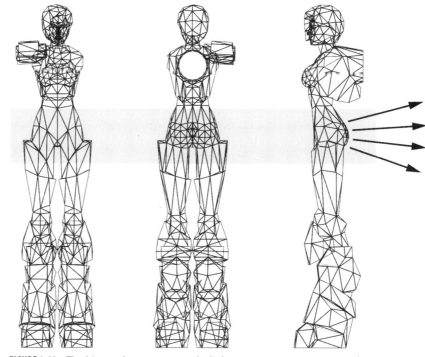

FIGURE 1.41   The hips and rear areas need a little extra geometry to support leg animations.

Never have the upper legs *join* in the groin area. Keep a gap at the groin to ensure the legs will look right when they're in motion. This is especially true for martial arts moves. Pay special attention, too, to the front part of the hips where the Biped upper leg attaches to the pelvis.

Elbows and Knees

Elbows and knees abide by the same rule: When the arm bends (or the leg bends), there has to be enough geometry to prevent it from collapsing in on itself (Figure 1.42).

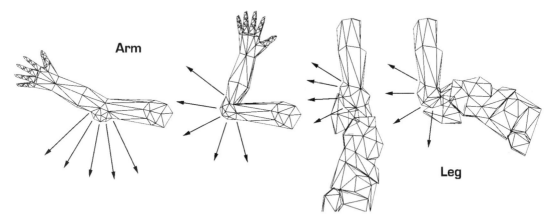

FIGURE 1.42 Keep the shape of the joint intact by using extra geometry that "fans" out when limbs bend.

Hands and Fingers

Actual fingers (that is, individual digits) are rare on real-time game characters. They're usually in the shape of "mitts" that can be textured to look like fingers (Figure 1.43).

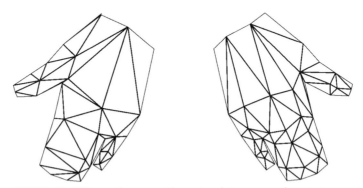

FIGURE 1.43 Mitts are the rage with most real-time game characters.

However, when you can add fingers, you must also add knuckles to accommodate animation, in the same way that elbows and knees need extra faces at the joint (Figure 1.44).

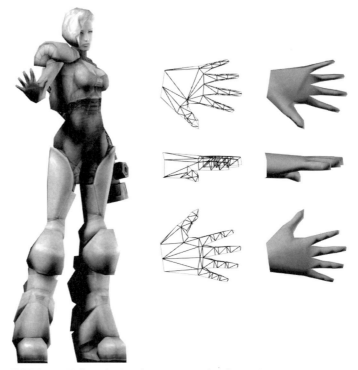

FIGURE 1.44 Talk to the hand . . . Betty's *five-fingered* hand, that is.

Wrists and Ankles

Wrist and ankles require very little extra geometry. There are usually plenty of polygons that enable them to keep their shape, and they can be forgiven if they deform incorrectly sometimes (Figure 1.45).

Sometimes, however, it's necessary to add an extra row of vertices along the top of the wrist if you find your character bending his hand down often. This is also true for the back of the ankle.

As you build your characters, always think about the areas that will be deforming as they animate. Ultimately, the best way to see which areas need extra triangles is to attach the mesh to a Biped, weight it, and animate it. Only after going through this process will you really understand the where, when, and why of how your model accommodates the animation.

Fitting the Biped

There's one last topic to cover when it comes to function: aligning your mesh to the Biped you'll be attaching it to. The joints of a Biped rotate on

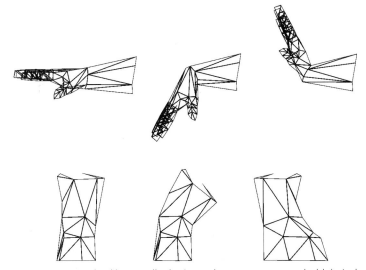

FIGURE 1.45   Wrists and ankles usually don't need extra geometry to hold their shape.

a pivot. The base of the fingers and the toes can be moved around and any of the limbs can be scaled to fit any geometric shape. But there's only so much you can do (and *want* to do) to the underlying skeleton. To assure proper function, sometimes it's necessary to adjust your mesh to fit the Biped. All this really entails is shifting some vertices around so they align with the joint they'll be affected by (Figure 1.46).

Because the Biped is created *after* the mesh is done, there's really no way to know what kind of "tweaking" needs to be done until the mesh is complete. However, never be afraid to make adjustments to your mesh during any part of the animation process.

TEXTURE: MAPS

Texture maps are another major consideration when ensuring a real-time character is "built to move," and they contribute significantly to the overall success of the character. Texture maps are the image files applied to the mesh to give the illusion of being a realistic character. There are two distinct elements that make up a good texture map: *UVW coverage* and the *quality of the texture*.

UVW Coverage

Mapping coordinates correlate to three spatial mapping axes that are known as *UVW*. (They could have been given any series of letters, but are

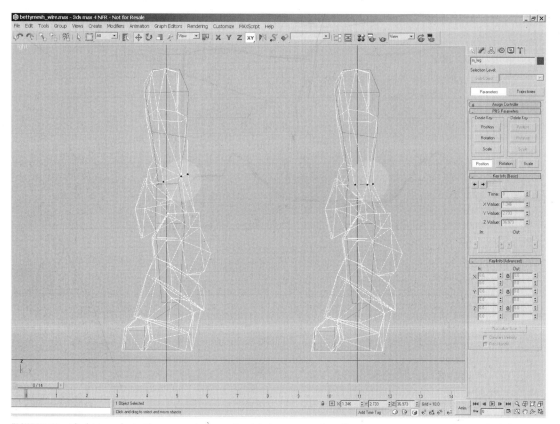

FIGURE 1.46   Slight tweaks to the geometry near the joints are occasionally necessary to ensure the mesh deforms correctly.

so named to precede XYZ in the alphabet. X, Y, and Z, of course, represent the three spatial axes of the Cartesian coordinate system.) No matter how good an artist you are, without the proper stretched canvas to paint upon, the work of art you strive for might not look even or square—the same is true for the real-time game character. You must ensure that the mapping coverage assigned to your character is complete, thorough, and efficient to give yourself the best canvas upon which to create your texture.

The following is just one way of many to apply mapping coordinates to a model. It's effective, but feel free to explore other techniques as well. First, visualize your model in pieces, seeing it as a collection of flat images arranged in 3D that approximate the look you're after. The flat images represent mapping *planes* or projections of the texture map that when merged together on one big sheet, are an "unwrapping" of your model.

ON THE CD   Load Head1.max from the Chapter1 directory on the book's CD-ROM (Figure 1.47).

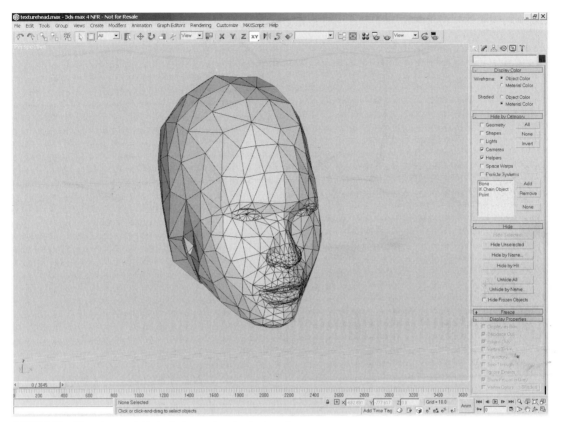

FIGURE 1.47   After the model is built, it needs to be textured.

The mesh shown in Figure 1.47 is the head of a higher polygon character model. Detach to Element has been applied to its faces; they serve as "sheets" of polygons that, in turn, represent a unique planar projection. The process of applying the mapping coordinates starts with making sure these elements are really detached and can be moved around (Figure 1.48).

Arrange all the elements so that they face the Front viewport with the maximum amount of exposure. This way, the viewport essentially becomes a planar mapping window. Use Snap (Snap to vertex) to put the elements in place, but be as careful as possible to keep the vertices aligned just as they were while whole.

It is very important to make sure you apply an Edit Mesh modifier before re-arranging the elements. This technique relies on the ability to turn the Edit Mesh modifier off *once the UVW Map and Unwrap UVW modifiers have been applied. It's easy to just start moving the elements around without applying an Edit Mesh modifier to the stack.*

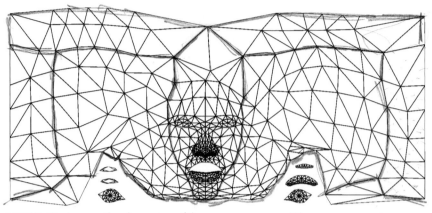

FIGURE 1.48   Arrange the elements as if they were unwrapped like an orange peel.

Next, select the vertices at the edge of those elements that you want to be joined to form a continuous surface. Then bring up the Scale Transform Type-In window by selecting and right-clicking on the Scale Transform icon (Figure 1.49).

FIGURE 1.49   The Transform Type-In menu is a great way to precisely scale, move, or rotate objects or sub-objects.

Enter 0 in the Offset Screen box and the selected vertices will instantly shrink in, occupying the same space *without* being welded. Unfortunately, you absolutely *cannot* weld or otherwise merge the vertices of the elements in this state; it would defeat the purpose of the technique because it changes the overall number and *numbering* of the vertices of the mesh. This ability to scale the vertices down by typing in a scale of 0 is one of the benefits of using this mapping technique instead of just the Unwrap UVW modifier. After the vertices are all scaled down and the elements are "joined" together, the mesh should look like Figure 1.50.

 Use multiple Edit Mesh modifiers to lay out the elements. Just make sure no sub-object is selected when the new modifier is applied—this would affect the end result negatively.

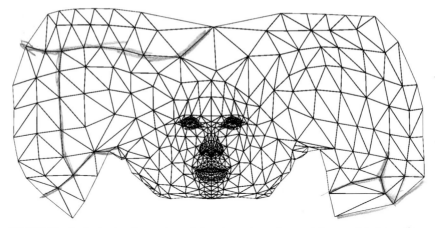

FIGURE 1.50   Scale the border vertices of the elements so the mesh is a continuous surface.

With the mesh now a continuous surface, there will be no seams in the texture coverage. However, the end elements are curved and also need to seam or "tile." To do this, simply slide the element on the right over to the left side along the X-axis, and scale the vertices where the two elements meet (Figure 1.51).

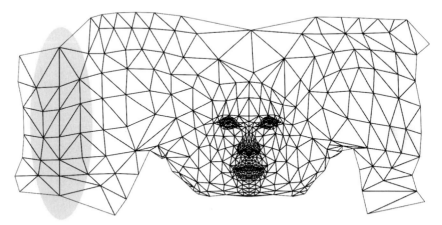

FIGURE 1.51   Align the end elements to make the mapping connect at the back of the head.

Finally, arrange the rest of the elements so the mesh has a completely tiled and covered mapping scheme (Figure 1.52).

Another advantage of this mapping technique is that you can assign a wireframe material to the mesh and render it to whatever resolution you want.

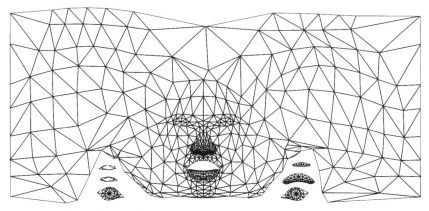

FIGURE 1.52   The mesh is ready to receive mapping assignment.

 When rendering a mesh that has a wireframe material applied to it, the edges need to be selected and made visible (Figure 1.53).

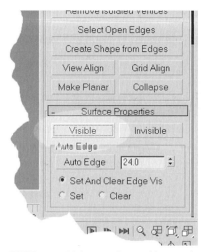

FIGURE 1.53   Make an edge visible in order to see it when rendering in wireframe.

With the mesh splayed out like a Mercator projection of Earth, it's time to apply a UVW Map modifier to the mesh. Change the mapping gizmo's dimensions to be square in order to accommodate an eventual 512×512 texture map (Figure 1.54).

The size of the image isn't really important at this point. The most important thing is the fact that the mapping gizmo is square. In other words,

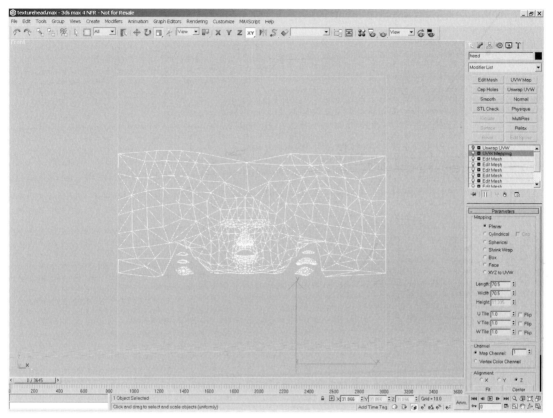

FIGURE 1.54   Apply the UVW Map modifier once the elements have been arranged.

by being square, the mapping will eventually be able to conform to the "powers of 2" rule (that is, a 512 × 512 or 256 × 256 texture page). Render at a high enough resolution to go *down* to the target resolution instead of *up*.

Once the map has been applied, apply an Unwrap UVW modifier to *lock* the mapping coordinates to the mesh. Render a wireframe image or make a snapshot of the screen in order to have a base image to apply to the mesh, and work from it as you create the real texture. Once the material is made, apply it, turn off all the Edit Mesh modifiers (leave the UVW Map and Unwrap UVW modifiers *on*, of course); the mesh snaps back to its original shape, yet keeps the new mapping coordinates. This allows you to see if there's any streaking in the mapping coverage. If there is, just turn the Edit Mesh modifiers back on and adjust (or simply adjust in the Unwrap UVW modifier). Once the coverage is good, it's time to start making the real texture.

Quality of the Texture

Achieving a great texture map when making real-time game characters is as subjective a process as they come. The truly great artists just start painting and don't stop until their digital opus is complete. Texture artists like John Mueller and Steve Garofalo of Epic Games have done (and continue to do) amazing work on character models for games like *Unreal Tournament* and the upcoming *Unreal Warfare*. Their innate ability to manipulate pixels and textures just as if they were painting with traditional color mediums is an inspiration to their peers.

Making a good texture means you know your mesh. In an ideal environment, you design the character, you build the character, you texture the character, and you animate the character. However, in the fast-paced world of making games and online content, it's rare to have the luxury (or the ability) to master all four areas. The more preferable scenario is one in which the artist who designs the mesh hands it off to a modeler to create; the modeler then hands it *back* to the artist who designed it so he can texture it. The modeler or another animator can be the one to rig, weight, and animate the character from there. This sort of "hand off" process is standard in Hollywood special-effects houses. Unfortunately, in most game development studios, *everyone* is expected to do *everything*. Specialization is generally discouraged, and all artists are supposed to be able to design, model, texture, and animate a character equally well. This is generally not a good situation, productively or otherwise, because it pits artist against artist, each one vying to be the best artist and the ultimate content-creation contributor. It's bad for morale, and it's bad for the health of any sneaky, ambitious types.

Every artist has his preference and area of specialization. Some are simply better at certain areas than others. Spreading yourself thin by trying to be a "perfect 10" at all levels of game art creation is an admirable goal, but ultimately a bad idea. Certainly you need to know all the areas in question and be competent in them, but this is where *teamwork* comes in. Four artists who excel at each of the four major areas individually create the best art team imaginable: designer, modeler, texture artist, and animator. A two-artist team, a designer/texturer and a modeler/animator, are a must. Each artist knows enough about the areas outside his expertise to make his partner's job easier, but focuses on making sure his responsibilities are met above and beyond expectation.

Regardless of who does the art, it needs to be as good as it can be and fit the real-time game character to which it's been applied. It has to fit on as few texture pages as can be managed, which reduces the strain on the game engine as it's loaded into a scene. It has to also make use of opacity,

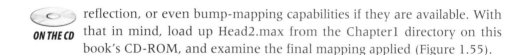

reflection, or even bump-mapping capabilities if they are available. With that in mind, load up Head2.max from the Chapter1 directory on this book's CD-ROM, and examine the final mapping applied (Figure 1.55).

FIGURE 1.55   Texture maps with opacity maps can create a convincing head and hairdo.

Note that the UVW coordinates have been changed to take advantage of the mirroring function within the Unwrap UVW modifier. In this case, the texture map applied to the head shows half the image in black because the rest of the character's texture will eventually have to fit on the texture page as well. Betty Bad's texture arrangement is similar and gives a look at how an entire character is mapped (Figure 1.56).

Both the textures shown in Figure 1.56 were created in Photoshop and applied to the meshes in iterative steps: Texture a little, see how it looks; tweak the map, tweak the mapping coordinates; repeat until done. Bouncing back and forth between Photoshop and 3ds max is easy if you have a powerful machine (or more than one machine), but keep in mind that using both programs at the same time will be a severe drain on your

FIGURE 1.56 Betty Bad's texture map efficiently fills the texture page.

system's resources. There are also 3D paint programs like Right Hemisphere's Deep Paint™ that can significantly help in the texturing process.

When it comes to the quality of the texture map, talent, thought, and sense of efficiency will determine the success of the art. Make sure the texture holds up while animating. Texturing a shadow on the inside of a character's thigh might look great in a static environment, but if it's lit and shaded dynamically (as is the case in most game engines), that same forced shadow can look out of place and affect the quality of the character.

SUMMARY

A great real-time game character can be broken down into five different elements: design, model, texture, animations, and sound. In order for the character to be *built to move*, its design, model, and texture have to succeed in specific areas. The design has to be well thought-out, unique, appropriate, and doable within the technological constraints of the game engine into which the character will be dropped. Then, a suitable and useful reference needs to be created and made available to the modeler so that the character can be taken from 2D to 3D.

When it comes to modeling, the success of the character's mesh relies on attaining superior *form* and *function*. Form is the integrity and artistry of the mesh, and it gives the impression of solidity and weight while adhering as closely as possible to the design. Factors to consider while striving for proper form are accuracy, efficiency, and surface quality. Because the character is built for a real-time game, polygon modeling techniques are best. Whether you start with primitives, use extrusions, Booleans, a higher resolution mesh as a template, or even patch modeling techniques, make sure every vertex is necessary to define the form—make every vertex count. Function is achieved when the mesh is broken down properly for both texturing and animation and it *accommodates* the animations imposed upon it by deforming correctly. Key areas like elbows, knees, and other areas of the body must have the right distribution of vertices and faces to support movement.

Finally, the texture has to be both technically correct and artfully done. The only way to end up with a great texture is to start with adequate and complete texture mapping coordinates. No matter which technique you use to apply the mapping coordinates to your character, make sure the canvas is big and laid out properly before painting your masterpiece.

CHAPTER

2

RIGGING YOUR CHARACTERS WITH BIPED

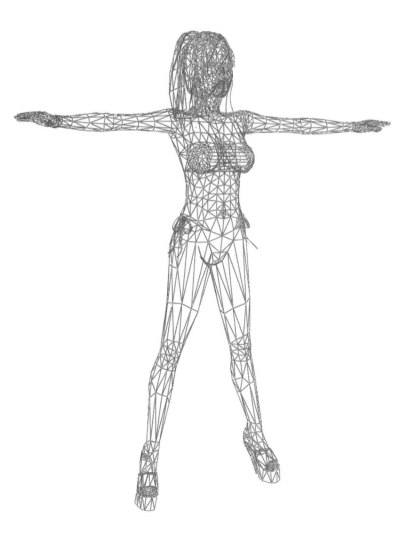

N early all real-time game characters are animated using some sort of skeletal animation system. This means the character has its geometry, or "skin," with an underlying "skeleton" to deform the "skin." Just as your skin doesn't move on its own, rarely will you animate a character's mesh on its own. Of the character studio package's two constituent parts, Biped and Physique, the former serves as the skeleton and the latter (in conjunction with the character's mesh) serves as the skin. The act of setting up a Biped to align correctly with and properly deform your character's mesh is commonly known as *rigging* your character.

SETTING UP A TYPICAL BIPED

In 3ds max, using a Biped is preferable to the indigenous bones, because it's a quick and easy way to create a character's underlying rig, complete with inverse kinematics (IK), joint constraints, and adjustable parameters for everything from number of fingers to adding a tail. The primary benefit of using a Biped, however, is *file-sharing*. This applies to its default pose as well as both keyframe and motion-capture data. It's a *huge* asset to be able to create that perfect pose, walk, run, or jump and then use it with any and all of your other characters.

Steps to Setting up a Biped Rig

1. Load your character's finished mesh and freeze it.
2. Create a Biped and put it into Figure mode.
3. Roughly align the Biped to your mesh by selecting and moving the Center of Mass (COM), making sure the pelvis lines up appropriately in all views.
4. Rename and adjust the Structure of your Biped.
5. Move, scale, and rotate the Spine objects into position in all views.
6. Hide all the limbs of one side of the character.
7. Adjust the remaining arm, starting with the clavicle and moving your way down.
8. Adjust the remaining leg by starting with the thigh and moving your way down.
9. Unhide all Biped objects, then copy and mirror the pose of the limbs to their unposed counterparts.
10. Save the character's pose as a .fig file.
11. Turn Figure mode off, and save the Biped's default position as a .bip file.
12. Your rig is now ready to be attached to your mesh.

Loading Your Character's Mesh

Load Betty04.max from the Chapter2 directory on this book's CD-ROM (Figure 2.1).

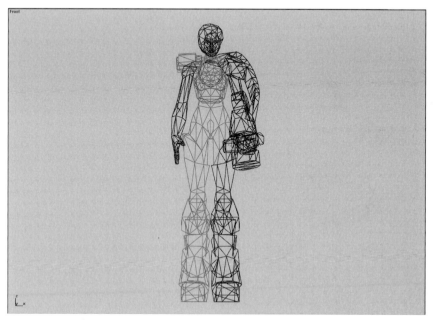

FIGURE 2.1   The first step to rigging your character is loading it into 3ds max.

There are several things you should note about the mesh. First, all the parts have been colored differently so you can quickly tell them apart, and their respective stacks have been collapsed. Also, the mesh objects are presumed to be the final version and won't be substantially altered in the future. This is very important, because once a mesh has been attached to a Biped, detaching it to make structural changes deletes any of the previous weighting information.

Even though it's best to have a completely textured, final mesh before attaching it to a Biped rig, more experienced modelers and animators always find it a good idea to do some test runs with the geometry before applying texture. Adding and deleting geometry to a mesh once the mapping coordinates have been applied sometimes makes a mess of those coordinates. Waiting to lay the UVWs in until you're sure the geometry is going to work will display prudence and foresight gleaned only through experience!

Note also that the names of the parts are descriptive: m_torso, m_headarmleg, m_gunarm, m_gun, m_energy, and m_fanvent. The "m_" in front of the object's name ensures that the mesh objects stay grouped together when bringing up a hit list. It also quickly differentiates a mesh object from a Biped object.

As mentioned in the previous chapter, game characters need to be made up of as few objects as possible to ensure the best performance by the game engine. Also, it behooves you to keep certain elements detached and spaced away from each other for easier access during the weighting phase of rigging your character. M_headarmleg is an example of how you can kill two birds with one stone and guarantee the best access to the vertices. It's a pretty unlikely mesh object, but it reduces the number of objects necessary for the character's mesh (Figure 2.2).

FIGURE 2.2 Sometimes unlikely elements form an object in a character's mesh.

Another reason to group certain elements together (or keep them separate) is to support materials/shaders. Some game engines can't handle a Multi/Sub-Object material, so some objects need to be separated by virtue of the material/shader assigned to them; this can be due to the desired shader effect, or to the fact that the objects are referencing different texture files (Figure 2.3).

In Betty's case, m_gun, m_energy, and m_fanvent are all detached, because they've all been assigned a material that uses a different texture file than the rest of the character. However, m_headarmleg, m_torso, and

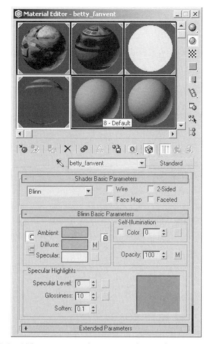

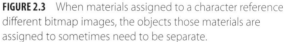

FIGURE 2.3 When materials assigned to a character reference different bitmap images, the objects those materials are assigned to sometimes need to be separate.

m_gunarm are detached purely for purposes of making life easier when weighting the character.

Unhide all the mesh objects and freeze them. Doing this always makes it easier to adjust the Biped you're about to make without inadvertently selecting the mesh you're fitting it to.

Creating Your Biped

Go to the Create panel, click on the   Systems icon and click the Biped button to activate it (Figure 2.4).

` Put the 3ds max arrow cursor at the frozen feet of Betty's mesh, hold the left mouse button down, and drag upward until the green box encompasses her head. Let go of the mouse button, and *voila!* You've made a Biped! (Figure 2.5)

In order to act as terminators for the IK solutions, Bipeds need dummy objects linked to the end of their fingers, the top of the head, and the ends of the toes. Whenever you create a Biped, these dummy objects are automatically hidden. However, if

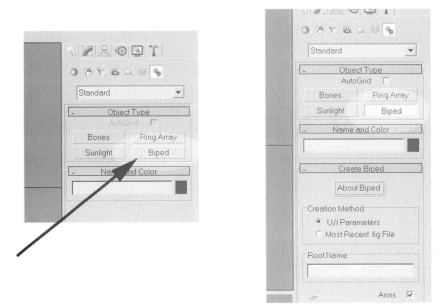

FIGURE 2.4   Creating a Biped is as easy as clicking on the Biped button.

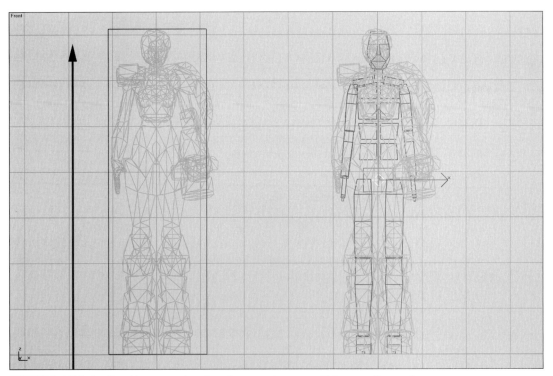

FIGURE 2.5   With the Biped button active, drag the green box up until it covers the mesh.

for some reason they're not hidden, go to the 🖼 *Display panel and check the Helpers box under Hide by Category (Figure 2.6).*

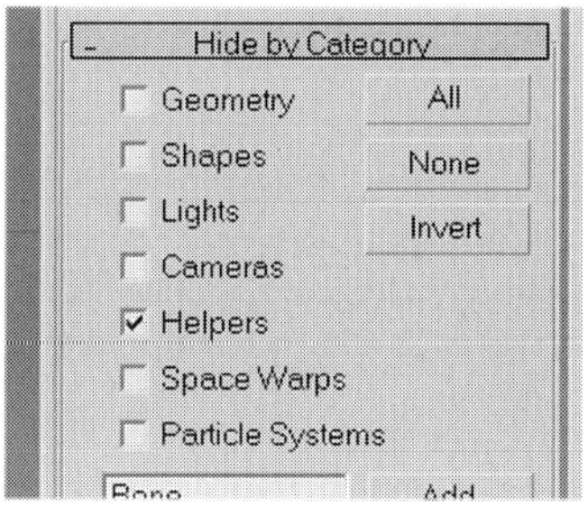

FIGURE 2.6   Keep a Biped's dummy objects hidden since there's never a need to animate these "Nubs."

Now, in order to fit the Biped precisely to your mesh, you need to put it into Figure mode. Think of this special state for a Biped as the default pose or "time-out" pose that is used to tweak the rig before, during, and after animations have been applied to it. Go to the ⊕ Motion panel and put your Biped in Figure mode by clicking on the "little man" icon, making it purple (Figure 2.7).

FIGURE 2.7   In order to fit your Biped to a mesh, it needs to be in FIGURE mode.

With no animations applied to the Biped, putting it into Figure mode has no noticeable effect, but now you have the ability to adjust its Structure to fit your mesh. To center the Biped in the world coordinate system (and over the character's mesh), select the root of the Biped, the COM object (the small, blue, diamond shape near the pelvis box), make the ✛ Move icon active, and right-click on it to bring up the Move Transform Type-In menu (Figure 2.8).

Double-click in the white portion of the ⊠ X-axis entry, type in 0, and hit Enter. If the number won't take and the Biped doesn't budge, make sure the active move axis is X (hit the F5 key), and try it again. With the Biped centered and nestled somewhat inside your character's mesh, you can begin. . .

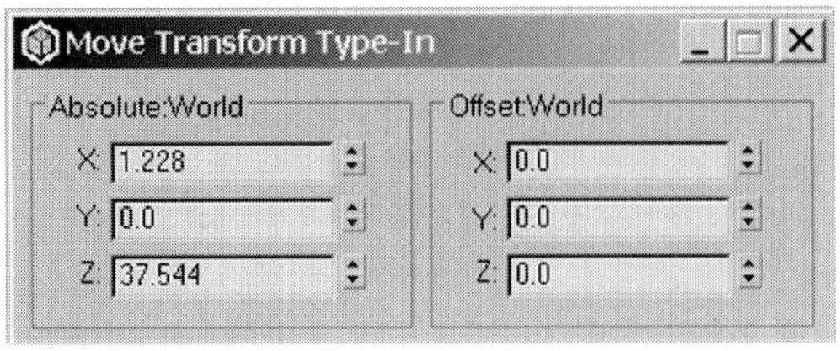

FIGURE 2.8 The Move Transform Type-In menu quickly and accurately moves objects.

Adjusting the Structure of Your Biped

Before adjusting the individual parts of a Biped (such as moving, rotating or scaling), you need to adjust its basic *Structure*. Begin by giving the Biped a name. Open the Structure rollout menu while in Figure mode. Go over to the Root Name box, select the name Bip01, and rename it to "Betty" (Figure 2.9).

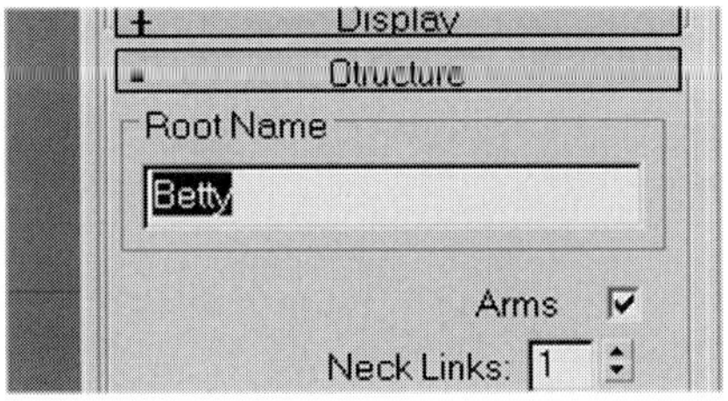

FIGURE 2.9 Any name you put in this field renames the COM and all its children.

While it's definitely not mandatory to name your Biped, it's a good habit to get into in case you have more than one in your scene.

Look over the rest of the Structure sub-menu and enter the values shown in Figure 2.10.

Unless your character doesn't need arms, leave the box beside Arms checked. The Neck Links value is usually 1 unless your character has a serpentine neck. The Spine Links values vary, but go ahead and stay with 4 (more on this later). Leg Link values are 3 by default (a value of 4 is supposed to support a tri-legged character—but more on this later as well).Keep Tail Links, Ponytail1 Links and Ponytail2 Links values at 0. Give Betty a Fingers value of 5 and Finger Links value of 3. Only give her a value of 1 for Toes and Toe Links (most characters only need one toe and one toe link). The Ankle Attach value is normally fine at whatever value it defaults to, but feel free to experiment with different values if you like.

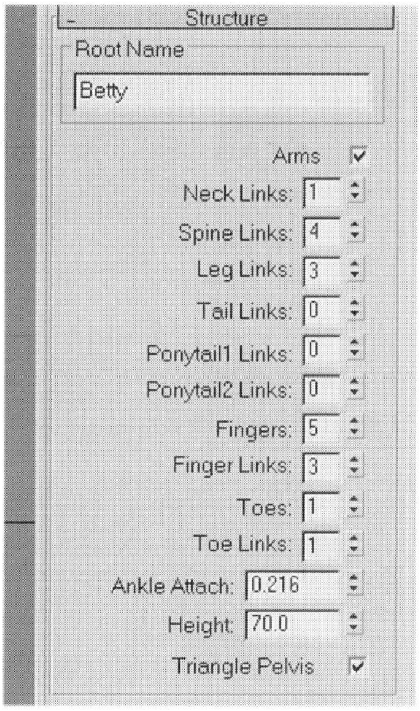

FIGURE 2.10   The Structure sub-menu controls the basic configuration of the Biped.

The Height value is basically irrelevant, because you've roughly pro-portioned the Biped to fit the mesh, but it is a good way to double-check your character's scale. Know beforehand how big your character will be in its game world, and adjust the height accordingly. As for the Triangle Pelvis box, just keep it checked.

Make sure that the height for both your character and Biped is correct before you go through the effort of attaching your mesh to its Biped rig. Adjusting the Biped height (especially with additional bones attached) after it's been attached doesn't uniformly scale the character down, but instead squishes it in an unacceptable (al-though funny) way.

Adjusting the Biped's Body and Head

With the basic structure now established, it's time to start adjusting the Biped so that it lines up with the mesh. Begin with the body's trunk areas since they drive and parent the limbs. Hide the arms (except for the clav-icles) and the lower leg objects of the Biped. Zoom in on the pelvic area, select the COM, and move it upward until the bottom of the pelvis lines up with Betty's groin. Make sure the thighs are relatively centered in the mesh legs (Figure 2.11).

FIGURE 2.11 Align the Biped's pelvis with the top of the character's groin.

The pivot point for the thighs are at their top, so envision your character's legs bending from these points. Widening the pelvis by applying ⬛ Non-Uniformly Scale to it along the ⬛ Z-axis; this makes the legs' attachment point move further away from the center accordingly.

💡 *Double-clicking any parent of a Biped causes all the children objects to be selected as well. This makes it very easy to select all the children in a limb hierarchy, for example.*

Next, select the four Spine objects, scale them down along the X-axis, and move them so the clavicles end up *relatively* near the shoulder juncture. Make sure the *top* of the first Spine object ("Betty Spine") is close to the point where the waist would normally bend. Go to the Right viewport, and apply the ⬛ Rotate function to the spine links, moving them until they conform to the posture of the mesh (Figure 2.12).

 The axis coordinate system for a Biped is unique in that it remains constant regardless of the coordinate system chosen in 3ds max. For most Biped parts, scaling along the X-axis lengthens the objects, scaling along the Z-axis widens it, and scaling along the Y-axis makes it thicker (as seen from the Front view). Rotating along the Z-axis results in a bending forward or backward for most Biped objects, but

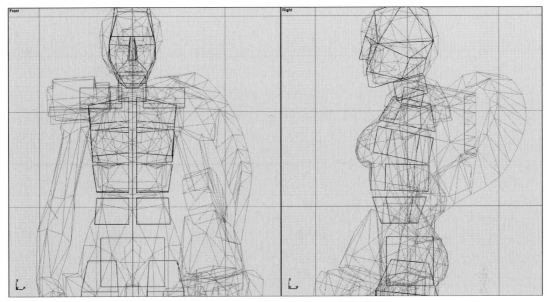

FIGURE 2.12   Make sure the Biped's Spine objects are aligned to the mesh in all viewports.

there are exceptions. Overall, this different coordinate system definitely (ahem) takes getting used to.

For the Head and Neck objects, just try your best to match their size and angle to the mesh, remembering that the head's pivot point is directly beneath it. When the trunk is done, it's time to move on to the arms and legs.

Adjusting the Biped's Arms and Legs

Unhide everything and unfreeze the mesh objects. Hide m_gunarm, m_gun, m_energy, and m_fanvent, then re-freeze m_headarmleg and m_torso. Hide all left-side limb objects, the torso, and neck and head objects of the Biped. In character studio, if your character has symmetrical limbs, you only have to pose one side, due to the plug-in's powerful capability to copy and mirror objects' positions. It's also always a good idea to keep your work as uncluttered as you can, so hide any extraneous geometry; this allows you to more quickly pose what *is* there (Figure 2.13).

 Before fitting the Biped to your frozen mesh, make sure the settings for the Biped arms and legs (fingers and toes, too) found under the Structure rollout menu are final. To see why, do the following: First, put your Biped in Figure mode. Second,

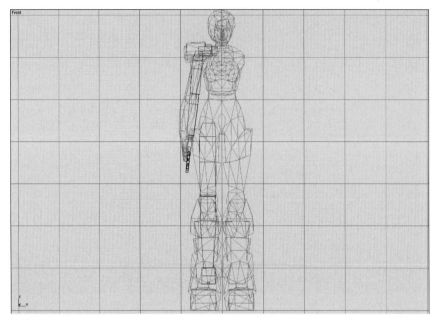

FIGURE 2.13   Hide any geometry and any objects that are unnecessary in posing one side of the character's limbs.

select and hide any arm or leg Biped object. Third, go to the Structure rollout menu and change the number of fingers or toes. Poof! *All Biped objects disappear.*

Start with the leg, since it's made up of fewer objects than the arm. Use the regular transform methods to scale and rotate it into place (Figure 2.14).

Character studio offers another way to adjust the knee, ankle, elbow, and wrist joints: Rubber Band mode. *To use it, just click the Rubber Band Mode icon to make it active, select the* parent *bone of the joint you want to move (for example, the upper arm Biped object for the elbow joint), and move the joint into place (Figure 2.15).*

Hide the leg and then adjust the arm, starting with the clavicle and working your way down. Since the clavicle is the root of the arm hierarchy, make very sure it's where you want it to be before moving on to the rest of the arm. To adjust the hand and fingers, select the hand, go to a Perspective view, and center the hand by hitting the ⬜ Zoom Extents icon. Then zoom in and adjust the fingers one by one, matching them up to the mesh (Figure 2.16, page 64).

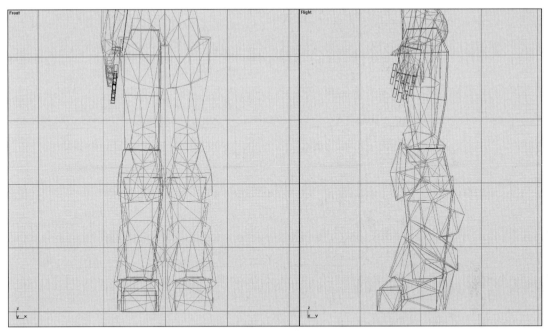

FIGURE 2.14   Align the leg to the mesh by scaling, rotating, and/or moving it into place.

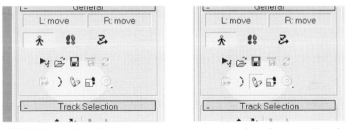

FIGURE 2.15   Rubber Band mode is another way to adjust the major Biped joints.

The first Spine object, as well as the Clavicle, Finger, and Toe objects, can be moved anywhere, because they take their pivot point with them. The rest of the Biped objects are anchored to their parent. This gets a little problematic with the Clavicle objects, because you're faced with the choice of moving them or rotating them to get the arm into the correct pose. As a general rule, it's best to rotate and scale them, rather than move them away from the neck.

Unhide everything hidden, re-freeze any character mesh objects, and then experience one of the coolest parts of character studio: copying and mirroring limb poses. Here's how it works. Double-click on the right (green) clavicle to select all the arm bones. Go over to the Keyframing

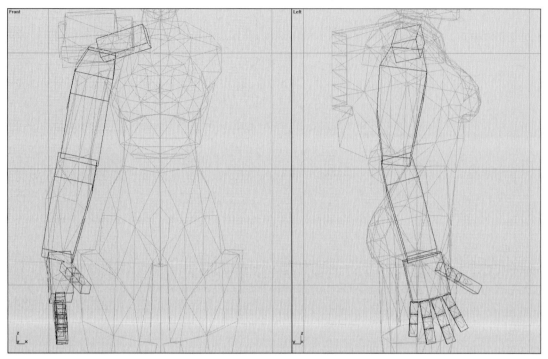

FIGURE 2.16 Adjusting the arm is easiest when the rest of the Biped objects are hidden.

sub-menu on the Motion panel and click on the ⬇ Copy Posture icon. As soon as you do this, the two icons below it will become selectable, because you've effectively pasted data onto your pose "clipboard" (Figure 2.17).

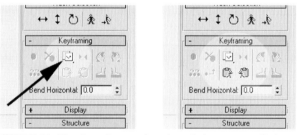

FIGURE 2.17 The Copy Posture function of character studio is a powerful animation ally.

Click the icon to the right (Paste Posture/Pose/Track Opposite) and the left arm bones assume the pose of the right arm bones. Double-click the right thigh, and repeat for the legs. As soon as your poses are copied over, you have a perfectly symmetrical stance (Figure 2.18).

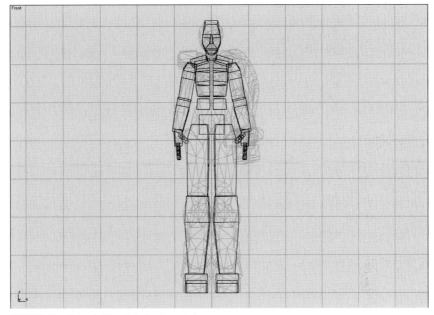

FIGURE 2.18   Betty's Biped rig is almost done.

Now, unfreeze the mesh objects, and hide everything but the Left Arm Biped objects as well as m_gunarm. Freeze the mesh object again, and rotate your view so you're looking at the left arm at the elbow, with the cylinder of her weapon arm seen from the side. Turn your grid off by hitting the G key so you can see your work more clearly (Figure 2.19).

With Betty's left arm, mirroring the pose of the right arm was close, but not exact. Because of the weapon system integrated into her armor, the elbow joint is encased in some sort of mechanical device, so the forearm has to travel as if it's locked into that mechanism. Thus, the elbow joint needs to originate from the center of the cylinder, as seen from the side in Figure 2.19 and Figure 2.20, and the arm itself has to line up more precisely with the orientation of the cylinder. Since the hand and fingers of the left arm won't be animated, ⬛, Uniformly Scale them down so they're very small. This will make it harder to inadvertently select them when visible (Figure 2.20).

That wraps up Betty's Biped adjustments. If you want to see what the final results should look like, load Betty05.max from the Chapter2 directory on this book's CD-ROM. Study the file and think about how you would approach your own unique character (Figure 2.21).

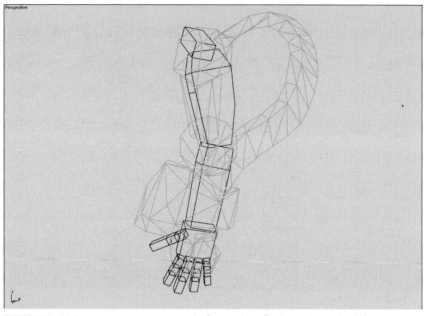

FIGURE 2.19   Hide unnecessary geometry before making final tweaks on the left arm.

FIGURE 2.20   Now the slightly asymmetrical left arm objects fit the mesh better.

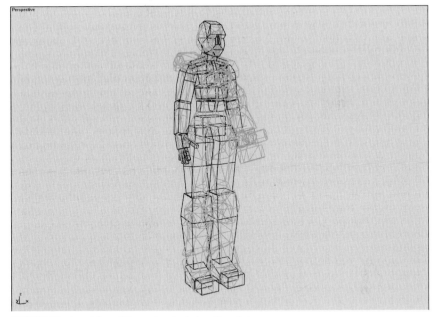

FIGURE 2.21   Load Betty05.max to study her Biped rig.

Saving the Biped's Pose

The final step in building that rig for your character is to save it. You should do this two ways, and in two character studio file formats. First, with your Biped still in Figure mode, go over to the Biped menu and click on the 💾 Save File icon. This brings up the Save dialog box, which allows you to save your Figure mode pose as a .fig file (Figure 2.22).

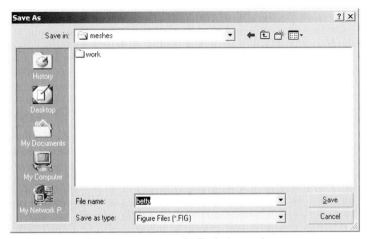

FIGURE 2.22   Make sure to save your .fig file for later reference.

Next, as added insurance, go out of Figure mode and save your current pose again, this time as a .bip file. Do this by once again hitting the Save File icon (Figure 2.23).

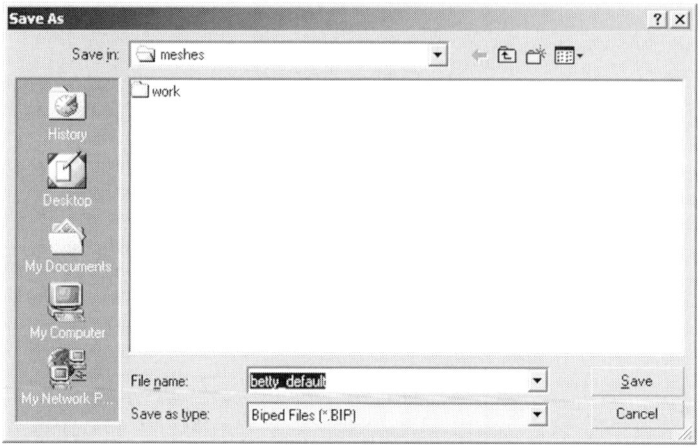

FIGURE 2.23   Saving the non-animated, posed Biped as a .bip file provides you with a handy reference pose.

That's it for a typical game character rig like Betty's. Now look at some other character types that can be rigged with Biped.

RIGGING A FOUR-LEGGED CHARACTER

Biped works great for a normal game character, but what about a four-legged, insectoid alien creature bent on the subjugation and consumption of mankind? In *Betty Bad*, our feisty, busty heroine must overcome the onslaught of an alien species as it tries to overrun a deep space asteroid mining complex, eating every miner in sight. A recurring and tough *hombre* is Widge. He and his cloned brethren are the main fodder for Betty's ZU88 OmniGun.

ON THE CD   Load Widge1.max from the Chapter2 directory on this book's CD-ROM (Figure 2.24).

Adjusting the Structure

In the Front viewport, create a Biped about 200 units in height that is placed to the side of Widge (Figure 2.25).

Since you're going to be scaling the Biped rather severely, don't worry too much about the base dimensions—the *composition* of the structure is

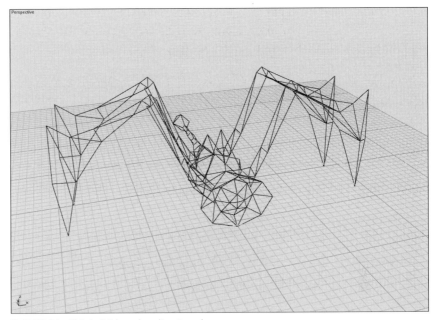

FIGURE 2.24   This is Widge, the alien invader.

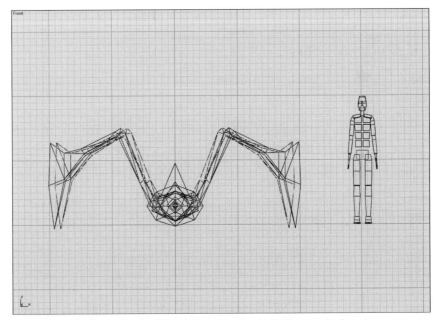

FIGURE 2.25   The basic Biped will be changed so drastically that its initial size is unimportant.

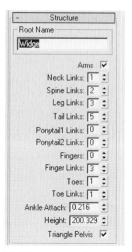

FIGURE 2.26   The structural configuration of a four-legged Biped is slightly different.

more important. Put the Biped into Figure mode and enter the values shown in Figure 2.26 in the Structure sub-menu.

Rename the Biped to "Widge." Of course the arms are necessary, so leave the Arms box checked. Widge's body bends in the middle only, so enter 2 for Spine Links. The Leg Links value is 3. *Tail Links* are necessary, so enter the maximum number of links you can have in a Biped: 5. Widge won't have hair, let alone ponytails, so leave the Ponytail boxes each set at 0.

The 3ds max tutorials, reference books, and even other third-party animation books suggest using Ponytail Links for a jaw or mouth rig. However, this is a bad idea because character studio is very demanding on your processor and RAM. Adding more indigenous bones to the Biped rig just makes the program work that much harder. Instead, create a box and link it to the Head object, since any objects in 3ds max can be used as bones and they are much less demanding on your CPU.

Adjusting the Body, Head, and Tail

Go to the Top viewport, freeze Widge's mesh objects, hide the Biped Arm objects, and begin adjusting his Biped by positioning and re-orienting the COM and pelvis (keep the legs unhidden to better see the pivot point where they meet the pelvis). Scale the pelvis so that the upper thigh attachments match the joints in the mesh. Go to the Right viewport, bring the Biped down so it's inside the mesh, then tilt the pelvis slightly by rotating the COM (Figure 2.27).

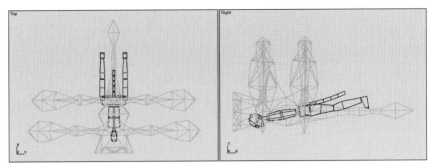

FIGURE 2.27   Begin adjusting the four-legged Biped by aligning the COM and pelvis.

Next, hide the legs so they're out of the way, and adjust the Tail object links so they correspond to the segments in the mesh. (Figure 2.28).

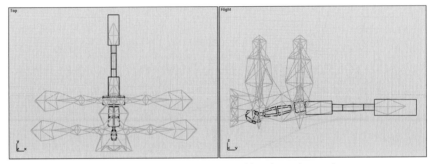

FIGURE 2.28   Align the Tail object links to the natural breaks in the mesh.

Next, adjust the Spine, Neck, and Head objects by scaling and rotating them into position. The neck really isn't important or necessary, so scale it down along the X-axis to make sure the Head object aligns with the head region of Widge. His head is just a termination of the body at the front, so it's okay to keep it facing downward (Figure 2.29).

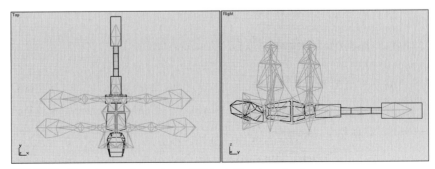

FIGURE 2.29   The strange dimensions of Widge's Biped continue...

Adjusting the Legs and Arms

Unhide all Biped objects, then rehide all but the right-side leg objects. Begin adjusting the leg by rotating the thigh 90 degrees along the Y-axis and 175 degrees along the X-axis (Figure 2.30).

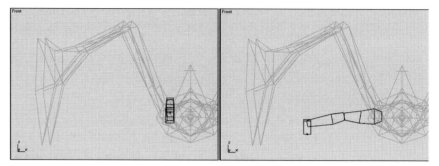

FIGURE 2.30   Rotate the leg along the X- and Y-axes.

Rotate and scale the leg into position, so it matches the geometry (Figure 2.31).

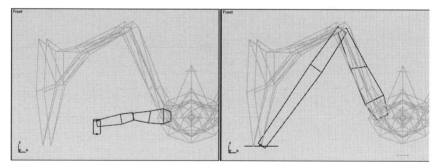

FIGURE 2.31   Scale and rotate the leg to further match the geometry.

The calf doesn't need to match the curved aspect of Widge's back forelimb, it just has to line up joint to limb-tip. The foot becomes nothing more than a handle for moving the leg, so flatten it to nothing and widen it for easier selection. The hand will be used in the same way as the foot, as a handle to move the leg around. (Figure 2.32).

Hide the leg, unhide the right arm objects, and match them up the same way you did using the leg objects. Remember that the point at which the hand meets the forearm (that is, the wrist) needs to line up with the end of the front forelimb (Figure 2.33).

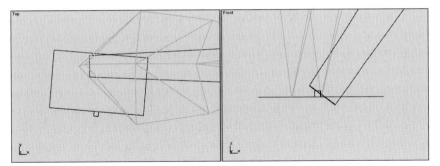

FIGURE 2.32   The foot is really just a handle with which to grab and animate the leg.

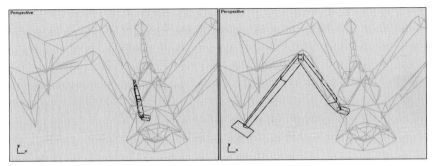

FIGURE 2.33   The arm objects are aligned just like the leg objects.

Now that the limbs on one side are complete, you can unhide the rest of the Biped, copy and mirror the limb poses, and you've got yourself a pesky alien critter rig! Feel free to load up Widge2.max from the Chapter2 directory on this book's CD-ROM if you want to look him over (Figure 2.34).

ON THE CD

OTHER TYPES OF CHARACTER RIGS

Biped can be used to rig almost any character type, from an evil alien to a giant bird to a tiny ant. To help you with some common deviations, this section will show you a few game characters that use a not-so-typical Biped rig.

A Dog

Dogs (and other four-legged animals) have a specific and unique musculature that requires careful consideration when setting up the rig. The knee, for example, is hard to see unless the dog is bending it. Instead of

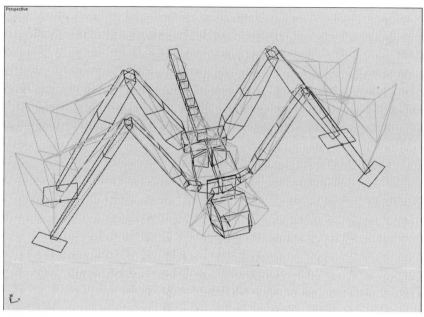

FIGURE 2.34 Widge's completed rig—one more ready-to-gib, four-legged bad guy.

walking around on its foot, it really walks around on its *toes*—the Biped needs to reflect this (Figure 2.35).

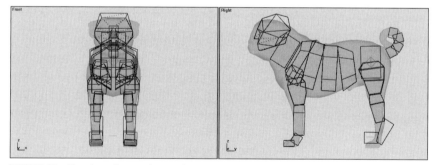

FIGURE 2.35 Biped can be used to make Rover . . . *sit*.

A Dolphin

If you've ever wondered why you would ever *uncheck* the Arms box in a Biped's structure, wonder no more. How about when you're animating a dolphin? It's a mammal, right? It probably shares our intelligence, why not our Bipeds? (See Figure 2.36.)

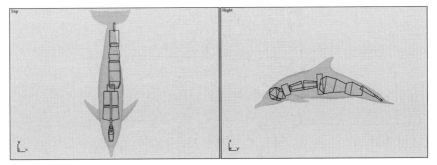

FIGURE 2.36   Finally, a reason for the option to not have arms!

While it's true the arms could have been kept *on*, to drive the flippers for example, it depends on how complex the animation needs to be. Only one leg is really needed, so the other one can be scaled down to nothing. The pelvis is placed in the center of the body, which facilitates flips and rolls through the water around that pivot point. However, the trickiest part about rigging a dolphin or shark with Biped is figuring out how to create parts like the dorsal fin. One solution is to add another bone; another is to be very careful when weighting the character's mesh so that it deforms properly.

A Goat-Girl?

Animating a tri-jointed legged character, like a chicken walker Mech (think AT-ST in *Return of the Jedi*), or a "Goat-Girl" demoness with goat's legs, is allowed for by the designers of character studio: there's a fourth leg link you can add to your Biped. However, using it is a bit problematic due to the way it recalculates the IK solution. Called a *horselink*, this fourth Biped object is supposed to help mimic the mechanics of a horse-like leg. Unfortunately, this extra bone added to the leg can never be a forward kinematic parent of the foot and is always slave to its inverse kinematics solution. Compare the following three leg configurations shown in Figure 2.37.

In Figure 2.37, Biped A is a normal configuration, Biped B uses a fourth leg link, and Biped C shows both thighs rotated 180 degrees along the X-axis. When animating a character with tri-jointed legs, start with a stance that is kind of a squatting position (it looks like zigzag, or a backwards Z). The deeper the squat, the more severe the zigzag. With Goat-Girl, there's at least three ways to give her a rig that supports her mesh. You can go with Biped A's design (a normal setup), ignoring the back joint altogether, and dial in the weighting to compensate. Or, you can

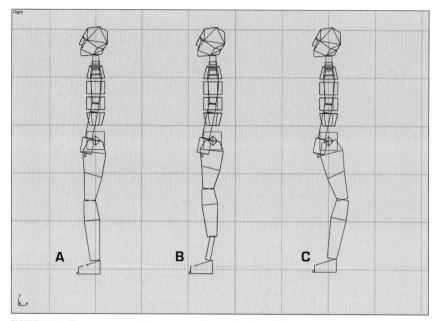

FIGURE 2.37 There are several ways to configure the Biped legs.

wrestle with that "horselink" and fit it to your mesh, as shown in Biped B. Your third choice is to go with Biped C's setup, flipping the legs around; this ignores the often unnoticeable knee joint above it and relies (like Biped A) on proper weighting (Figure 2.38).

The benefit of the third solution is that you can plug in normal .bip — they are reversed only in regards to the knee. Try this technique to animate a character that moves solely by walking on his hands!

FACIAL RIGS

In a rendered character situation, you typically use *morph targets* to animate the face. Morph (short for *metamorphosis*) targets are posed head and face shapes that are used as keyframes for emotion and phoneme recognition for lip-synching. Unfortunately, in most real-time game situations, characters can only have animated faces if they use some kind of a bone system. While Biped doesn't have any automatic facial-rig solutions, it's easy to add bones and link them to the Biped Head object. The type of facial rig you use depends on how detailed the facial animations need to be and how high the mesh's resolution is. For example, the dog head mesh shown in Figure 2.39 has enough polygons to support almost any level of facial animation.

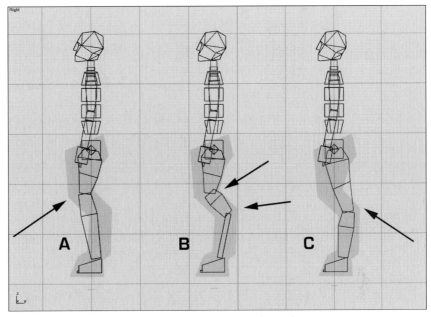

FIGURE 2.38   Choose from three ways to skin that goat-legged cat.

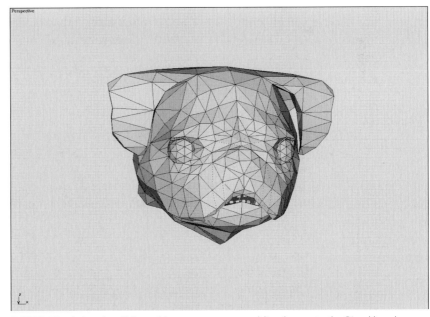

FIGURE 2.39   Animating Fido reciting poetry means adding bones to the Biped head.

As mentioned, when using Biped to animate your characters, you have to add bones to it in order to create a face rig. In 3ds max, adding bones is as easy as linking a box to the Biped. Of course, controllers and other more complicated elements can be thrown into the mix, as well.

For a real-time game character, you have about four levels of rig setup to accommodate options from a low-res, low-poly case to a high-res, high-poly case. For lack of better terminology, call them *Face Rig Level 1* through *Face Rig Level 4* (this section will cover the first three levels).

Face Rig Level 1

- Single jaw bone (with Nub)

Known as the "muppet" approach, this rig is used frequently with game characters, because a hinged jawbone can be moved programmatically to key off sound wave amplitude. The reasoning is that a character has to open its mouth wider when speaking loudly. Simply create an equal-sided box, sized to fit within the mesh. Center the pivot point on the box by going to the ⚒ Hierarchy panel, click Pivot, click Affect Pivot Only, and then click on Center Pivot To Object. Create a dummy object by clicking on the ▫ Helpers icon, making the Dummy button active, and clicking anywhere in an orthogonal (F, K, L, R, T, B) viewport. Place the dummy object in front of the jaw (and the mesh), and link it to the box you created earlier by clicking the ⬚ Select and Link icon active, clicking on the dummy object, and dragging the dashed Link line to the box. Rename the box as "Jaw" and the dummy as "Jaw Nub" (Figure 2.40).

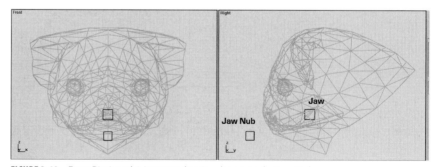

FIGURE 2.40   Face Rig Level 1 just needs a jaw bone and a jaw Nub.

 Character studio needs the Nub not only to act as an end effector for an IK chain, but also to supply a link in Physique to which vertices can be assigned. The advantage of using a dummy object and naming it "Nub" conforms to the system already

established by Biped. It also helps that all dummy objects can be hidden with the checking of the right box in the Display panel.

Face Rig Level 2

- Single jaw bone (with Nub)
- Eyelids that can blink
- Eyes that move

At Face Rig Level 2, the facial rig involves animating the eyes and therefore requires some forethought when modeling. The eyes should be closed when Physique is applied, because it's easy to deform the mesh *opening* the eyes rather than *closing* them (think blink). A simple patch with geometry can serve as an eye by including something distinguishable as an iris (a few vertices will work), and a G-Sphere (or partial G-Sphere) of moderate resolution can serve as an eyeball *bone* (Figure 2.41).

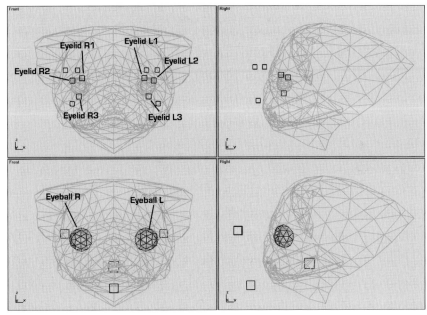

FIGURE 2.41   Face Rig Level 2 has bones to blink and move the eyes.

Eyeballs are made of fluid and are very malleable; it would take an impractical amount of geometry to represent the viscous liquid found in your peepers. Form-fitting a curved sheet of triangles is the best way to represent an eye object.

Keeping left and right facial bones symmetrical (even in naming) helps you keep track of what's where much more easily. Even though the eyeballs are partial objects, their pivot points are the same as if they were centered on a whole G-Sphere.

Face Rig Level 3

- Single jaw bone (with Nub)
- Eyelids that can blink
- Eyes that move
- Eyebrows that move
- Articulate lips
- An articulate tongue

Moving up to a Face Rig Level 3 means adding the final components that give any character realistic phonemes and emotions: *eyebrows*, *lips*, and *tongue* (Figure 2.42).

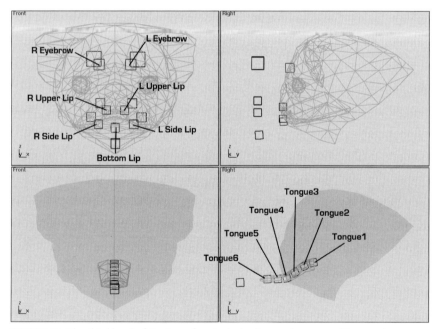

FIGURE 2.42   The third level of rigging a face includes lips, eyebrows, and tongue bones.

In Figure 2.42, the tongue is shown separately for clarity's sake; really it is inside the mouth, intersecting the head geometry. This is because you always have to link a mesh to a skeleton in its *extended* state. Like a tail or a loincloth that is rarely fully straight and extended, the tongue is posed only *after* it's been attached to its bone.

If you were to continue to the fourth level of face rig, it would include even more bones that could be used to deform areas of the face like cheeks, ears, more eyebrow areas, and so on—but this is enough for now. To further examine the relationship between the linked bones of the face and Biped, load up Doghead.max from the Chapter2 directory on this book's CD-ROM.

ON THE CD

A Higher-Resolution Character Rig

Most typical real-time game characters are made up of anywhere from 500 to 1,500 polygons. While that number increases every year as the hardware and rendering technology evolves, any character over 2,000 polygons can be considered a *high-polygon* character. Resolution obviously has an impact on the speed of gameplay when the character is implemented. It also has an impact on the type of rig you use.

Ta Da Vinci or Not Ta Da Vinci?

In 1490, Leonardo da Vinci made a famous sketch based on an architectural book by Vitruvius. The illustration attempted to verify the mathematical formulas that Vetruvius proposed to describe the proportions of the human figure (Figure 2.43).

Betty wasn't in this da Vinci pose when you built her Biped rig earlier, because of her resolution. Since she comprises about 2,000 triangles, she is still low-poly enough to warrant the *manually* assignment of weighting values, which can be done in a relatively short amount of time. Her pose isn't as important, so her model was built in a more casual stance. The opposite would be true if she were a higher polygon character like the one shown in Figure 2.44.

This character is in a da Vinci pose because she has 5,663 polygons. She's built for a real-time application—not a game—that incorporates dancing to music via music-playing plugins like WinAmp (a demo version can be found on this book's companion CD-ROM). Her resolution demands that she be in this pose, because it's the best way to allow for automatic generation of weighting values based on influence envelopes. In other words, the jumping-jack position keeps the main bones of an underlying skeleton far enough away from each other that the surrounding vertices are influenced by the right bone.

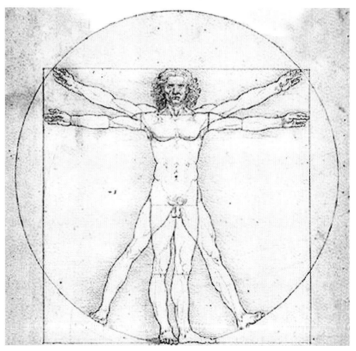

FIGURE 2.43   The pose of da Vinci's "Vitruvian Man" illustrates the relative proportions of the human form.

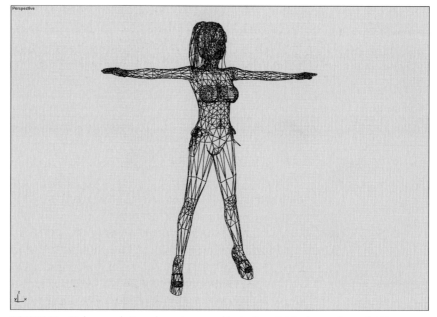

FIGURE 2.44   Higher resolution characters need to be in a da Vinci pose for weighting.

While it is crucial that your character model be in some sort of default pose that makes it easy to texture (don't hand a texture artist a character in an action pose and expect him to create the mapping coordinates from it!), the da Vinci pose is an unnatural position that most characters would never be in. However, like the tongue example mentioned earlier, it represents the extreme pose a character would be in, thus making any pose up to that point not only possible, but realistic as well. Figure 2.45 shows the rig for the mesh shown in Figure 2.44.

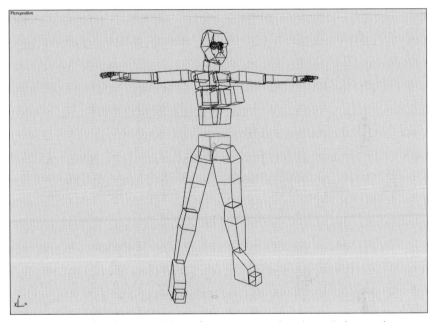

FIGURE 2.45   A rig for a hi-res mesh has a few more extras than the typical game character.

A Face Rig for a Higher-Resolution Mesh

Because of the way she's implemented, the face rig of the character shown in Figure 2.46 only needs to support an ability to *show emotion*. She has eyebrows, eyeballs, eyelids, jaw, and lips, but she doesn't need a tongue.

The other reason she doesn't have a tongue is that there is a clipping issue that is an unfortunate limitation of the rendering engine. At the distance she's seen on-screen, only one or two pixels of pink from a tongue would be displayed. The renderer doesn't know whether to display the white pixel of her teeth or the darker one of her tongue—the latter mightmake the character look like she's missing a front tooth! Thus, she never does more than part her lips as she's boogying to the beat.

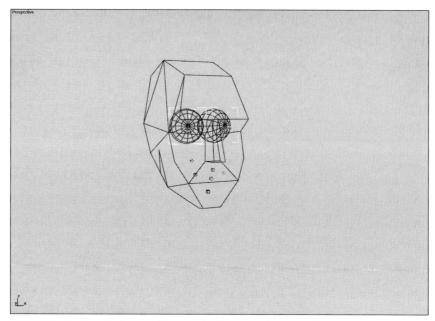

FIGURE 2.46 A closer look at the face rig of a higher resolution mesh.

Adding Bones and Using Different Controllers

In addition to the extra face bones, this character also has objects attached to her torso that simulate her breasts realistically moving as she dances (Figure 2.47).

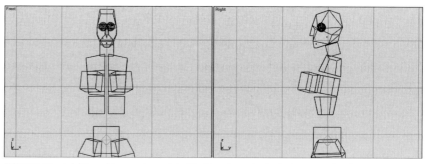

FIGURE 2.47 Additional bones are added to the character's rig to move her breast geometry realistically.

ON THE CD

Once the box objects are oriented and aligned to the mesh, they can be assigned a *Spring* controller to give them ancillary motion as the character dances (Figure 2.48). Load Bikini1.max from the from the Chapter2 directory on this book's CD-ROM.

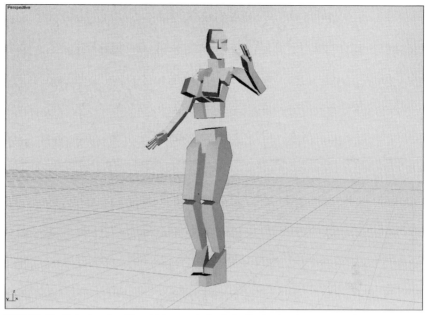

FIGURE 2.48   This dancing Biped is in need of a little "Spring" to her step—a Spring controller.

The Biped already has a dance animation applied to it. Hit the ▶. Play Animation button to the lower right of your screen and watch the animation. The blue boxes don't move aside from being attached to the spine. Now select either box, go to the Motion panel, and select the Position track so it's highlighted and the ▶ Assign Position Controller button becomes selectable (Figure 2.49).

Click on the green arrows to bring up a list of controllers you can assign to the Position track of the object (Figure 2.50).

Select Spring and hit the OK button. You've just assigned a Spring controller to the object. Now, under Properties, give it some Spring Dynamics values that will cause it to bounce as the character moves: Enter a value of 500 for Mass and 0.3 for Drag (Figure 2.51).

Close the dialog box, and assign a controller with the same values to the Position track of the other object.

Always close the Properties dialog box after entering values in the Spring controller dialog box for the first time. If you don't, and then you click on another object, the dialog box stays up; it may make you think a controller's been assigned to it already.

FIGURE 2.49 Access animation tracks that can have controllers assigned to them in the Motion panel.

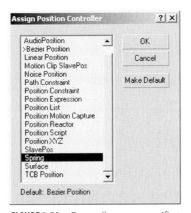

FIGURE 2.50 Controllers are specific to the animation track selected.

Once both objects have Spring controllers assigned to them, deselect everything, close any dialog boxes, and hit the slash (/) key as a shortcut to Play Animation (Figure 2.52).

Feel free to experiment with different values for Mass and Drag, but as a general rule of thumb, make the objects heavy enough to be noticed when they move (500 is a good number to start with). The higher the value for Drag (given the same value for Mass), the *less* the amount of bounce there will be. Again, try different variations, and even mess with

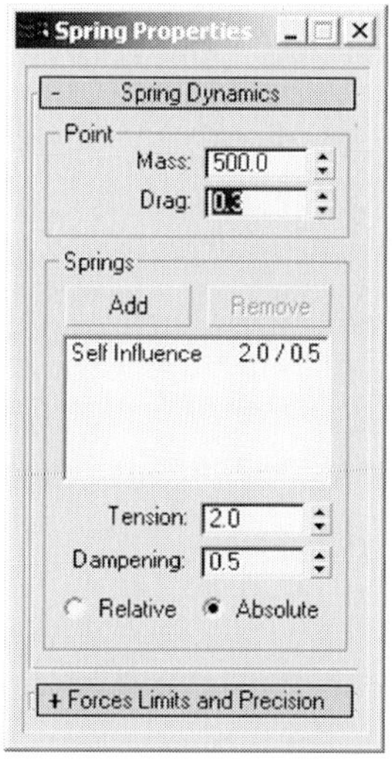

FIGURE 2.51   A Spring controller needs enough Mass to be noticeable in its effect.

FIGURE 2.52   Now the dancing Biped enjoys a bit more bounce in her motions.

Tension and Dampening if you want. However, keep in mind that in order to change those values, you first have to have the Self Influence line in the dialog window selected (Figure 2.53).

FIGURE 2.53 Self Influence must be highlighted before Tension and Dampening can be adjusted.

 Once a Spring controller has been applied to an object, you can access the dialog boxes for it on the Motion panel itself, or right-click on the Position track, and click on Properties (Figure 2.54).

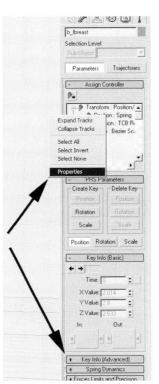

FIGURE 2.54 There are two ways to access the Spring controller parameters.

SUMMARY

Of the two parts that make up the character studio plug-in, Biped and Physique, Biped is the half that provides a quick and easy way to get a character's underlying *skeleton* built, complete with IK, constraints, and pose sharing. Almost any character imaginable can be rigged with Biped. The greatest benefit of using it is that you can use the rigging for a similar character later on.

To rig your character, load the character mesh you'll be fitting the Biped to, and freeze it. Create a Biped, put it into Figure mode, and move, rotate, and scale your Biped to fit it. Start with the root, or Center of Mass (COM), move to the pelvis, and then to the spine. Adjust the limbs, beginning with the thigh and the clavicle. However, if your character has a *symmetrical* set of arms and legs, only pose one side or the other, then copy and mirror that pose to the other side. The base pose that your character and Biped assume for the default position depends on the resolution of the character's mesh. The "da Vinci pose" should be used for higher resolution characters that are too time-consuming to weight manually, vertex by vertex. It's up to you to decide whether or not to build a lower resolution character in a da Vinci pose.

Since most real-time game engines don't support morph targets to animate talking and other facial expressions, bones have to be used to deform the face. For facial rigs, you have to build and link objects to the Biped's Head object (any object in 3ds max can be used as a bone). The type of facial rig you use depends on how many polygons are in the face and the amount of animation required. Finally, assign *Motion controllers* to the bones attached to the Biped; this gives extra, ancillary motion to them that is calculated automatically by 3ds max at playback.

3

WEIGHTING A CHARACTER USING MANUAL VERTEX ASSIGNMENT

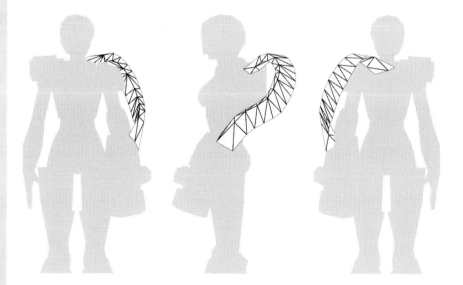

Once you have your mesh fitted with a Biped, you need to apply Physique to it. Again, the analogy behind Physique's role in animating your real-time game character is that it turns your mesh into a "skin" that the Biped "wears." Animating the Biped deforms the mesh, because vertices of the mesh are linked to one or more of its underlying "bones." When exported into a game engine, the Biped is invisible in the final animation, so it appears that only your mesh is animating. The controls and parameters of Physique give you the ability to dial in the best ratio of *influence* that the Biped links will have over the vertices of the mesh. Getting this *weighting* of the vertices right is a major factor in making your animations look great.

A TYPICAL GAME CHARACTER

A typical game character is one that comprises up to 2,000 polygons and has to perform a range of animations and functions. For most of these characters, the lower number of triangles makes them candidates for *manually* assigning vertices to links, rather than for using envelopes. This allows the greatest control over a character that has relatively little real estate to manage. It also places less of a constraint on the initial pose of the mesh and doesn't require you to build it in the restrictive "da Vinci pose." Still, manually assigning vertices is always going to be a slower process than using envelopes, but it teaches you the fundamentals of weighting and links. The fact that the vertices of real-time characters need to be assigned as *Rigid* also makes manually assigning them desirable—and easy. Like anything else, once you get used to it, assigning vertices manually really isn't so tough.

Steps to Applying Physique

1. Select all the mesh objects that make up the character.
2. Apply Physique to the mesh objects.
3. Attach to Node by clicking on the pelvis of the pre-fitted Biped.
4. Select Rigid under Vertex – Link Assignment.
5. Take the Biped out of Figure mode and apply an animation to it.
6. Adjust the weighting of the character by adjusting the Envelope settings under the Physique Sub-Objects rollout menu, and adjusting individual vertex weighting assignments.
7. Toggle Initial Skeletal Pose on and off to see the effects of the weighting.
8. Save the weighting as a .phy file.

Applying and Initializing Physique

Load Betty06.max from the Chapter3 directory on this book's CD-ROM, put her Biped into Figure mode, hit the H key to bring up your "hit list," and select all the m_ objects (Figure 3.1).

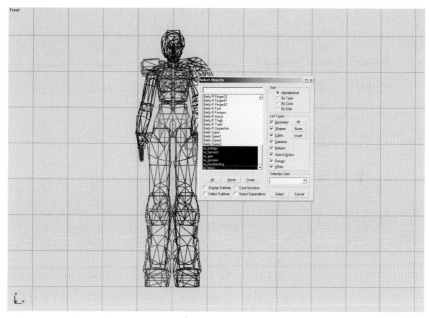

FIGURE 3.1   Select all the mesh objects that will have Physique applied to them.

Assigning Physique to all your character's mesh objects at once is helpful, because adjusting the parameters of Physique for one object is reflected in all the objects to which the modifier was assigned.

Once they're all selected, go to the Modify panel and assign the Physique modifier to them. Initialize Physique by clicking the Attach to Node button on the Physique rollout menu so that it's active (Figure 3.2).

Now zoom in so that the pelvis of the Biped can be easily clicked on. Click on it, and the Physique Initialization dialog box will come up. Leave everything as is, except for the Vertex – Link Assignment selection. Change it from Deformable to Rigid (Figure 3.3).

Even if Deformable is chosen, the envelopes, links, or vertices can be changed to Rigid afterward. Choosing Rigid during initialization saves time.

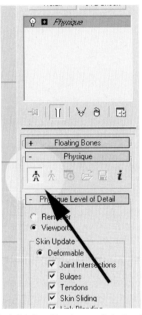

FIGURE 3.2   To initialize Physique, click the Attach to Node button to make it active and click on the Pelvis Biped object.

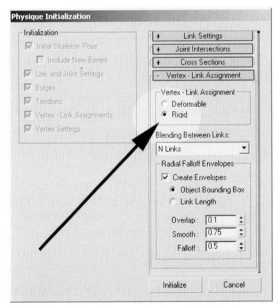

FIGURE 3.3   Most of the preset values in the Physique Initialization dialog box are acceptable when you begin weighting your character.

Click Initialize; you may have to wait a few seconds as character studio works out the weighting solutions. When it's through, a gold stick figure will appear inside your mesh (Figure 3.4).

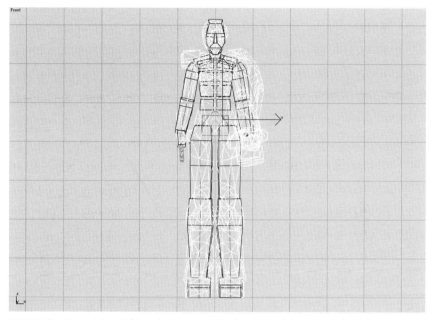

FIGURE 3.4   The gold stick figure inside your Physiqued mesh is really all the links being displayed.

Real-time game engines cannot take advantage of assigning Deformable vertices to your mesh and will usually convert them to Rigid upon export from 3ds max. Also, because of this limitation, Physique's spline-based deformation parameters found in the Link, Bulge, and Tendon Sub-Objects settings cannot be utilized in the same way as in a strictly rendered character.

Right-click anywhere in your viewport, and click Hide Unselected from the Quad menu; this gets rid of everything but the mesh objects (Figure 3.5).

Assigning Vertices to a Link

It's always best to start with the easier objects (or elements of an object) that can be weighted and then hidden—*easy* just means the object should be isolated, and the link the vertices need to be assigned to should be readily apparent. In Betty's case, m_gun is the first lucky candidate.

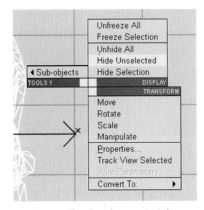

FIGURE 3.5 The Quad menu in 3ds max is a quick and easy way to hide or freeze objects.

Select it, and hit the small plus (+) sign beside Physique in the modifier stack; this opens up the available sub-objects. Select Vertex, change N Links to No Blending under Blending Between Links, and click the Select button to make it active (Figure 3.6).

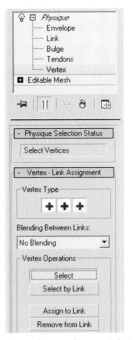

FIGURE 3.6 In order to adjust weighting values, you have to be in one of Physique's Sub-Object menus.

Select all the vertices of m_gun, click the Assign to Link button to make it active, make the Vertex type *Rigid* (green), and click on the left forearm link to assign the vertices to it (Figure 3.7).

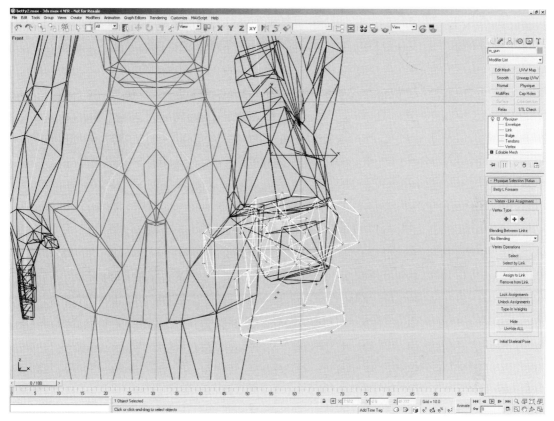

FIGURE 3.7   With the vertices selected, just click on the link to which you want to assign them.

To complete the vertex re-assignment, you need to click on the Lock Assignments button. Locking the vertices ensures they stay assigned to the link you want them assigned to, even if you adjust the envelope or values for other links (Figure 3.8).

Hide everything but m_headarmleg, and you can begin adjusting its weighting.

With the Vertex sub-object selected on the Physique menu, right-clicking to bring up the Quad menu doesn't work. You have to be out of Sub-Object mode, so click on the word Physique to make it the active level in the stack. Then, right-clicking will bring up the menu again.

FIGURE 3.8   It's very important to *lock* the vertices after manually assigning them to a link.

Start with the head element of the mesh, since it's easiest. Select all its vertices, making sure No Blending is up instead of N Links, and assign them to the Betty Head link (Figure 3.9).

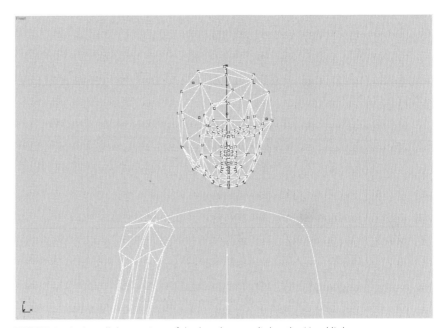

FIGURE 3.9   Assign all the vertices of the head to one link—the Head link.

Next, move on to the toe of the boot shape and assign the vertices to the Betty L Toe link. Use Arc Rotate to make sure you assign the vertices to the proper link (Figure 3.10).

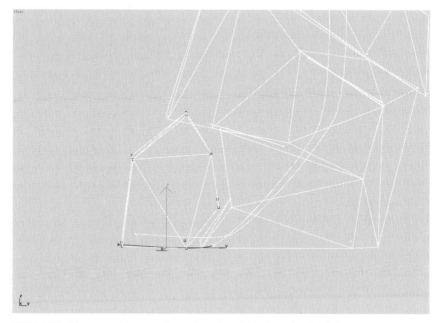

FIGURE 3.10   The toe vertices can be assigned exclusively to the Toe link.

When going through the weighting process, it helps to hide *the vertices of the mesh that have been assigned. This way, you can tell what has to be weighted next, and it un-clutters your work area (Figure 3.11).*

So far, you've manually assigned vertices to specific links, but more often than not, you'll need to have vertices assigned to *more* than one link. To do this, you have to learn about . . .

Typing in Weighting Values

Select the vertices of the foot shown in Figure 3.12 by dragging your selection fence across them.

Assign them to the Betty L Foot link, and then select only the vertices near where the ankle would be. Click on the Type-In Weights button on the Vertex menu to bring up the Type-In Weights dialog box (Figure 3.13).

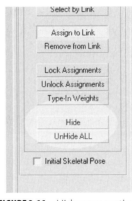

FIGURE 3.11 Hide your vertices once they've been weighted.

FIGURE 3.12 Select and assign the vertices of the foot.

By default, only the links that the vertices have been assigned to are shown. To see *all* the links, you need to click All Links. Do so now, so you can assign the ankle vertices to both the Foot and the Calf links. Simply highlight Betty L Calf by clicking on it, and enter a value of 1 in the Weight box (Figure 3.14).

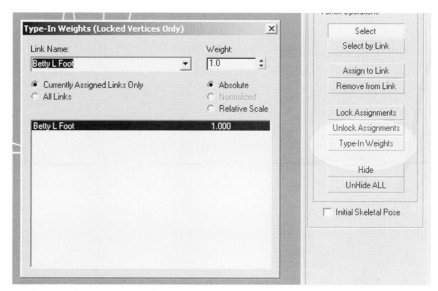

FIGURE 3.13   The Type-in Weights dialog box can only be accessed if the vertices are locked.

FIGURE 3.14   You can share influence on a vertex among as many links as you want.

 When sharing influence between links, the values can be anything you want them to be. Instead of 1 and 1 for example, two links can equally influence a vertex by having values of 0.5 and 0.5. However, if you assign weighting to a link, or number of links, and the sum doesn't add up to 1, Physique will automatically add influence to one link or the other so that the total weighting does equal 1.

Unhide Betty L Foot, and rotate it along the Z-axis to test the weighting (Figure 3.15).

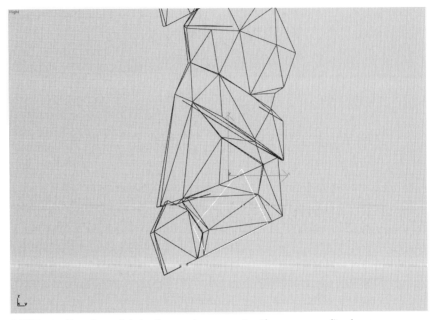

FIGURE 3.15   Test the weighting by rotating or moving the corresponding bone.

Hit Ctrl-Z to "undo" the foot rotation and re-hide it. Select all the vertices of the lower leg from above the ankle to mid-way at the knee, and assign them to the L Calf link (Figure 3.16).

Zoom in on the knee area and select the line of vertices where the Thigh and Calf links meet. Bring up the Type-in Weights dialog box again, and enter a value of 1 for the parent Betty L Thigh (Figure 3.17).

Unhide Betty L Calf to bend the lower leg and test the deformation of the knee geometry (Figure 3.18).

It looks acceptable, but it could look better with some further modification. Assign the values shown in Figure 3.19 to the indicated vertices of the knee.

Now when the leg bends, the geometry deforms better, holding the shape of the knee more fully (Figure 3.20).

Don't be afraid to spread influences across as many vertices and as many links as you need, above or below the link, to achieve the proper deformation. Now, select the rest of the vertices on the left leg, assign them to the Thigh link, lock them, and then hide them.

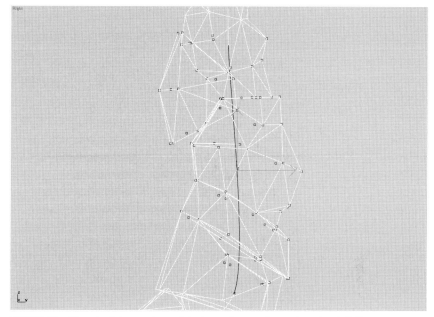

FIGURE 3.16   Almost all the vertices of the lower leg can be assigned to L Calf.

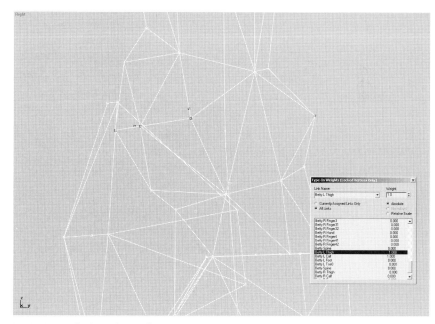

FIGURE 3.17   The knee has to feature shared influence by both the Thigh and Calf links.

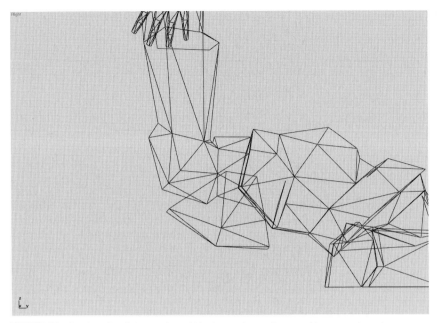

FIGURE 3.18 Testing the deformation of the knee shows the need for more tweaking.

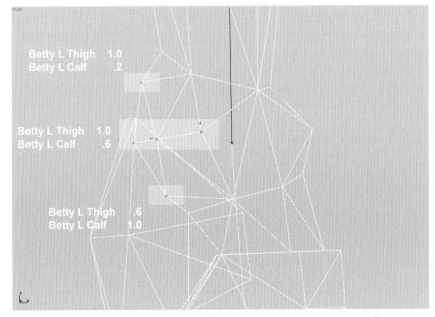

FIGURE 3.19 Including more vertices to be shared by the thigh and calf makes for better results.

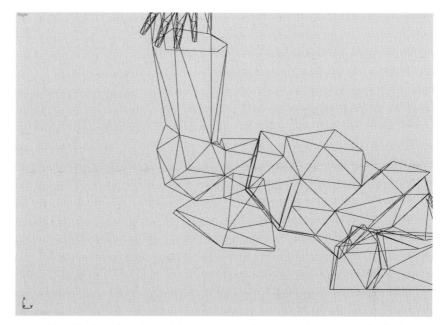

FIGURE 3.20   The knee bends much better now, and retains its shape more effectively.

 If, in the course of testing your weighting, you somehow screw up the pose of the limb you're moving, simply unhide the other limb, and copy/mirror its pose on the one that's screwed up.

Removing Vertices from Links

With the left leg and head taken care of, it's time to weight the arm. First, though, you'll try a different approach to testing the weighting, by animating the arm bones. Unhide all the Biped objects that make up Betty's right arm. Click on her forearm, and turn Figure mode off. Make the Rotate Transform active, and while at Frame 0, hit the Set Key button on the Biped menu to set a keyframe for the rotation track of Betty R Forearm (Figure 3.21).

Next, turn the █ Animate button on (make it red), go to Frame 5, and with the forearm still selected, rotate it –75 degrees along the Z-axis (Figure 3.22).

Obviously, there are a few things wrong with this picture. Go to the Front viewport and select the character's mesh again. Go to the Modify panel, and select all the vertices of the right arm element. Click the

FIGURE 3.21 The Set Key button sets a keyframe for the selected Biped object.

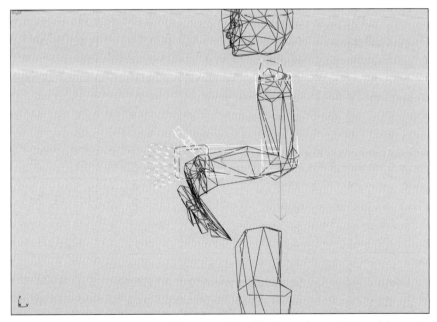

FIGURE 3.22 Bending the arm out of Figure mode will help test the weighting of the mesh.

Remove From Link button to make it active, drag your selection fence across the leg and torso links, and let go (Figure 3.23).

As they're removed from the influence of the incorrect links, the vertices of the arm that were all stretched and deformed now snap to their proper position. Hide everything but m_headarmleg again, and make the Vertex sub-object of Physique active.

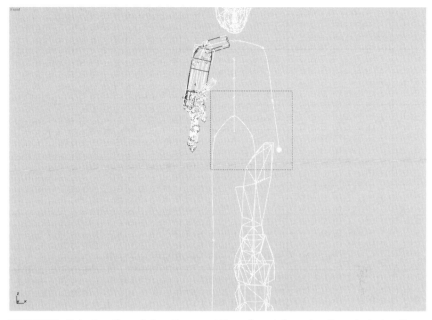

FIGURE 3.23   Selecting these links will prevent them from influencing the selected vertices.

Another way to test the weighting of a character's mesh is to drop an animation into the Biped, and see where the problem areas are when the mesh is deformed through the movements. Bending the arm like you did earlier is a step in that direction. However, if the animation doesn't have an "at rest" frame like you set at Frame 0 for the arm, there is another way to toggle the character's mesh back and forth from animated to non-animated: Uncheck and check the Initial Skeletal Pose checkbox (Figure 3.24).

Click on the checkbox to turn *on* the Initial Skeletal Pose, and continue weighting the right arm. Start by assigning all of the upper arm vertices (down to the bottom of the elbow) to the Betty R UpperArm link (Figure 3.25).

Adjusting the Elbow Area

Since Betty has big shoulder pads, there doesn't have to be too much effort put into a normally time-intensive area: the shoulders. However, the elbow still needs to go through a trial-and-error process to see what the weighting values should be. Near the center of the elbow, the influence should roughly be equal to, or slightly biased towards, the UpperArm link

FIGURE 3.24   The Initial Skeletal Pose option helps you go from an animated to unanimated state.

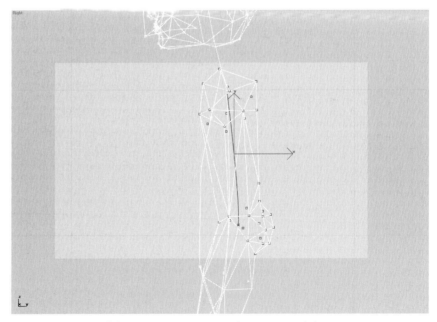

FIGURE 3.25   Assign all the upper arm vertices to the UpperArm link.

(think knee and thigh). Vertices that are farther above the elbow will be less influenced by the forearm, and vertices below the elbow will be less influenced by the upper arm.

Whenever it's a certainty *that two links will be influencing a set of vertices like the elbow, go ahead and assign them all an equal weighting (1 to the parent link and 1 to the child link). Of course, these values won't stay that way for all the vertices, but it's a quick way to assign them to the right links simultaneously, causing the default Currently Assigned Links Only to be a boon and not a handicap when tweaking the values.*

Zoom in on the elbow area, and only select those vertices that make up the elbow. Bring up the Type-In Weights dialog box, click All Links, and assign the vertices to Betty R Forearm by clicking on it and typing in 1 (the vertices will turn dark green). Toggle Initial Skeletal Pose back and forth by unchecking and checking its box to see the effects the weighting change has on the elbow (Figure 3.26).

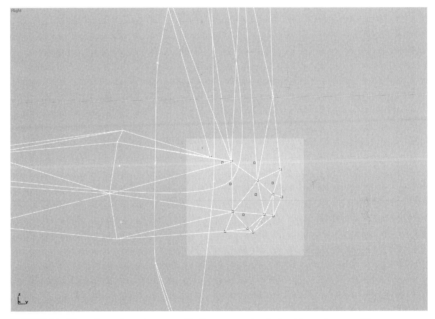

FIGURE 3.26   The elbow here has equal influence on both the UpperArm and Forearm links.

Unfortunately, the Forearm link does not immediately follow the UpperArm link in the Type-In Weights dialog box. Several links that are children *to the Forearm appear first. Be careful not to accidentally assign weighting to a Hand link when you think you're assigning it to the Forearm (Figure 3.27)!*

While the weighting doesn't look bad, giving all of the vertices equal influence from both links detracts from the intent of the geometry, which

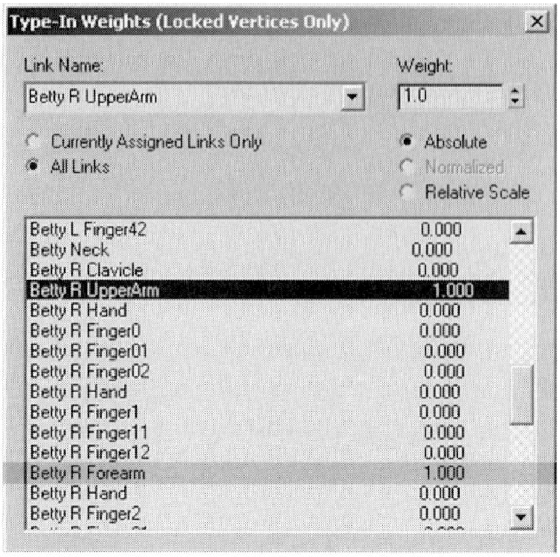

FIGURE 3.27   Beware the confusing out-of-order Forearm link.

is to portray a thick elbow pad. Therefore, a few adjustments need to be made. By toggling the Initial Skeletal Pose box on and off, you can get a rough feel for what the values of the vertices should be changed to. For example, the vertices at the top of the elbow need to be influenced less by the forearm so the elbow can retain more of its shape, but the vertices at the bottom of the elbow don't need to be changed as much. Turn your Initial Skeletal Pose back on, and try the values shown in Figure 3.28 for the elbow area.

Now when the elbow is bent, it looks better and keeps the shape of the elbow pad intact. (Figure 3.29).

That solution solves the problem with the back of the elbow, but the front of the joint (the bottom of the bicep area) needs to be tweaked as well. With a weighting of 1 and 1, the arm crimps enough to make the bicep shrink, instead of remaining the same or bulging. However, if you bias the vertices more toward the UpperArm link, the forearm geometry will look strange (Figure 3.30).

A solution to the forearm deforming the way it does is to lessen the contrast of the elbow juncture; transfer some of the influence from the forearm vertices over to the UpperArm link. It doesn't have to be much, and can vary from character to character. Select the three vertices at the top of Betty's arm in the bent position, lock them, and add the Betty R UpperArm link to the links that influence the vertices. A value of 0.1 should work fine (Figure 3.31).

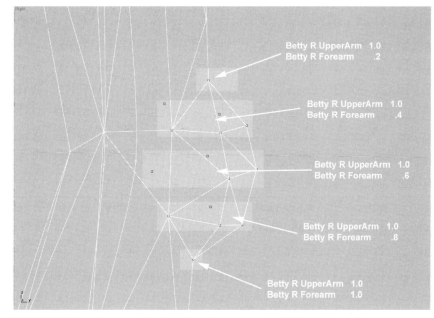

FIGURE 3.28   The elbow needs to be biased more toward the UpperArm link.

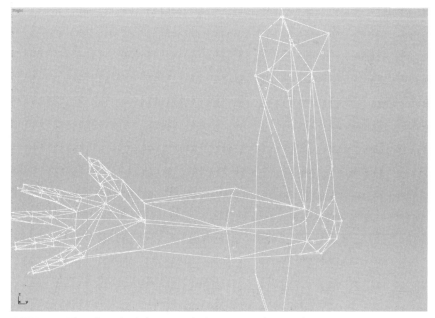

FIGURE 3.29   The elbow looks better with the new weighting values.

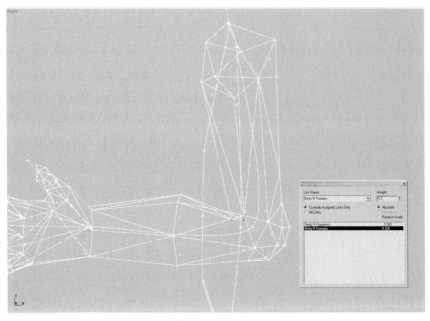

FIGURE 3.30 Biasing the front of the elbow joint to the UpperArm link causes a strange deformation.

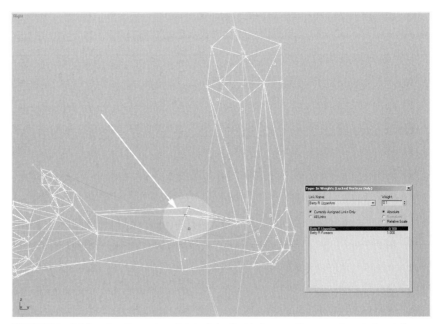

FIGURE 3.31 Adding the UpperArm link to links that influence these vertices helps deform the forearm better.

This juggling of weighting influence between adjoining links is necessary to get around the limitation, which is a drawback of most generic weighting algorithms found in most programs like Physique. Only with a true "sliding skin" weighting system can areas like elbows, knees, wrists, ankles, necks, and even shoulders and hips be 100 percent accurate in the deformation of polygonal skin. However, keep in mind that this only applies to real-time games; movies featuring CG-rendered characters employ all kinds of complex skeletal and musculature algorithms to simulate skin and muscle movement.

Working on the Hand and Fingers

While most real-time game characters have mitts for fingers and clubs for fists, Betty has the full use of five digits on her right hand. The weighting for wrists is somewhat similar to that for ankles; select the vertices at the joint, and give them equal influence by both Forearms and any of the internal Hand links.

 To avoid too extreme a deformation at the wrist area, sometimes it's a good idea to build your character with the palms facing forward instead of downward. This may be as simple as turning the hand geometry, and then turning any bad edges (Figure 3.32).

The fingers need to share influence between links at the knuckles. Starting at the end link of the finger, and working your way towards the

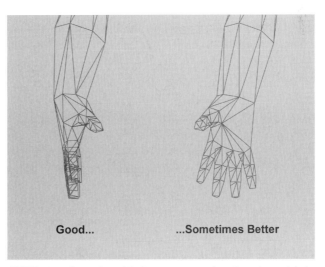

Good...   ...Sometimes Better

FIGURE 3.32   Sometimes it's the *geometry* rather than the weighting that needs to be tweaked to ensure proper deformation.

hand, select and assign the vertices to each link along the way (including all knuckle vertices), locking them as you go (Figure 3.33).

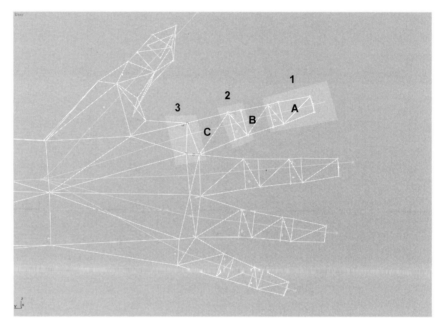

FIGURE 3.33   Assign the vertices of the hand by starting with the fingers.

As you can see in Figure 3.33, the vertices highlighted in Group 1 are assigned to Link A. Vertices in Group B are assigned to Link B, and those in Group 3 are assigned to Link C. The quickest and easiest way to complete the weighting is to go back and select only the knuckle vertices, and share influence with the link that is the *parent* of the assigned link.

 Whenever the Type-In Weights dialog box is brought up and All Links is chosen, the link to which the selected vertices are assigned will automatically be highlighted, to make it easier to see against all the other links. However, when the link selected is far enough down the overall list, character studio displays it by dropping it to the bottom of the display window. By assigning vertices to the end link of the fingers, and moving inwards towards the parent, the parent link that needs to share influence over the vertices selected will be visible and on top of the selected link when the list of links is displayed. If the vertices had been assigned to the parent first, the child would be below the displayed list, and you would have to scroll down to see the child of the selected link (Figure 3.34).

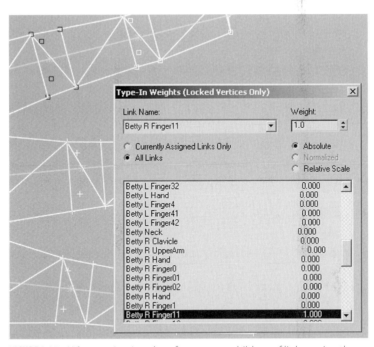

FIGURE 3.34   When typing in values for a parent-child set of links, assign the vertices to the *child* first, not the parent.

Character studio duplicates the naming of links so that each character can have a number of Hand links. The best way to tell them apart is to look below each link in the list of links. For Betty's uppermost knuckles, share influence with the Hand link *above* the link the vertices have been assigned to.

Often, when weighting vertices by hand, you'll select a set, enter their values with the proper links, and then select another set, keeping the Type-in Weights dialog box open all the while. One quick way to isolate a link when "off screen" is to toggle back and forth between displaying All Links and Currently Assigned Links Only. Doing this immediately lines up the selected vertices' link at the bottom of the long list and saves you from scrolling up or down to find it.

For the thumb, rotate your view so you can see it in profile, and select and assign its vertices (Figure 3.35).

All the vertices in Group 1 are assigned to Link A, Group 2 to Link B, and Group 3 to *Link D*. Share influence with the proper links, and the thumb is weighted. The vertices in Group 3 that are assigned to the Betty

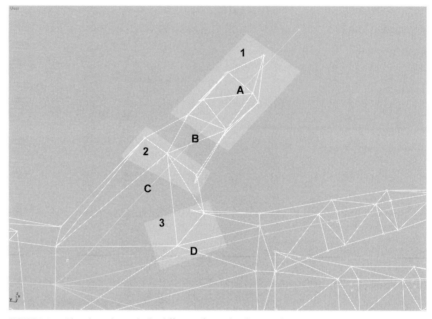

FIGURE 3.35   The thumb is a little different from the fingers, but you assign the vertices in the same way.

Hand link (Link D) can share influence with Betty R Finger0 (Link C). Un-hide all the Biped Finger objects of the right hand to test the weighting.

Saving Your Weighting Values

Most of the time, the best way to save your weighting values is to save it-erative versions of your mesh as you work. You can also easily reuse or recover your weighting by saving the .phy file. Do this by clicking on the Save Physique (*.phy) File icon (Figure 3.36).

FIGURE 3.36   Save your Physique file for additional insurance or later reference.

Keep in mind that when re-loading a physique file into one character or another, the Biped structure has to be the same, with the same added bones (if any) assigned to it.

When working with older Biped or 3ds max files, Biped will sometimes revert to the previous version of character studio's naming convention. This means that all Biped links will be named after their child (one link below) instead of the actual bone they correspond to.

Assigning the Neck, Shoulders, and Torso

Hide m_headarmleg, and unhide m_torso, m_energy, m_fanvent, and all the Biped Spine objects, and go to the Right viewport (Figure 3.37).

FIGURE 3.37   Even torso mesh objects are supposed to be heavily armored (that is, *rigid*).

Start with the neck. Since the head is a separate object, it's easier to weight both it and the neck. When the neck is joined to the head, it requires more polygons and more time to set up the weighting. Zoom in to the top of the neck, select the vertices there, and assign them to the Betty Head link. Unhide the Biped head and m_headarmleg to test the deformation (Figure 3.38).

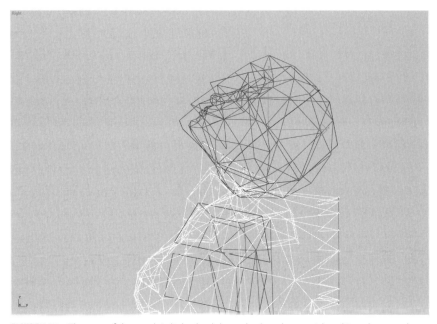

FIGURE 3.38   The top of the neck is linked solely to the head to avoid making the gap there visible.

Since there's no geometry at the top of the neck, the line of vertices there has to move with the head. Now, undo any rotations you did, and re-hide m_headarmleg and Betty Head. Hide the assigned neck vertices, go to the Front viewport, and select all the vertices near her right shoulder geometry. Don't include any of the rear backpack geometry (for example, m_fanvent or m_energy), but assign them instead to the Betty R Clavicle link (Figure 3.39).

Linking the shoulder to the clavicle gives you a small amount of mobility, but because Betty is supposed to be wearing heavy armor, the shoulder will remain almost motionless throughout her animations. Hide those assigned vertices, and go back to the Right viewport. Make sure all three of the mesh objects are selected (m_energy, m_fanvent, and m_torso), and assign the vertices of the backpack and upper torso to the Betty Spine2 link (Figure 3.40).

All the vertices are assigned to the second spine link instead of partially to the third, because the backpack and upper body armor need to appear hard and inflexible. Assigning as many vertices as possible to one link achieves this look. However, because there are four links, some of the lower backpack and torso vertices can be assigned to Spine1, the parent of Spine2 (Figure 3.41).

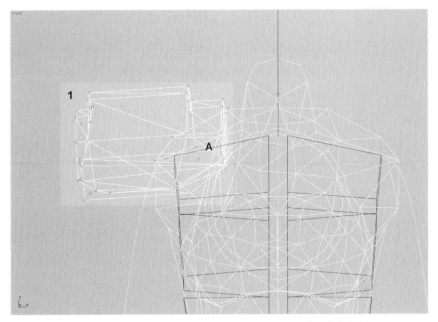

FIGURE 3.39   Assign the shoulder pad vertices (1) to the Betty R Clavicle link (A).

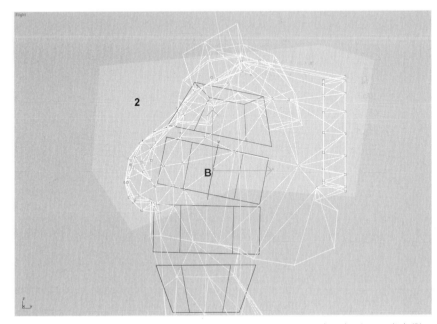

FIGURE 3.40   The backpack and upper torso vertices (2) are assigned to the Spine2 link (B).

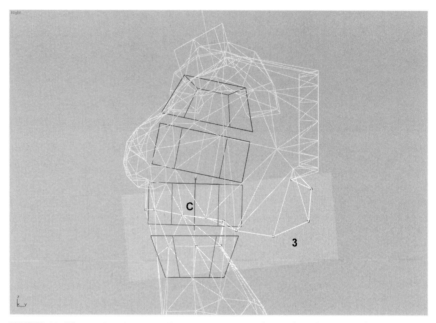

FIGURE 3.41   The vertices in vertex Group 3 are assigned to Link C, the Spine1 link.

 Earlier, Spine2 was chosen as a link for the backpack vertices, because Spine1 would have vertices assigned to it as well, and Spine2 was a better choice over Spine3 due to its proximity to the next bone in the hierarchy.

Next, the vertices near the waist need to be tweaked further, to make sure they deform smoothly when the torso bends and twists. Select only the vertices that make up the two rows you just assigned to Spine1, bring up your Type-In Weights menu, and assign the vertices to the Betty Spine link as well. Make sure you *don't* assign any backpack vertices to the second link (Figure 3.42).

Weighting the Other Leg

Assign the vertices of the right leg to their proper link by *referencing* the first leg you spent time weighting. First, assign the Toe vertices of the leg element of m_torso to the Toe link, and hide them. Then unhide m_headarmleg, and go to the Front viewport. Select both m_torso and m_headarmleg. Click on the Select by Link button on the Vertex menu to the right (Figure 3.43).

Click on the *left* Foot link and study the vertices selected (Figure 3.44, page 122).

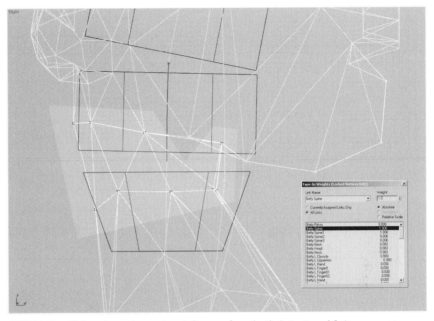

FIGURE 3.42   Giving the waist vertices influence from both Spine1 and Spine ensures smooth deformation.

FIGURE 3.43   The Select by Link button selects all vertices assigned to a link.

Using Select by Link is a quick way to see which vertices you previously assigned and how. Because of the pose of the Biped rig, some of the vertices of the right foot geometry are included in the vertices assigned to the left Foot link. Ignoring this temporary weighting, select all the vertices of the right foot geometry that mirror the left foot geometry. Assign them to the Betty R Foot link; then, using the left foot vertices as a guide, type in matching values for the right foot vertices (Figure 3.45).

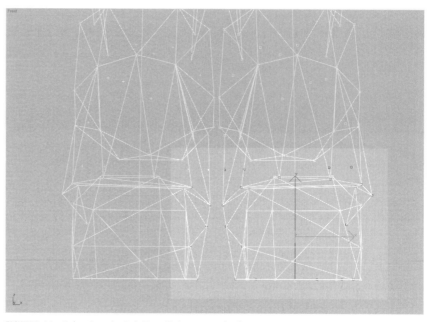

FIGURE 3.44 Selecting the left Foot link to see which vertices are assigned to it also selects some vertices of the *right* foot geometry.

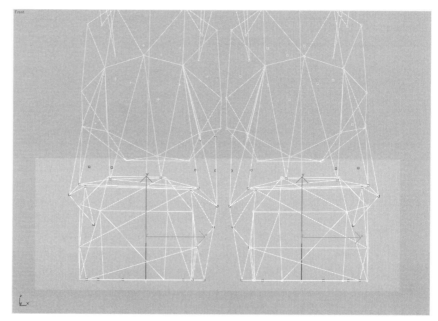

FIGURE 3.45 Using the vertices of one foot for reference, the other one is easily and quickly weighted.

Use this same technique to weight the right knee and rest of the right leg geometry. When you get up to the thigh area, hide m_headarmleg, and make sure to assign the left thigh vertices to the Betty L Thigh link (Figure 3.46).

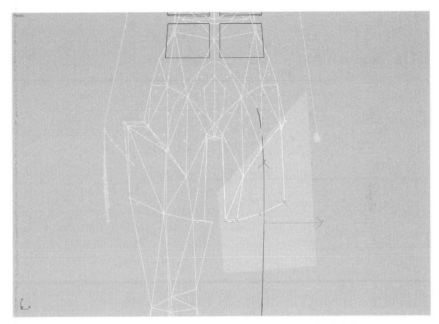

FIGURE 3.46   Don't forget to assign the left thigh vertices to the L Thigh link.

Loading a .Bip File into Biped

Before moving on to weight the hips, you need to apply a run animation to the character to see the effects of the weighting as you make adjustments. The rest of the character could have benefited from a full animation as well, but for the hips, it's especially important to see the character's mesh deform while adjusting it. A run or walk animation is perfect for this.

Hide everything but Betty Spine and m_torso. Select Betty Spine, and go over to the Biped menu on the Motion panel. Make sure you're out of Figure mode. Click on the ◎ In Place Mode icon (it turns purple). Now the character will stay in view, even if the animation translates it through space and it's supposed to move off-screen. This mode is great for fine-tuning animations for real-time characters, which, by nature, usually need to be animated "in place" for implementation in a game.

Click on the Load File icon (Figure 3.47).

FIGURE 3.47 Click on the yellow Open File icon to load a .bip animation into your character.

ON THE CD

Find Run.bip in the Chapter3 directory on this book's CD-ROM, and load it into your character's Biped. Click on the Time Configuration icon located near the bottom of the screen to the right (Figure 3.48).

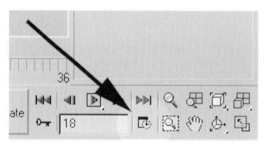

FIGURE 3.48 The Time Configuration icon brings up the menu that controls the number of frames displayed.

Once the Time Configuration menu comes up, establish the number of frames in the active animation range by setting the Start Time to 0 and End Time to 18 (Figure 3.49).

Changing the length of the animation to match Run.bip allows you to play it in an endless loop if you want. Hit OK, and as you slide the Time Slider or advance through the animation frames, the mesh deforms with the run animation.

Advance forward through the animation one frame at a time by hitting the period (.) key. Go back a frame at a time by hitting the comma (,) key. Play and stop the animation by hitting the slash (/) key.

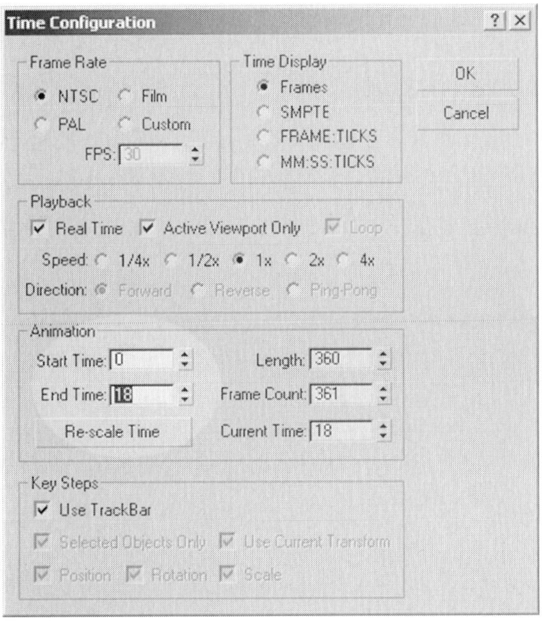

FIGURE 3.49 Set the animation Start and End time to 19 frames (0–18).

With the animation applied to the Biped, you will find it easier to see the deformation on all parts of the mesh. With the In Place mode active, the character won't run *away* as you try to weight it.

The In Place Mode icon has a fly-out menu that allows you to restrict the movement along the X-axis only, Y-axis only, or both simultaneously (the default). Just hold down the mouse button with the cursor over the icon, and drag down to bring up the other options (Figure 3.50).

Tackling the Hips

The hips are one of the most difficult areas to weight, second only to the shoulders. Usually, even when weighting vertices manually, it's a good idea to see how closely the default initialization weighted the hips before dialing them in by hand. Put Betty in her Initial Skeletal Pose, and select all the vertices around her hips. Click the Remove from Link button to make it active, go to the Front viewport, and drag your selection fence across all the links on either arm.

FIGURE 3.50 These are the options for the In Place Mode icon's fly-out menu.

 Whenever you use Remove from Link, you must *select the right type of three avail-able vertices. Since you're dealing solely with rigid vertices, make the* green *plus sign active, or the removal won't take. Also, under the Blending Between Links menu, choose No Blending (Figure 3.51).*

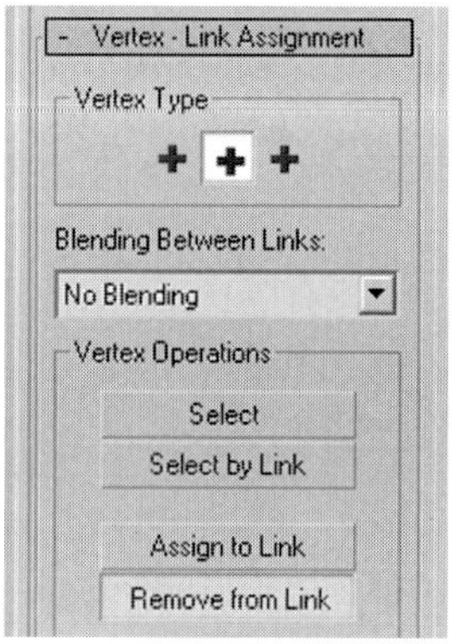

FIGURE 3.51 Under Vertex Type, select the color of the vertices to which you're applying Remove from Link.

Drag the selection fence across the upper body Spine links, as well. Lock the vertices, and play or frame forward through the animation. The front part of the hips look good, and the posterior looks nice except for the bottom two rows of vertices of her rear. When Betty takes a step, you can see those vertices have too much weight assigned to the leg links, so they need to be corrected.

Turn on the Initial Skeletal Pose again, and, on Betty's right buttock, select the nine vertices shown in Figure 3.52. Unlock them, and assign them a weight of 1 for both the Betty R Thigh link and the Spine link that appears just above it in the Type-In Weights dialog box (Figure 3.52).

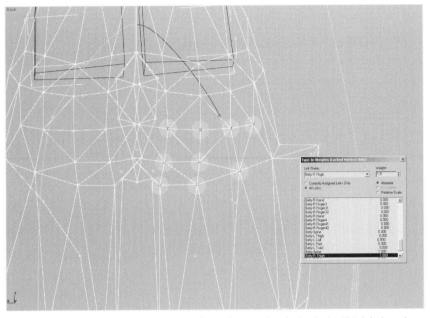

FIGURE 3.52   Assign these vertices an equal weighting value for both the Thigh link and Spine link above it.

 If you had not checked Triangle Pelvis under the Structure sub-menu on the Biped rig, you wouldn't have the two additional Spine links to help hold the hips together (Figure 3.53). As you'll see later, these two Spine links will often supplant the Pelvis link—if not replace it entirely—to hold the hip shape together.

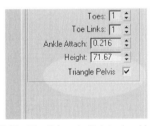

FIGURE 3.53   The Triangle Pelvis checkbox *is* pretty useful after all.

Turn off Initial Skeletal Pose again, and see how the area deforms. Everything should look good now, except for the three vertices *above* the ones just corrected. Select these three, unlock them, and assign them to the Spine link above the Thigh link (Figure 3.54).

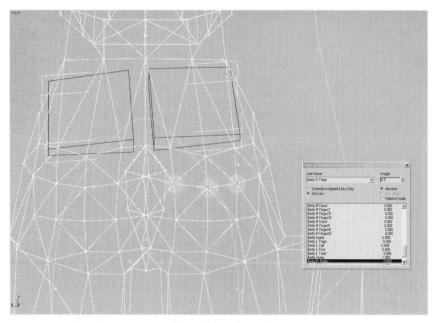

FIGURE 3.54   These three vertices still need a bit of an adjustment to their weighting.

After you've assigned them to the Spine link, give the vertices a shared value of 0.5 with the Betty R Thigh link. Turn Initial Skeletal Pose off once again, and check how the right buttock deforms from all views as she runs. Do the left buttock as well, using the right as a guide. They should look fine—the hips are done.

Adjusting the Gun Arm

Hide everything, and then unhide the m_gunarm mesh object. Go to the Right viewport. From the looks of it, this object needs a little help (Figure 3.55)!

Select the object, go to the Vertex Sub-Object menu under Physique, and put the object in its Initial Skeletal Pose. Select all of the vertices that make up the left forearm elements of the mesh: hand, gun body, and even the cylinder that covers her elbow. Rotate your view as necessary.

 If you have Initial Skeletal Pose checked, and you then select another object in your scene, and go to the Physique root or even to another Physique sub-object, the mesh will remain in its Initial Skeletal Pose.

Don't select any of the vertices belonging to her upper arm element, and only select the first few vertices of the belt that feeds into her back-

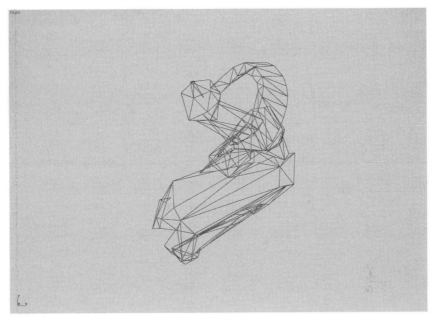

FIGURE 3.55   What is it?

pack. Assign all these vertices to the Betty L Forearm link, and turn the Initial Skeletal Pose back off to see the results (Figure 3.56).

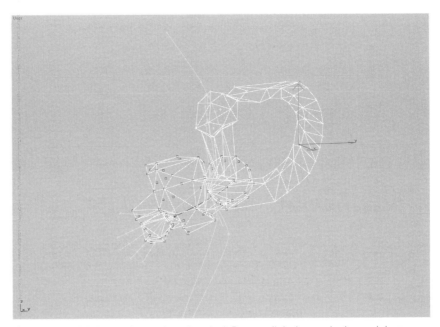

FIGURE 3.56   With the vertices assigned to the L Forearm link, the arm looks much better.

Hide the vertices assigned; select and assign the upper arm element vertices to the Betty L UpperArm link. Once they're assigned, hide them as well, and you can then begin work on the *real* problem area: the belt feed.

The shoulder for the left arm is a different design from the right one and can move around with the arm. The only time it will look a bit odd is when Betty's arm goes very far up or very far back.

The belt feed geometry is a looping structure that goes from back-pack to forearm. Unfortunately, an extra set of bones couldn't be linked to the Biped to serve as a weighting link for the geometry. If the bones were linked to the back or shoulder, they wouldn't move with the arm. If they were linked to the arm, they wouldn't stay linked to the back (Figure 3.57).

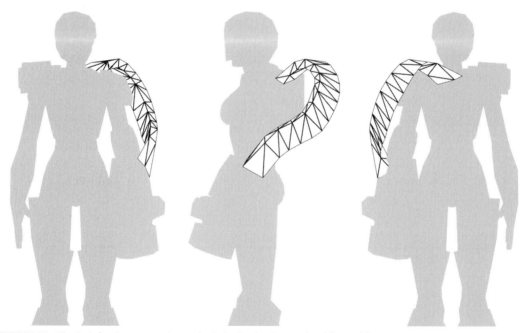

FIGURE 3.57   The belt feed geometry has to be linked to both rear shoulder and forearm.

The solution to this weighting dilemma isn't adding extra bones, it's carefully sharing the weighting between Betty L Forearm and Betty L Spine2—bypassing Betty L UpperArm altogether. Rotate your view so you're looking down on her left side, and advance to Frame 6 in the animation. Select all the remaining vertices of the object and assign them to Betty Spine2 (Figure 3.58).

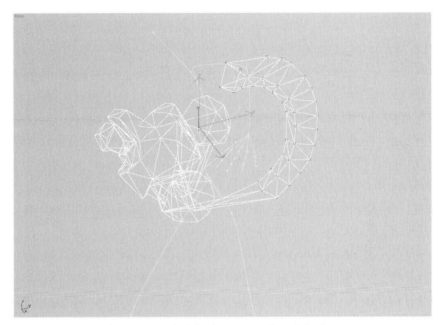

FIGURE 3.58   Assign the remaining belt feed vertices to Betty Spine2.

Keeping selected all but the four vertices that touch the backpack, bring up the Type-In Weights menu, and assign those vertices an *additional* weighting value of 0.5 to the Betty L Forearm link (Figure 3.59).

 Deselect vertices from a selection set by dragging your selection fence across the vertices while holding down the Alt key.

Obviously, the geometry can't stay that way, but at least the two links to which the vertices need to be assigned are now ready to be dialed in and their respective influences adjusted. Put the mesh back into its Initial Skeletal Pose, and begin at the row of vertices that starts at the top of the feed belt near the shoulder. Rotate your view so you're looking at the row of vertices "edge-on," and change their value from 0.5 to .05 (Figure 3.60).

Work your way over and down to each row of vertices until you have the values for them shown in Figure 3.61.

Note how the forearm is given progressive influence over the feed belt. This will result in a smoother deformation of the geometry. Now,

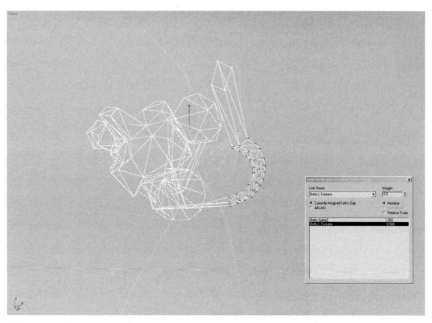

FIGURE 3.59 Being equally influenced by both the Spine2 link and the Forearm link is a start.

FIGURE 3.60 Rotate your view so you can clearly see the row of vertices to be adjusted.

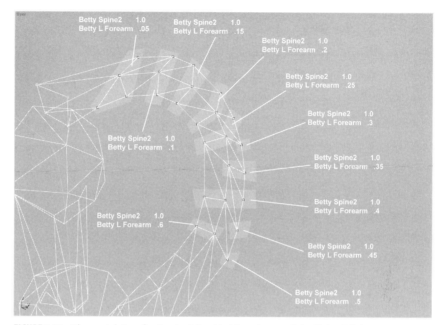

FIGURE 3.61   The weighting for the belt feed is biased toward the Spine2 link.

unhide the three vertices that are part of the belt feed where it nears the forearm and that were hidden before. Rotate your view to see the remaining vertices better. Assign them the values shown in Figure 3.62.

Unhide the rest of Betty's mesh objects, and watch her jog a nice steady pace (Figure 3.63).

ON THE CD

Load Betty07.max from the Chapter3 directory on the companion CD-ROM, and compare your results to the figure in this file.

While it takes a lot of trial and error to get the weighting of an object like Betty's weapon belt feed to deform correctly, the only way it can be done is to type the values in. The rest of her is composed of a low enough number of triangles to also allow a vertex-by-vertex weighting approach.

SUMMARY

Getting the weighting values right for your real-time character's mesh means the difference between average animations and *great* animations. Without proper weighting, all that hard work spent on the design, model, texture, and rig is wasted. Physique allows for quick and easy adjustment of your character's "skin" by giving you access to individual vertices and

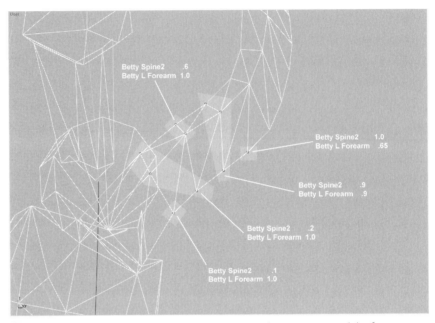

FIGURE 3.62 The rest of the feed belt geometry starts to bias more toward the forearm.

FIGURE 3.63 Betty is ready for *action*!

groups of vertices via *envelopes*. For typical game characters that are less than 2,000 polygons, manually assigning the weighting values to the mesh objects is the best way to ensure proper deformation.

When applying Physique to your mesh, initialize it by activating Attach to Node and clicking on the pelvis of the Biped, then select Rigid as the vertex link assignment, with N Links for envelope creation/calculation. While it's recommended that you manually assign the vertices their weighting values, it doesn't hurt to try using envelopes to see if they work. Begin the weighting process with objects that are easy to weight, so they can be hidden and removed from the work area. Pay particular attention to the shoulder and hip areas of the mesh, and make sure the deformation is correct in a variety of poses. Check the effects of the weighting values by loading a simple animation into the Biped and toggling back and forth between the Initial Skeletal Pose and the animated state. Finally, save your Physique settings for reference in case the mesh needs to be detached and reattached to the Biped.

WEIGHTING A CHARACTER USING ENVELOPES

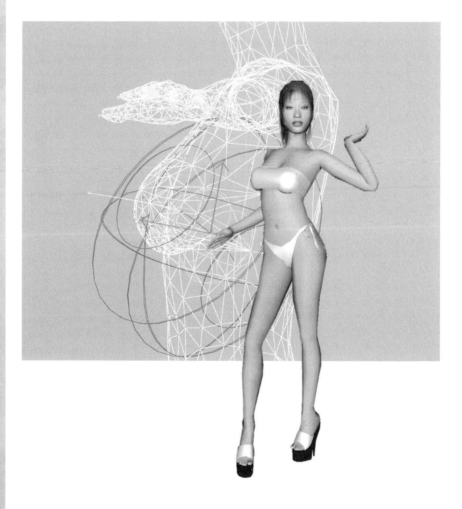

C haracters that can be used on many of the consoles today like Nintendo's GameCube™ and Microsoft's Xbox show a substantial increase in the number of polygons available for their models. Other real-time applications, such as those with dancing characters for a music visualization plugin, also use higher polygon meshes. These characters still need to have rigid vertices and be as polygonally frugal as they can be, because they're 3D and considered "real-time."

CONQUERING ENVELOPES

Figuring out how to use envelopes in character studio isn't easy. It takes many hours of practice to make them a useful part of your weighting process. However, you *must* conquer them when working on high-poly characters. While manually assigning the weighting assures you the most control, *time* is your enemy. It takes 50–100 hours to manually assign the vertices of a mesh with 6,000 or 7,000 triangles. Compare that with the 50–100 *minutes* it takes to weight a character using envelopes. You owe it to yourself and the project you're working on to conquer envelopes if your characters are high-res.

Steps to Applying Physique

The steps to applying Physique to a character when using envelopes are similar to those taken when assigning vertices manually:

1. Make sure all mesh objects have their stacks collapsed and are ready to go.
2. Build a Biped rig and put it into Figure mode.
3. Apply Physique to the mesh objects.
4. Activate the Attach to Node function, and then click on the pelvis of the Biped.
5. Select Rigid under Vertex – Link Assignment.
6. Take the Biped out of Figure mode and apply an animation to it.
7. Adjust the weighting of the character by adjusting the Envelope settings under the Physique Sub-Objects menu, and typing in individual vertex weighting assignments.
8. Toggle Initial Skeletal Pose on and off to see the effects of the weighting.
9. Save the weighting as a .phy file.

However, using envelopes makes it necessary to pay closer attention to the seventh item in the preceding list. The order in which you *adjust* the weighting of a character that primarily uses envelopes is:

1. Turn off any unnecessary envelopes.
2. Adjust the Radial Scale of the envelopes.
3. Adjust the Parent/Child Overlap of the envelopes.
4. Copy and paste any appropriate envelope settings to symmetrical limbs.
5. Remove any vertices from the appropriate links, *and then . . .*
6. Use Type-In Weights to finish the weighting for any remaining vertices.

You save yourself the most time by adjusting the envelope settings *first*, because they affect all the vertices of all the mesh objects to which you've assigned the Physique modifier. This is the benefit of using envelopes—the pure speed at which you can weight a character. Manually typing in the value of vertices is the last step in weighting a higher resolution game character, because (as mentioned before) it is the most time-consuming process.

Turning Off Unnecessary Envelopes

ON THE CD

Load Bikini2.max from the Chapter4 directory on this book's CD-ROM (Figure 4.1).

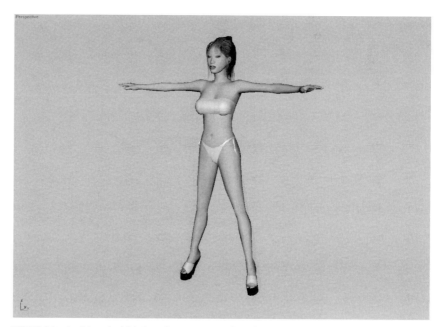

FIGURE 4.1   A girl and a bikini—what more needs to be said?

This character, Bikini, weighs in at 5,663 triangles. Take a moment to study the mesh, and the first thing you'll notice is that all the Biped objects and the bones attached to the Biped have been assigned a zero opacity material. This is so the mesh can be seen in shaded mode without being obstructed by the solid Biped objects. While there are other ways to make the Biped object transparent, this way is the most reliable (more on this in Chapter 6).

Another way to make your Biped less obtrusive when viewing your mesh is to select all Biped and bone objects, right-click on them, click on Properties, and check the See-Through box under Display Properties (Figure 4.2).

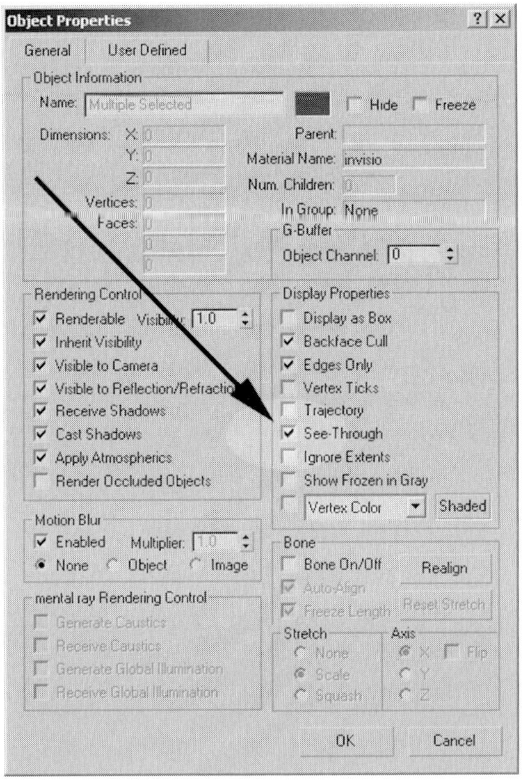

FIGURE 4.2 Turning on the See-Through option is another way to make Biped objects less obtrusive when viewing your mesh in a shaded viewport.

While this does make the objects transparent, their opacity is controlled by 3ds max, not by you. Still, it is an option. You could also assign a *wireframe* material to the objects and see them as shaded wireframes, even when in a smooth-shaded view. Another way to change the appearance of *just* the Biped objects is to go to the Display sub-menu for Biped, click *on* the Bones button, and click *off* the Objects button (Figure 4.3).

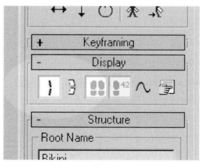

FIGURE 4.3   Turning Bones on and Objects off is yet another way to make your mesh objects easier to see in a shaded viewport.

The only problem with this sort of display arrangement is that when you click on one of the colored stick figure "bones" that are now representing your Biped objects, you are actually selecting the *child* of that bone. It's also harder to isolate a bone in order to click on it (unless the mesh is frozen).

Another thing you may notice is there are only three Spine links. This is due to the way the motion capture (*mocap*) data used for the .bip file was captured. The motion just works better with three links instead of four.

Select all the mesh objects (m_*) for the character, and apply the Physique modifier to them. Go to the Right viewport, make Envelope the active sub-object under Physique, and zoom in to the head area. Carefully select *all* the links of the head, except for Bikini Head (Figure 4.4).

When dealing with the plethora of links that can result in a facial rig, the best way to make sure all the links are selected, excluding *the head link, is to select everything from the neck up; then, hold down the Alt key and select the Head link, thus deselecting* it.

Next, go over to Active Blending in the Blending Envelopes rollout menu, and *turn off* the links selected by unchecking the Rigid box (Figure 4.5).

It may take a while for 3ds max to process the action, but once it turns the envelopes off, switch to the Vertex sub-object for Physique, and

FIGURE 4.4   Select all the envelopes of the head links, except the Head link.

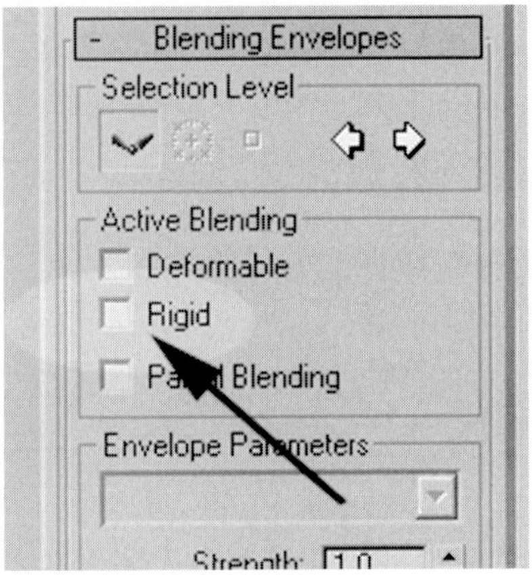

FIGURE 4.5   Turning off envelopes is as easy as unchecking a checkbox.

select the vertices of the head mesh. They're now effectively within the influence of the Bikini Head link.

 Another way to remove vertices from the influence of an envelope is to select the envelope, go to the rollout menu, and enter a value of 0 for Strength under Envelope Parameters (Figure 4.6).

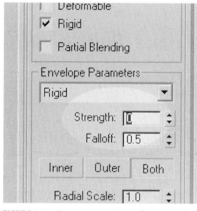

FIGURE 4.6   Entering a value of 0 is another way to effectively "turn off" an envelope.

If you ever find yourself dialing an envelope's strength down to nothing, or close to nothing, just turn it off. It saves processing time and effort to have as few active envelopes as possible.

The reason why you just turned all those envelopes off is because envelopes will be useless even in a face of this resolution. Manually assigning vertices is the only way to get the weighting just right. Pan down to the end Breast links and turn them off, too (Figure 4.7).

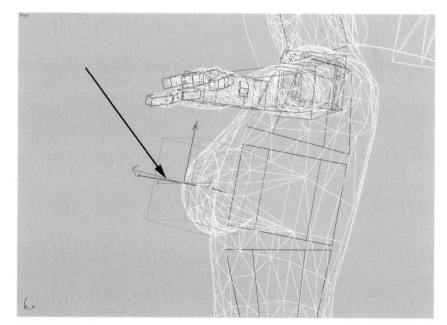

FIGURE 4.7   The Breast envelopes aren't necessary, either.

It's true the breasts are highly malleable by nature, and could be weighted using envelopes, but assigning them manually ensures the right amount of deformation to achieve a realistic look.

 If the Breast objects hadn't had dummies (Nubs) linked to them, this link wouldn't exist, and the movement of the breast boxes couldn't affect the geometry.

The last envelope to turn off is the Pelvis link. Go to the Front viewport, use Arc-Rotate to rotate the view slightly so you can see the small link underneath the Spine link; select the link, and turn it off (Figure 4.8).

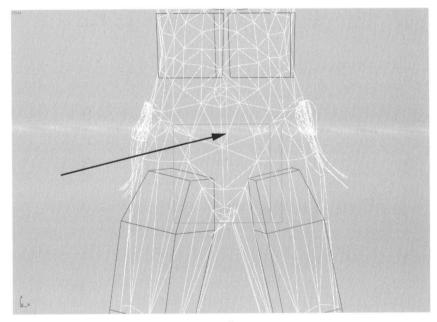

FIGURE 4.8   The Pelvis link can also be turned off.

 The best reason to turn off the Pelvis isn't an aspect of weighting, but an aspect of the game engine into which the character is exported. For some reason, many real-time game engines have problems with this particular link. Besides, by having Triangle Pelvis active in the Structure of the Biped, the need for a Pelvis link is moot.

Adjusting the Radial Scale of the Envelopes

If an envelope doesn't encompass a vertex, it won't influence it. Thus, sometimes you have to increase, decrease, or alter the envelope so it includes (or even *excludes*) certain vertices. In areas like the shoulders and hips, envelopes work best when several of them encompass the same vertex or vertices. Everything you need in order to adjust the basic shape and setting of an envelope can be found in the Envelope Sub-Object menu under Physique.

First, click on the Physique modifier at the top of the stack, select one of the Biped objects, and turn Figure mode off. Select just m_body, go back to the Modify panel, go to the Envelope Sub-Object menu, and scroll down to the bottom and check on the Initial Skeletal Pose box (Figure 4.9).

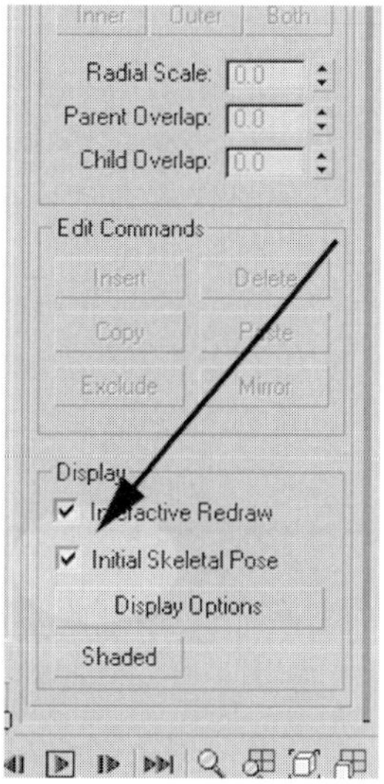

FIGURE 4.9   The Initial Skeletal Pose checkbox is available in the Envelope sub-menu, too.

Right-click in your scene and choose Hide Unselected to clear your workspace. Then select the two Breast links that are parents to the end links you turned off earlier (Figure 4.10).

Go to the Envelopes sub-menu and type in a value of 0.4 for Radial Scale. Make sure the Both box above it is active and purple (Figure 4.11).

When Both is active, the number entered in the Radial Scale box acts as a *multiplier* to the original value assigned to *both* the Inner and Outer range of the envelope. The default value is set at the time of initialization and typically is 1 for the Inner and 1.75 for the Outer settings. Thus, when a value of 0.4 is entered, a decimal multiplier is applied to the outer and inner envelope settings; the size of the envelopes selected visibly shrinks (Figure 4.12).

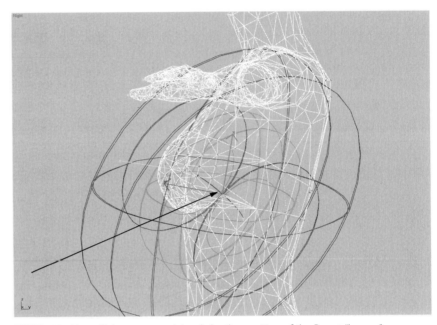

FIGURE 4.10 These links are created simply by the position of the Breast "bones."

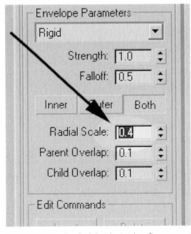

FIGURE 4.11 Radial Scale is the first step in adjusting the influence of an envelope.

While these links could have also been turned off, keeping them on at a lower setting turns into a serendipitous cosmetic trick. As the character bends and gyrates while dancing, these spheres of influence will press in upon the vertices at the waist, keeping the area looking tight, yet feminine and sexy.

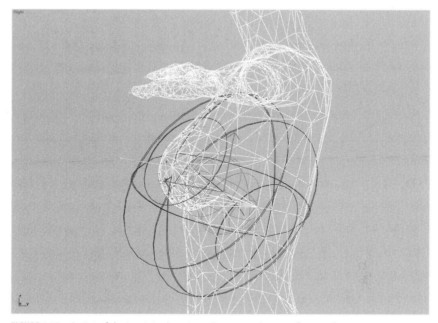

FIGURE 4.12   At 0.4 of their original setting, these envelopes influence fewer vertices.

Next, go to the Front viewport and select the Bikini Spine2 link found just below the neck. Go to Frame 430 by moving your Time Slider, and turn the Initial Skeletal Pose off. Hit the P key to go to a Perspective viewport, and rotate around to see the left shoulder area (Figure 4.13).

The hardest thing about Rigid weighting is accommodating the shoulders of a mesh like this when the character is in an arms-raised position. An arms-back position looks a bit rough too, but there is a way to alleviate the ugliness of the deformation. With Spine2 selected, enter a value of 0.8 in the Radial Scale box. Now the shoulder area on the left looks a bit more like a real deltoid (Figure 4.14).

There are more links that need their Radial Scales looked at, but since you're working on the shoulder, it's a good time to learn about the next kind of envelope tweaking: adjusting the parent/child overlap of the envelopes.

Adjusting the Parent/Child Overlap of the Envelopes

While entering a lesser value for the Radial Scale for the Spine2 link helps the shoulder maintain it's shape, one more step needs to be taken while that envelope is being adjusted. Go to Frame 260, and rotate your view so you can still see the back of the mesh (Figure 4.15).

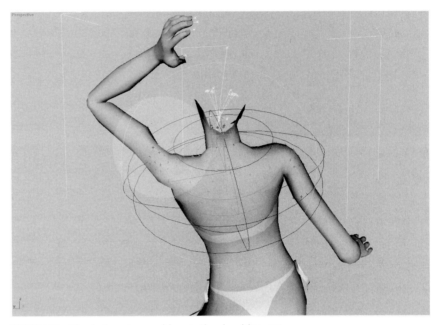

FIGURE 4.13   Clearly there is a problem in the shoulder area.

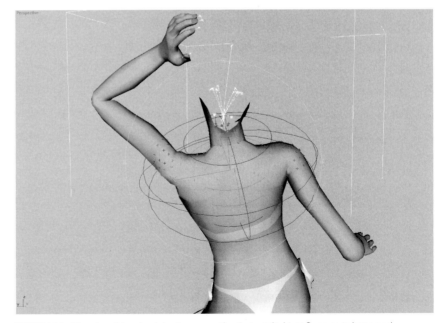

FIGURE 4.14   The shoulders look better once the Spine2 link's influence is lessened.

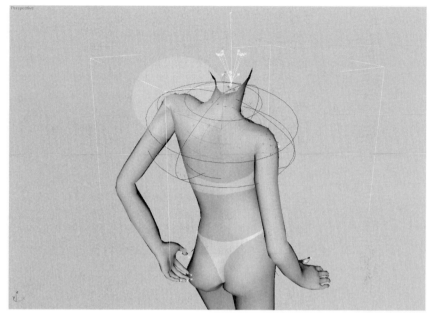

FIGURE 4.15   The shoulder still needs one more adjustment to be complete.

Go to the Envelope sub-menu again and enter a value of 0.4 for Child Overlap (Figure 4.16).

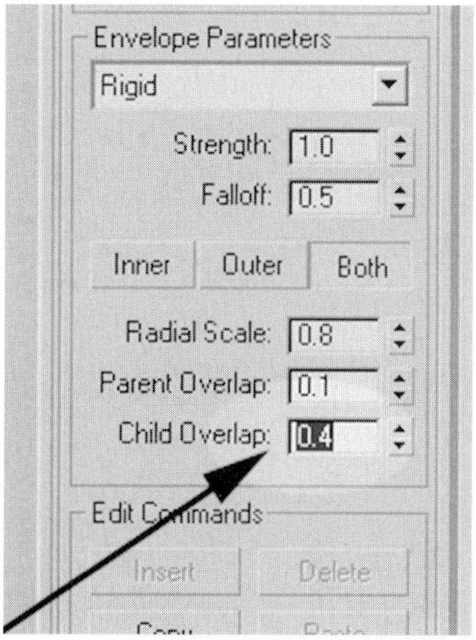

FIGURE 4.16   Child Overlap and Parent Overlap are crucial settings for envelopes.

This value extends the envelope into the next link below the selected link in the hierarchy of the links; it extends it more than the default 0.1 and smoothes out the roughness previously seen in the shoulder (Figure 4.17).

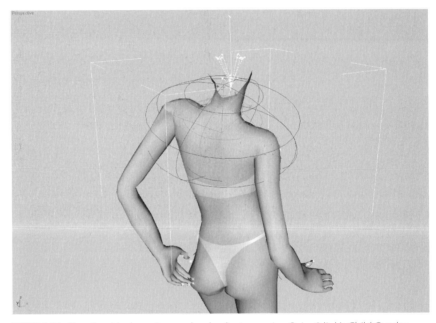

FIGURE 4.17   The shoulder loses its rough edge by increasing Spine2 link's Child Overlap.

Sometimes, however, instead of increasing the Child Overlap, it's better to *decrease* it. Go to Frame 110, and look at the left arm (Figure 4.18).

To fix the elbow area, type in a value of 0 for the Bikini L UpperArm link's Child Overlap—and *voila* (Figure 4.19)!

Of course, the type of rig you have created for your character dictates how much to increase or decrease the Child or Parent settings; however, as a general rule, increasing the child overlap of the top Spine link and decreasing the child overlap of the UpperArm link ensures the best deformation in the shoulder and elbow area. So, with the Bikini L UpperArm's envelope set, is there a way to copy the settings to the Bikini R UpperArm link? Of course there is!

Copying and Pasting to Symmetrical Limbs

The task of adjusting your envelopes involves a very nice tool in character studio: copying and pasting link settings. It's very simple to use. With

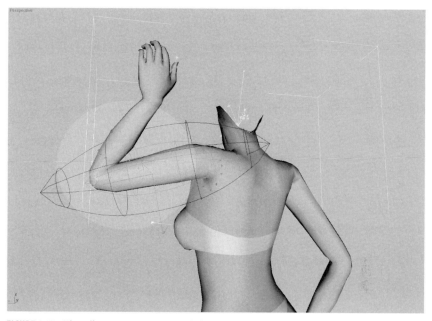

FIGURE 4.18   The elbow appears crimped due to too much influence from the UpperArm envelope.

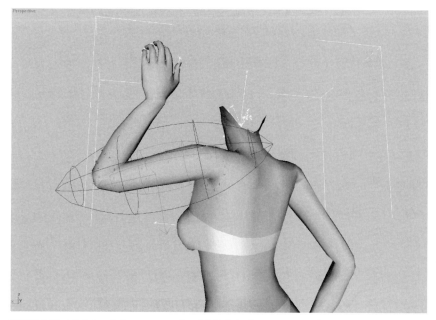

FIGURE 4.19   With less influence over its child's link, the upper arm doesn't crimp the elbow joint when bent.

the Bikini L UpperArm envelope still active, go to Edit Commands in the rollout menu to the right, and click on the Copy button (Figure 4.20).

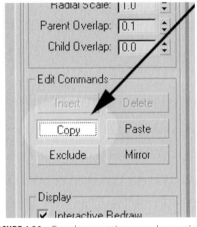

FIGURE 4.20   Envelope settings can be copied and pasted to other links/envelopes.

To paste the envelope setting, simply click on the Bikini R UpperArm link and hit the Paste button, found beside the Copy button you just hit.

 When modifying arms and legs, go ahead and select both of the symmetrical links at the same time. Entering a value in the Envelope menu while more than one link is selected will change all the selected links to the new value. This method is an alternative to copying and pasting link/envelope settings.

While it shouldn't really cause you much trouble to redo your tweaking on an envelope-by-envelope basis, the copy and paste functionality of character studio helps more when you have entered multiple settings that have taken a long time to complete. This brings up another way to adjust envelopes: Cross Section and Control Point (Figure 4.21).

Cross Section offers a way to move the cross section of an envelope up and down the length of a link. To access this feature, click on the Cross Section icon to make it active instead of the default Links; select a cross section on a selected link, and move it around. Control Point offers a way to grab and move the control points of a cross section. Click on its icon to make it active, then click on a control point and you will be able to move it where you want, along whichever axis you want.

While useful for extremely high-resolution meshes or very strange shapes, these two added layers of refinement can usually be skipped with a real-time game character. Definitely give them a try, however, as you

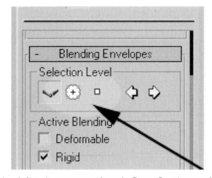

FIGURE 4.21 Adjusting an envelope's Cross Section and Control Point are additional ways to change an envelope's shape and subsequent influence over vertices around a link.

may find them to be useful tools for quickly achieving the right weighting. Do make sure the results are truly worth the extra effort. Now let's cover the next step in weighting your character with envelopes: removing vertices from links.

Removing Any Vertices from Links

While envelopes serve you well with certain types of characters, Removing Vertices from Links offers another way to quickly achieve the weighting you want. Turn Initial Skeletal Pose back on, go to the Top viewport, and pan or zoom until the right hand of the mesh fills the screen. Select all the vertices of the index finger, starting with the second knuckle (Figure 4.22).

With the vertices selected, click Remove from Links to make it active, make sure Rigid (green) vertices are selected under Vertex Type, and drag your selection fence across all the links of the hand, except for the last two links of the index finger just *below* the selected vertices. Lock the vertices after you've removed them from the unwanted links, and repeat the process for the other fingers (don't do the thumb yet).

Turn the Initial Skeletal Pose off, and you'll see the fingers deforming correctly as they bend (Figure 4.23).

Weighting the Waist, Hips, and Legs

Weighting the waist is fairly simple. The only thing you generally need to do is to reduce its Radial Scale a bit, and extend the first Spine link into its parent, the pelvis. In the Front viewport, put the character in its Initial

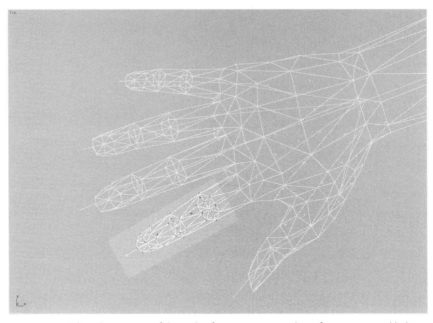

FIGURE 4.22   Select the vertices of the index finger to remove them from unwanted links.

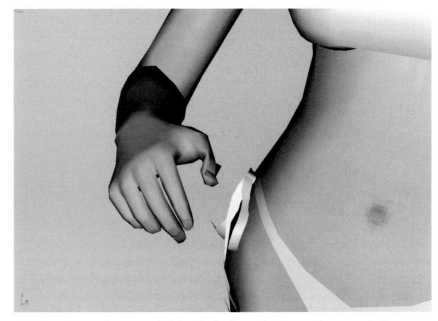

FIGURE 4.23   Except for a crumpled thumb, the fingers look great after strategically removing vertices from links.

Skeletal Pose if it isn't already, select the Bikini Spine link, reduce Radial Scale to 0.8, and enter a value of 0.3 for Parent Overlap (Figure 4.24).

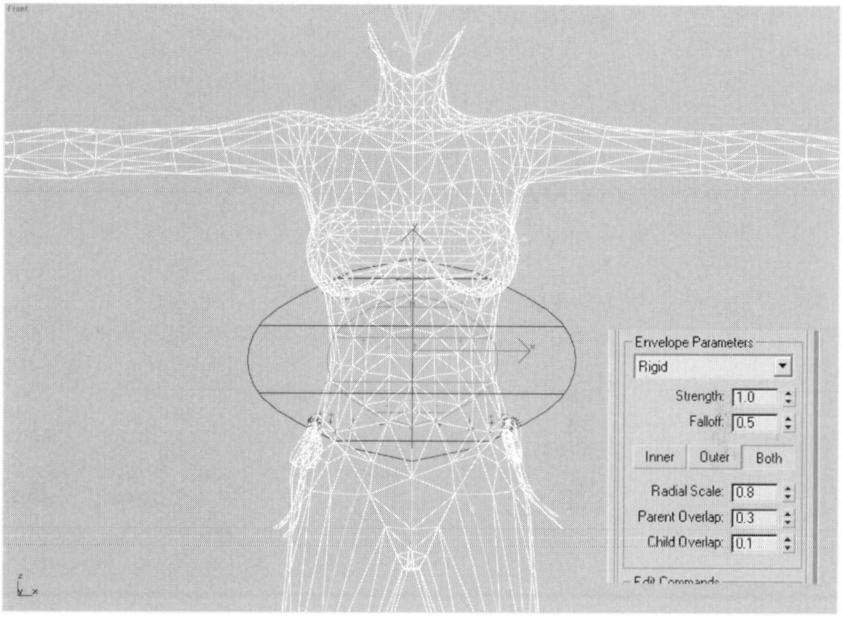

FIGURE 4.24   The waist area needs to extend slightly into the pelvis.

Extending the Spine envelope down into the pelvis area helps compensate for the Pelvis link being turned off. The two links that connect the Spine link to the Thigh links are also called *Spine links*, but they really serve as left and right Pelvis links.

While the naming convention for links in character studio 3 is better overall than in character studio 2, the decision to allow redundant naming is puzzling. Equally perplexing is the decision to call the links directly above the thighs and, in fact, inside the hips area 'Spine.' Why not L Hip and R Hip?

These two overlapping "Spine" envelopes need to not only maintain the shape of the hips, pelvis, and rear, but they need to also overlap the Thigh links. Select the two links that appear just above the Thigh links. Leave their Radial Scale and Parent Overlap as is, and increase their Child Overlap to 0.7 (Figure 4.25).

Moving down to the thighs, several adjustments need to be made. First, the Radial Scale needs to be reduced to 0.8 so that the left thigh envelope reaches less of the right thigh vertices, and vice versa. Next, to

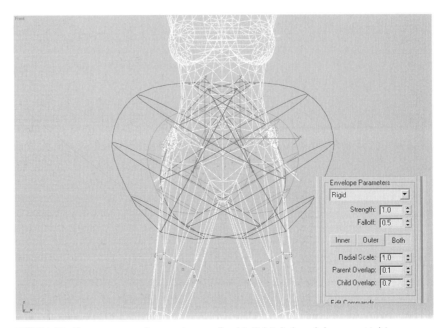

FIGURE 4.25   These two envelopes take over for the Pelvis link and do a great job!

avoid influencing too much of the rear geometry, the Parent Overlap can be reduced to 0. Just like the UpperArm link, the Thigh link needs to leave the Forearm link alone, so enter a value of 0 for the Child Overlap as well (Figure 4.26).

Finally, the Betty L Calf and Betty R Calf links are taken care of with the same sort of child/parent adjustments. Reduce the Radial Scale to 0.8, leave Parent Overlap the same, and change Child Overlap to 0 (Figure 4.27).

You can now work on the feet. The bottom edge vertices of the feet need to be rigid. They make contact with the ground and don't need to deform, other than allowing for the Toes to bend when appropriate. In the case of Bikini, her toes can't bend, so all the vertices lower than the ankle can be assigned solely to the Foot link (Figure 4.28).

RESORTING TO TYPE-IN WEIGHTS

Finally, as a last resort, type in the weights for areas of the mesh that can't be fixed by any other quick envelope tweaking. The thumb is a great example of a mesh area that needs to have weights entered manually. The trick is to divide it up into *zones* that correspond to the underlying links,

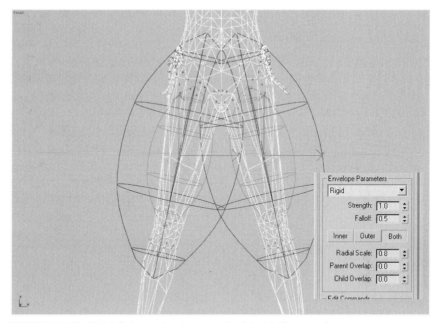

FIGURE 4.26   The Thigh links need to have much of their influence taken away.

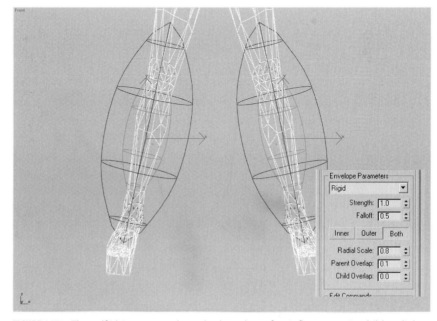

FIGURE 4.27   The calf/shin area needs to also have less of an influence on its children links.

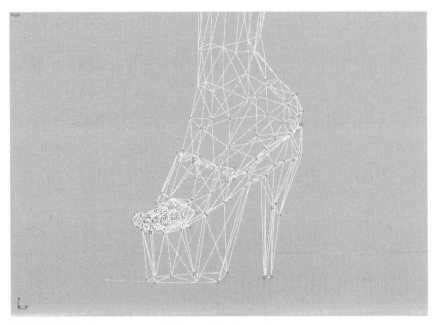

FIGURE 4.28   The feet need to be rigid at their bottom edge.

and assign the vertices to those links. Vertices that are right on the line between links will, of course, get equal influence from each link. For example, links A through E would have all the vertices inside their grid "borders" assigned to them, with vertices close to the edges of border getting equal influence (Figure 4.29).

You can spend as much or as little time as you care to with the fingers and thumb. Generally, they won't be an easily recognized detail in a real-time game character.

Assigning the Breast Vertices

The breast area also benefits from manually assigning the vertices. As the breasts move and bounce, via the Spring controllers assigned to the breast "bones," the mesh needs to deform appropriately and look realistic. Assigning the vertices manually means the breast shape maintains the appropriate form while animated.

Go to the Right viewport, zoom in to the chest, and select the vertices around the breasts, hiding all the other vertices of the mesh so that you have a clear workspace (Figure 4.30).

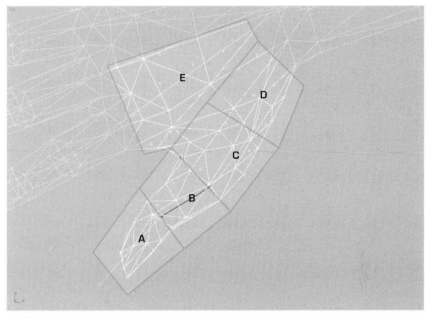

FIGURE 4.29   Zone off the thumb area in order to weight it properly.

FIGURE 4.30   Begin weighting the breasts by hiding all the other vertices of the mesh.

Whenever a majority of vertices need to be hidden, take advantage of Select Invert. Simply select the vertices you want to remain in view, go to the Edit pull-down menu, and click on Select Invert. Then the selected vertices become unselected and the formerly unselected vertices become selected, allowing you to hide them (Figure 4.31).

Edit	Tools	Group	Views	Create	Modi
Undo Select			Ctrl+Z		
Redo			Ctrl+A		
Hold			Alt+Ctrl+H		
Fetch			Alt+Ctrl+F		
Delete			Delete		
Clone					
Select All					
Select None					
Select Invert					
Select By			▶		
Region			▶		
Edit Named Selections...					
Object Properties...					

FIGURE 4.31   Select Invert is the fastest way to select and hide a large group of vertices.

Next, rotate around to the front of the mesh, then select and hide any vertices that are part of the torso and that are not supposed to move with the breasts. An exception to this would be the cleavage area—it will move with the breasts to avoid bad deformation (Figure 4.32).

Once the immobile torso vertices are hidden, go to the Front viewport again, and select all of the vertices of the right-side breast geometry, *including* the cleavage vertices of the left-side geometry. Make sure Rigid is selected as the Vertex type. Under Blending Between Links, choose No Blending, and assign the selected vertices to the b_rbreast_nub link at the end of the right breast's bone chain (Figure 4.33).

The center vertices that make up the cleavage can really be assigned to either the left or right link. Including them in this step saves time. Hold down the Alt key and *deselect* all the vertices you just selected; bring up your Type-In Weights menu, and enter 1 for b_lbreast_nub to share influence over these cleavage vertices (Figure 4.34).

Select the remaining vertices on the left side and assign them to the b_lbreast_nub link at the end of the left breast's bone chain. Now comes the trial-and-error phase of trying some weighting values for the vertices that tie into the rest of the torso at the top of the breast areas. Select only the vertices that are above the breasts and below the armpits, and add the Bikini Spine2 as an influential link (Figure 4.35).

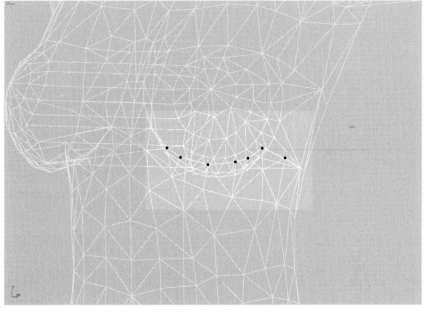

FIGURE 4.32   Select and hide vertices that are part of the torso lying *behind* the breasts.

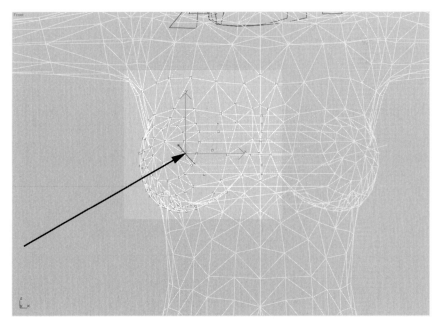

FIGURE 4.33   Assign all the vertices within the box to the b_rbreast_nub link.

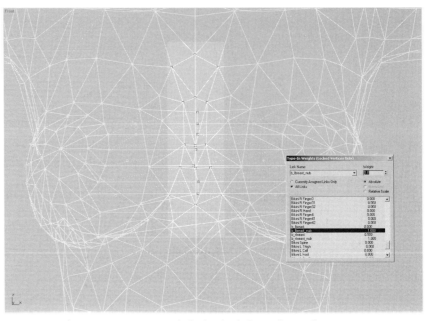

FIGURE 4.34   These center vertices are linked to both Breast "bones."

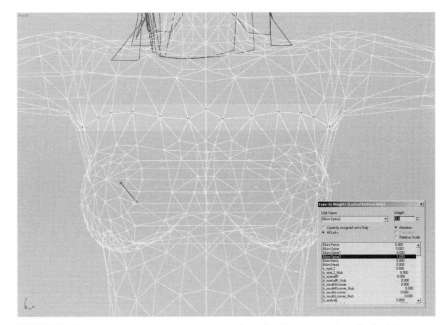

FIGURE 4.35   Partially assigning these vertices to Spine2 will dampen the effect of the breast links, resulting in better deformation.

That will ensure the breasts don't stretch unnaturally as they move around. To further help this area, add influence from Spine1 to the torso vertices at the side of the breast (Figure 4.36).

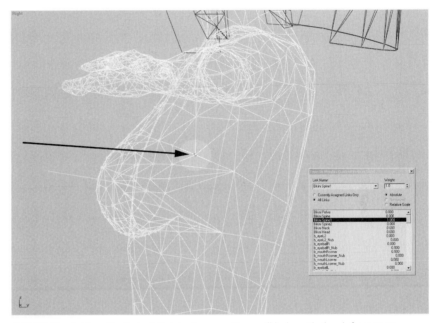

FIGURE 4.36   Adding the Spine1 link to these vertices will help with the deformation.

Turn the Initial Skeletal Pose off and go to a shaded viewport. Scrub the Time Slider back and forth to see how the mesh deforms as the character moves. When you're satisfied that the breasts are moving more naturally, it's time to move on to adjusting the head and face.

Adjusting the Head and Face

With a character like Betty Bad, the head geometry doesn't have any moving parts and is assigned fully to the Head link—nice and simple. For a character like Bikini, on the other hand, there usually is some sort of facial rig. With the addition of a more elaborate hairstyle, there could also be bones attached to the head (like a ponytail) that would require more thought and effort put into the weighting of the head. Then it's just a matter of manually typing in the weighting values again. However, now that you have the basic understanding of how to do that and how to adjust envelopes, take a break from trying to follow along and simply study the finished product.

Load Bikini3.max from the Chapter4 directory on the companion CD-ROM. Select the head geometry and go to the Vertex Sub-Object menu under Physique (Figure 4.37).

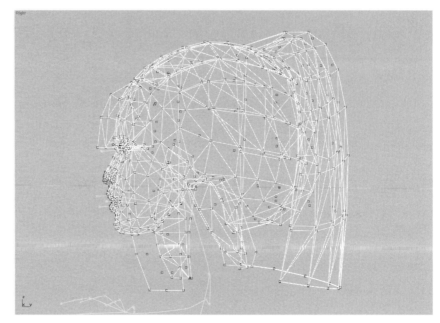

FIGURE 4.37   Nearly all the vertices of this character's head are assigned to the Head link.

Note that most of the vertices are only assigned to one link and that there are very few blended dark-green ones. The vertices at the base of the neck have to share weighting with the Neck link, of course, because the head fits exactly on top of the body (even though it's detached). The vertices by the mouth and eyes are weighted to more than one bone, because that's what is required to accommodate the basic facial rig attached to the character: moving eyes, blinking eyes, and parting lips.

The important thing to remember is to begin weighting the head by simply assigning *everything* to the Head link. This cleans up any stray weighting or unwanted envelope influence over the geometry and provides a basic starting point. Then, if there are multiple objects that make up the head, as with this character, start with the geometry that can be weighted fastest and then hidden out of the way. In this case, the hair was first. All of it was assigned to the head, even the geometry that was near the shoulders and neck (in this case, no one will miss any *swish-swish* of the ponytail mesh) and the mesh object was hidden. The m_mouth geometry was next (Figure 4.38).

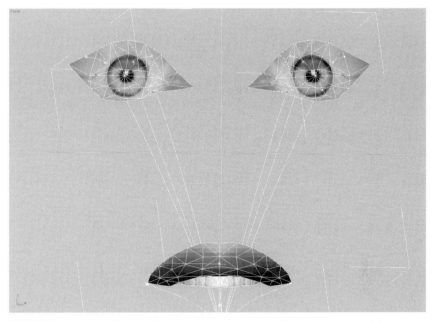

FIGURE 4.38   Geometry is sometimes kept detached purely for access when weighting.

The eyeball elements are weighted mostly to the Head link, while the circular arrangement of triangles in the center of the eyes are weighted to the eyeball bone links. This makes it seem like the whole eye is moving, even though it's just the iris. The lips and teeth are assigned to the Head link, too, because of the minimal amount of animation required for the character's mouth.

Keeping the lips of your character detached as an element within the mesh, even if they're low-res, helps keep a nice line for that part of the mouth and prevents smoothing from adding ugliness to the geometry's surface.

After m_mouth, the head itself was weighted, starting with the neck-line. This was done by adjusting the values of m_head and m_body at the same time (Figure 4.39).

The vertices of the neck highlighted in Figure 4.39 are where the Biped's head meets the neck; they are equally influenced by both Head link and Neck link. The vertices just below them are given a weighting of 1 to the Neck and 0.5 to the Head, to ensure the area deforms smoothly as the head turns from side to side. The vertices *above* the head bone's pivot point are actually influenced by Neck, Head, and *Jaw* links. The hair

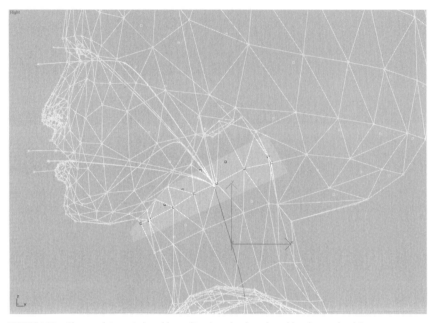

FIGURE 4.39   The neck is weighted by adjusting the head and body mesh objects simultaneously, because the vertices lie flush with each other.

mass can be assigned just to the Head link. Speaking of the jaw, these vertices are assigned partially or fully to the Jaw link (Figure 4.40).

The extra link at the end of the jaw isn't really necessary, but it makes the link easier to select than if it went directly to the lower lip "bone." Its main purpose is to further deform the bottom lip, if necessary. The corners of the mouth are weighted to allow the bones there to create a pout or a smile. The rest of the face, up to the eyes, is weighted to the head.

Next, work on the eyes. The two bones that control each eyelids are all that are necessary to make the character blink (Figure 4.41).

When creating a character that has to blink, it's easier to weight and animate the geometry when starting in an eyes-closed position. When using bones, an eyes-open pose is more difficult to weight and animate to appear closed than the other way around.

These vertices share influence with the Head link and the individual *eye bone* links (not the *eyeball* bones). If the character required more

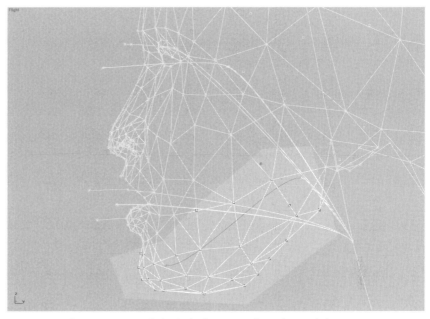

FIGURE 4.40   These vertices are linked wholly or partially to the Jaw link.

FIGURE 4.41   The eye geometry is built with the eyelids *closed*, to allow for weighting.

expressions, additional bones would need to be added for eyebrow movement. Once the eyelid geometry has been weighted, you can bring back the hair geometry, with the eyelashes attached, and give them the same weighting that you did for the eyelids (Figure 4.42).

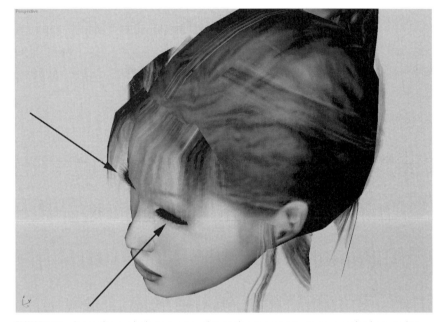

FIGURE 4.42 Since the eyelash geometry shares the same texture map as the hair, it also shares the same mesh object.

That wraps up weighting a higher resolution real-time character. Remember to make envelopes do as much of the work as you can, before getting your hands dirty at the manually-weighted vertex level. It will save you many hours of work and effort (Figure 4.43).

SUMMARY

Adjusting envelopes is the best way to tackle the weighting of higher resolution real-time characters. The base pose of a character that will be relying on envelope weighting needs to be well thought out. By putting the character in the "da Vinci pose" (arms out, feet apart), the limbs are separated enough so that so that the envelopes generated avoid influencing the wrong geometry.

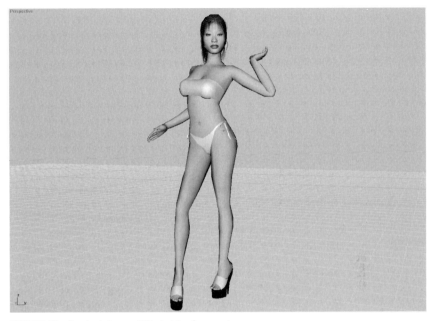

FIGURE 4.43 Say *buh-bye* to Bikini girl—for now!

The order in which you apply Physique and adjust weighting is also more important when primarily using envelopes. If Physique is applied to all the mesh objects of a character at the same time, then any envelope settings are applied across all the objects, even if they're hidden or unselected. For that reason, when dealing with a higher resolution character, you need to achieve as much of the weighting via envelopes as possible before resorting to manually entering the weighting values. It saves time and effort.

THINGS TO CONSIDER BEFORE YOU ANIMATE

I f you go to *www.dictionary.com*, the definition of *animation* you'll find is: "The act, process, or result of imparting life, interest, spirit, motion, or activity." In order to fully understand that definition, in order to "impart life" into your characters, you need to be alive yourself. You need to have the innate ability to recognize what looks right and what doesn't look right when a character is moving around. You need to *breathe* life into your characters—they're not going to take on life by themselves. Do this by opening your eyes to everything and everyone around you. Watch movies with the sound off, to better concentrate on movement without the distraction of noise. Grab a book on stage-acting or even body language, to see how physical movement becomes communication. Take the act of animation *seriously*. This attitude, this mental aspect of animating characters, may feel a bit melodramatic, but it's *required* if you want to stand out from the pack. So, take a moment to consider some of the elements to be thought out before animating your real-time game characters.

Know Your Character

Successful character animation, whether it's for rendered or real-time purposes, relies on many factors: the skill of the animator, the complexity of the character being animated, the time available to do the animations—the list can go on. However, the most important thing to remember when animating a character is simply to *know it*. Knowing your character is the first step towards bringing it to electronic life. Thinking of the character as a real person or creature and animating it in a way that's consistent with its nature will result in believable animation. Think of yourself as both puppet master and puppet, or director and actor. Achieve the performance you're after in your animation by constantly asking yourself, "Is this something the character would do, and is this how they would do it?"

Knowing your characters requires in-depth study and an intuitive sense of what they're about. While creating a written description and sketching the physical appearance can ensure you know your characters on the surface, your translation of those inputs into *action* requires that you know the characters completely. Don't be satisfied with just a one-to-one processing of the information at hand. Strive to rise above mediocre, lifeless animation, and search for some sort of *uniqueness* and individual quality to inject into your characters' movements. Make their animations not only adhere to and reinforce their identity, but make them stick in the mind of the person viewing those animations as something *cool*.

Appearance Dictates Identity

The first step in knowing your character is to look at the model and any "action" sketches done in pre-production. This will spark your imagination and begin to give you ideas for how the character should move. For example, consider Widge. As a bad guy in *Betty Bad*, he's an evil alien bent on defeating mankind—but he's also a soldier. He isn't too smart, and it's not even known if *he* is actually a "he." One thing is for certain, though—he's *nasty* (Figure 5.1)!

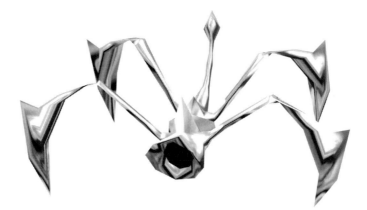

FIGURE 5.1   Widge is not a nice guy (or really even a *guy*, for that matter).

Why is he nasty? Well, he looks it, for one thing. He's all spiny and angular, and his metallic skin is intended to make him even more of an unfeeling, *inflexible* character who is entirely single-minded: He wants to eat you. Even his eye is red, to let you know he's a bad guy and he's dangerous. His physical appearance is based on a written description that says: "Widge is the fodder for the game. He's mean, nasty, and travels in packs."

This isn't much to go on, but combined with the model, it's enough to inspire thought about the character's animations. While it's important to adhere to the initial description, you need to give it a little more depth, even if it's only in your mind. He's a bad guy without remorse. He's a little "Terminator," who won't stop until he's been obliterated. Maybe he's a bit too eager sometimes, and trips. Maybe when he gets knocked back, he tumbles, rolls, and then comes right back at you because he's so anxious to eat you (Figure 5.2).

Fill in the character's gaps—whatever it takes. The duty of the character animator is to use your imagination to give the character a personality,

FIGURE 5.2   Widge is feisty, nasty, and mean, and his animations reflect it.

providing an identity template to follow while animating the character. If no detailed background on the character exists, then create one. Don't straddle the fence on a character's mannerisms or characteristics. Decide what they are, and commit to them while putting it through its paces. It will make a difference in the character's overall impact in the game.

The game *Betty Bad* is supposed to be light-hearted fare. It's not serious entertainment, just a little diversion to have fun with. So despite Widge's nasty demeanor, he can't be all salt and vinegar. He needs to reflect a little of the *game's* attitude, as well. So take another look at his design. He has a fairly flexible tail that's probably for balance, but then again, maybe he's like a dog and exhibits emotion through the appendage. Or maybe he's like a cat and swishes it from side to side, right before he's ready to pounce! How you treat just one design element of a character, like Widge's tail, can make all the difference in the attitude and nature of the character. The geometry of the character can inspire as well as direct the animations, even if it isn't written down for you.

Uniqueness Required

While *uniqueness* was mentioned earlier, it was meant to be a motivational suggestion to bring something to a character's motions that's not mundane. It also applies to individual characters when compared to other characters in the same game. Give them a limp, or a lean, or something that helps identify them in a line-up with the other characters in a game. Give them a consistent aspect to their animations that keeps them in character. While uniqueness also means trying to inject something different into your characters' movements to make them stand out, try also to animate them so they are interesting and fun to watch.

Widge, for example, is always hungry. It's a very powerful driving instinct that compels his species to attack and conquer. He lives to feed. Naturally, therefore, he will eat almost anything—including a fallen comrade (Figure 5.3)!

FIGURE 5.3   Scoop, lift, and swallow—the observed eating habits of an evil alien.

The animation for Widge's feeding changed the game's design and affected the gameplay, because everyone on the Betty Bad team thought it was so cool. It also provided a reason for the character to stop and occasionally be an easier target for the player. This sort of improvisation and experimentation frequently happens during the animation phase and can positively impact a game. Therefore, even though it was kind of weird, the feeding animation for Widge made it into the game primarily because *it's what the character would do*. He stayed true to his perceived character, and the action made a twisted sort of sense. Remember, making sure your character stays in character can only happen if you *know* your character.

THE ANIMATION SET

A character's *animation set* is the sum total of all his animations that are required to be a part of the game. The number of animations, and kinds of animations, depend on many things. When determining a character's animation set, the genre, point of view of the game, its environment, any file-size limitations, gameplay mechanics, and how the characters are implemented within the game's core technology are all factors to consider.

Genre

There are lots of genres of games available today: action, strategy, puzzle, racing, fighting, adventure, and so on. There are even sub-genres, like first-person shooter (FPS) action games and third-person shooter action games, "top-down" view racing games, and "in the car" racing games. When you think "real-time characters," you mostly think of those found in action games like *Quake*™, *Unreal*™, or *Betty Bad*. But even Luigi of Nintendo's GameCube game, *Luigi's Mansion*™, and an X-Wing fighter from the Star Wars™ game, *Rogue Squadron II: Rogue Leader*™ are real-time game characters.

The animation sets for each character will differ solely in the way they're implemented to support their genre. For example, in a typical FPS, the characters run around a visually rich world, jumping, strafing, and blowing things up with bright, satisfying explosions. They zip around at superhuman speeds and make slippery and elusive targets for the player behind the mouse. However, to make these characters come to life, an artist has animated them, then programmed them to respond to input from the person playing the game. The basic animation set for games of the *Quake* and *Unreal* genre are basically made up of the following actions:

- Idle
- Run
- Backpedal
- Walk
- Jump
- Crouch
- Crouch walk
- Strafe left
- Strafe right
- Shooting attack
- Melee attack
- Change weapon
- Taunt
- Pain
- Death

Idle animations are what you see when the character is inactive and waiting for input. This could really be nothing more than one frame of being "ready" to go into action. The other animations are either locomotive in nature (attack or response from an attack) or getting temporarily knocked out of action ("death" or recovery animation). This list supports a character's movements based primarily on the demands of fast, responsive input from the player. In other words, it supports the basic gameplay requirements of an FPS: evade, attack, and die.

During the development of Quake II *and* Quake III Arena (Q3A)*, it was suggested several times that the ideal deathmatch character would be just a box with the player's face on it. It would keep the character's file-size to almost nothing and reflect just how much hardcore deathmatchers cared about the aesthetics of regular real-time game characters.*

These animations are the meat and potatoes of the FPS character, but what about the third-person action game? In a game like those in the *Lara Croft Tomb Raider*™ series, Lara Croft runs, jumps, flips, and generally shows you her shapely posterior during the entire game. She climbs, scoots, and straddles her way through very complex and very demanding levels. For a third-person character like her, the animations set is decidedly more comprehensive.

Environment

A game's environment also affects a player's animations set. Will the character fly? Is there water to swim in? Are climbing up ledges even part of the game dynamics? Is rope-climbing or rope-swinging required (Figure 5.4)?

FIGURE 5.4   A swim animation is only required if there's something to actually swim *in*.

Game design will answer these questions. The level designer, project leader, or art director will usually determine and clarify the issues. The bottom line is that genre greatly affects many elements in the game design, especially the animation set.

Size Still Matters

Once the genre and game design elements are considered, the amount of memory a character takes up also comes into question, as does the assessment of how many animations there will be and what type of animation will be required. For example, a ceiling of 2 megabytes might be set for a game character for in-game use. The mesh might take up 100 kilobytes, the texture another 300 kilobytes, and the sounds 400 kilobytes. That would only leave about 1.2 megabytes for the animations! This allocation affects the creators' approach when determining not only the animation set, but the length and playback speed as well. It means that an extra-long death animation must instead become about 10 frames showing the character doing a face-plant, and the frame-rate is reduced from a lush 30 frames per second (fps) to a potentially ugly 15 fps. Sometimes, however, characters require a large list of animations just to function within the game (Figure 5.5).

FIGURE 5.5 In *Betty Bad*, the main character has nearly 3,000 frames of animation.

While all game characters need to be frugal with their frames, multi-player games are particularly sensitive to the number and length of their characters' animations.

Multi-player characters like those seen in Quake *or* Unreal *need to consume as little memory as possible, due to the nature of playing games online. As players duke it out in their favorite deathmatch level, feedback information is sent back and forth invisibly between players' machines. Characters with large animation sets, large numbers of polygons, and large texture maps not only make it hard to support a multi-player environment, but slow a game down noticeably because of the work involved in processing the data that represents the character.*

While the main character of a single-player game usually has the most number of animation frames, sometimes other characters that are used frequently have just as many (if not more) animations. In Gray Matter Interactive Studios' *Return to Castle Wolfenstein™*, the main character is never seen outside of scripted cutscenes and option screens, so his animation set is subsequently lower than most of the other characters in the game.

Another reason a character's animation set could be larger than another's is a matter of utility. To save memory and maximize assets, some characters can easily be turned into *other* characters by scaling them up or down programmatically and adding or subtracting "accessories" to the character at predetermined points. To add to their effect and distinctiveness, the characters will exclusively use select animations as well as share animations from a larger animation set. In *Return to Castle Wolfenstein*, the designers and artists employed an excellent system of one body and multiple heads; to make the oft-seen Infantry and Elite Guard soldiers appear as different characters, heads and accessories are randomly swapped. These characters referenced difference animation sets based on their configurations.

In contrast to the main character and the "fodder" characters that pop up frequently, the "Boss" or major bad-guy characters (usually seen at the end of levels in most games) have hardly any animations at all. Those they do have are mainly attacking, showing pain, and then the payoff when you defeat them: a big, elaborate death animation.

Game Controls

The game controls that drive a character also play a role in deciding the number and types of animations a character needs. In *Betty Bad*, when a change of direction is sudden enough, Betty performs another animation that reinforces the suddenness. For example, when strafing left or strafing right, Betty shuffles left or right appropriately. When going side-to-side fast enough, she will perform a dramatic cartwheel motion that covers more distance and looks really cool (Figure 5.6)!

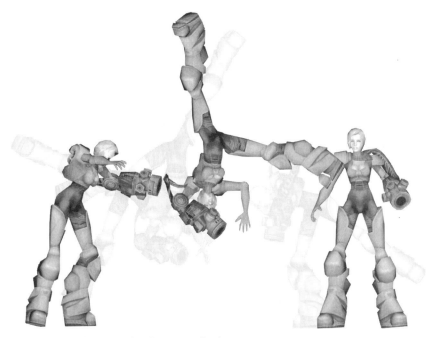

FIGURE 5.6 See Betty run. See Betty *cartwheel*!

In Quake, *the first, highly successful* three-dimensional *FPS, instant weapon switching was a feature. This meant that when you chose a different weapon,* poof! *It appeared. During the development of* Quake II, *a lengthy and ongoing debate developed over the amount of time a character spent changing weapons and whether or not it was even necessary. People complained that it was too slow, and the arguments that resulted boiled down to the difference between* tenths of seconds. *When Q3A was made, the decision to animate the weapon switch by flicking the arm down and away from the body also caused a controversy about whether to perform the action in 0.6 seconds or 0.9 seconds. The shorter length of time won, and players around the globe rejoiced.*

Game Technology

A character's animation set can change a game's core technology, but more often than not, it's a slave to it. In *Quake* and *Quake II*, the characters had no animations to support turning or looking around. During deathmatch, if you were to see another player "free," looking around, you would see the character in a single action pose, rotating and moving while frozen in that pose. During the development of *Q3A*, a new animation system was implemented to support not only "looking around," but also to portray character movements more realistically. The characters' animations had to be divided into three parts: head, torso, and legs. When given input from the player moving his mouse, the head would respond, then the torso, and then the legs. All three would be involved if moving while shooting or gesturing.

While creating the new animation system in Q3A, *a side-to-side shuffle animation was tried to simulate strafing. It wouldn't work because the game engine didn't support smooth blending between animations. The solution was to turn the character's legs at a 45-degree angle while strafing left or right, with the upper body pointing wherever the player pointed. This helped keep the animation set low, but it wasn't very accurate or realistic.*

The decision to divide the characters into three distinct parts for *Q3A* was made because regardless the action, character animations can be roughly grouped into three different categories (Figure 5.7):

- Lower body (running, jumping, etc.)
- Upper body (shooting, weapon changing, etc.)
- Full body (deaths, taunts, etc.)

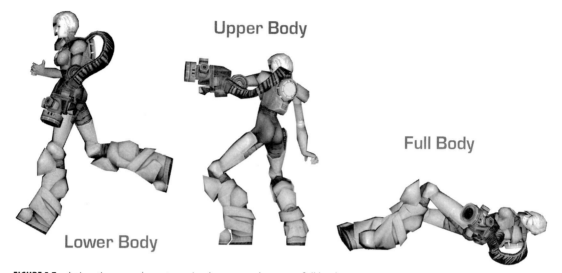

FIGURE 5.7   Animations can be categorized as upper, lower, or full body movements.

Q3A takes the categorization literally because it has to support the game's technology and animation system. However in Betty Bad's case, *all* her animations involve her full body, because the animation system didn't support segmented body parts like in *Q3A*. Instead, the game technology requires unique animations for any given situation. This technological difference resulted in Betty's huge animation set, and was due to redundancy and covering every animation situation throughout the game. For example, in order for Betty to run in the game, she had to have *four* different animations: her normal run, her run while shooting, her run while shooting going diagonally to her right, and her run while shooting going diagonally to her left (Figure 5.8).

Involving the full body in all the animations makes them richer—they simply look better. The fact that *Betty Bad* is a third-person game also required that more attention be placed on the aesthetic value of the main character, since she's fully on screen at all times.

Once all the factors have been taken into consideration and the animation set for a character is roughed out, the next real question to consider before animating your character is what technique to use—keyframe or motion capture.

KEYFRAME OR MOTION CAPTURE?

As a character animator, it's very important to understand the timing necessary to simulate realistic and exaggerated motion. The biggest

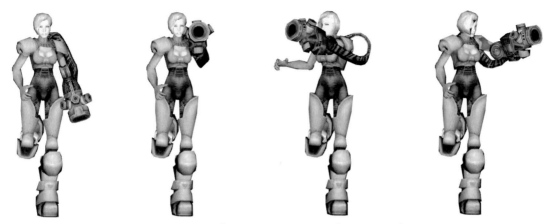

FIGURE 5.8 Betty's run animation has to be in four versions to support the game engine.

question you always need to ask yourself is, "Does this look right?" Does the animation succeed in its intent? More important, does it fit the character?

When it comes to character animation, there seem to be two approaches to take: keyframe or motion capture (*mocap*)—that's "*seem to be*," because in reality, all your animations are keyframed. You simply can't animate a character without dealing with keyframes. While some opponents of motion capture decry its validity (it's not "art"), it's just a tool like any other plug-in, bought mesh, or scanned texture you would use. Many purists feel it has to be one or the other, keyframe or mocap. However, mocap is merely a *starting point* to animate characters, not a replacement for keyframing. The truth is that when animating real-time game characters, using a combination of both keyframe and mocap is an excellent solution for achieving great animations *quickly*. However, there is no doubt whatsoever that your first step to mastering character animation is learning how to *keyframe*.

Keyframing Defined

Keyframe animation is the act of posing an object or character at time intervals or at different "frames," and allowing the computer to fill in the gaps between those intervals, simulating motion. In regular cel animation, senior artists make keyframes while junior artists fill in the "tweens" (cels between the keyframes).

The steps involved in keyframing in 3ds max are:

- Turn on the Animate button (it becomes red).
- Select the object you wish to animate.

- Select the Move or Rotate Transform icon.
- Move or rotate the selected object, thus "setting" the keyframe.
- Advance forward in time and set another keyframe.
- Scrub the time slider back and forth between keyframes to review the animation.
- Make adjustments as necessary.

When to Keyframe

It's true that all of the animation for a character (*any* character) can be done solely by keyframing them. In fact, if you're completely new to character animation, it's a good idea to animate at least one character solely by keyframing all its moves, before you ever touch a mocap file. However, this isn't a hard and fast rule and like all other rules ("Clean your plate," "Color within the lines," "Finish every book you start" . . .), is meant to be taken for its intent and acted upon only if *you really want to*. The important thing about keyframing is to understand how to do it, so when and if mocap is used, it can be tweaked and *augmented* as necessary with keyframes.

There are some animations that are better suited for keyframes than for mocap, though. As a general rule, when animating a character with a typical animation set, the idle animations, upper body animations, and hard-to-mocap moves, like swimming, are usually best done by keyframing them. This is more for expediency's sake than anything else. The idle animations are particularly better suited for keyframing, because they're generally very slight and very subtle. The exception to this is when the character has to do a special idle animation, like breaking into a fancy dance or lying down to take a nap.

In Betty Bad, *if you sit idle for too long, the heroine of the game will turn around and do a bit of hip-hop before* demanding *that you get on with playing the game. This sort of "conditional" idle is a way to give a character more personality.*

Of course, motion capturing four-legged animals to apply to a four-legged character is hard to come by. Usually these types of characters are animated solely through keyframing. So, that covers when to use keyframes, but when do you use motion capture?

When to Use Mocap

Motion capture is the process of capturing movement from a real object or person and using the data generated to animate a computer-generated object or person. Special markers are placed over the joints of actors, and special hardware then samples the position and/or orientation of those markers in time, generating a set of motion data.

Mocap is ideal for animating real-time characters, because it adds realism to a fantastic setting. Looking at a lower-poly character, you can tell whether it's computer-generated. If the animations aren't very good, the structural failings are even more apparent. With mocap, the movements make you suspend your disbelief and let the character *in*. But motion capture is nothing more than a tool to the animator.

Mocap is ideal for lower body animations and full body animations like deaths and massive knockbacks. Animations like jumps are perfect for mocap, because the nuances and subtleties of adjusting one's weight after recovering from the impact of landing are hard to simulate through keyframes. Complex cutscenes where multiple characters interact are also great for mocap, if for nothing else but the speed with which the animations can be captured and implemented. Studying mocap is also a great way to improve your animation skills. The neck and shoulders are particularly interesting to watch in a mocap animation, since they're not often animated when keyframing.

Tips on the Mocap Process

As great as it is, and as much as it helps achieve quick, realistic animations, mocap isn't for every project. It's a little more costly than keyframing (that is, if your artist is a fast keyframer), and the wait time to get the motion back from the service chosen to do the mocap is sometimes longer than desired. However, if you decide to go the motion capture route, here are some time- and money-saving tips:

Be prepared. This can't be stressed enough. A solid animation list is required in order to obtain a bid from a potential service bureau and is crucial for you to refer to when the shoot takes place. Try to cover all the bases; know exactly what's needed and how you want it broken down. For example, will there be any props (that is, will the character be carrying a weapon or something)? Most mocap houses have a veritable tool chest of ready-made props, but knowing what they are beforehand ensures they'll be available when the time comes. Most mocap studios also have specific naming conventions they adhere to, so come up with a basic naming convention for the animations that is flexible and easy to change.

Shop around for the right service. Call and speak with several studios before committing to one. Consider travel, lodging, and the logistics of the whole process, and make sure that's factored into the bid as well as the actual cost quoted. In most cases, an optical system like Vicon is more preferable than magnetic-resolution or other "suit and cable" systems. Suits are far too restrictive to the actors wearing them, and certain actions like jumps or other moves where the actor leaves the ground can be problematic. Still, these systems usually offer cleaner data and a quicker turnaround time to get your moves. When going with an optical system, make sure the studio has at least eight cameras. This compensates for "losing markers" when a reflective marker is blocked or occluded by a body part or prop. Other factors to consider when choosing the right mocap house are their knowledge of tools you use (such as 3ds max and character studio), past customers of theirs, and their overall attitude toward you, the customer. Some studios, like House of Moves, BioVision, and Loco-Motion, have tons of motion capture files in ready-to-sell libraries. Character studio comes with a substantial motion capture library. However, nothing compares to getting the data you want by setting up a mocap session.

Hire good talent. While it may be tempting to suit up and do the motions yourself, *don't*. It's very important that you hire someone else to have the fun and pain of doing the animations. The most important reason, however, is the performance itself. You have to be able to *see* the actor do the moves and then nicely guide them into doing what it is you really want. Studios like House of Moves have casting calls to show you potential actors. Find someone who fits the bill and is comfortable performing. During the shoot, they will look to you or whoever is directing them for guidance and comments on their performance, so be critical when putting them through the animations. Just don't be insensitive to an actor who's trying to get it right.

Rehearse the motions before the shoot. The week before, the day before, the morning before, and during the session itself, run through each animation before capturing it. The more times you do this, the easier and the *sooner* you will get the motions you want. In *Star Wars: Episode I* and other movies that feature big fight scenes, the actions are rehearsed up to a hundred times before committing to film. Take your job seriously—rehearse!

Have the animator direct. The animator that will be using the data needs to be at the motion capture session—directing the shoot, if possible. To direct, all you have to do is focus on the performance of the talent and, as you do each take, make suggestions to get the motion right. Be very precise in your comments and give tangible suggestions for improving the move. If you're too shy to direct, have someone who is more qualified do the directing, but be there watching the process. A producer and his assistant are great for doing what they do back at the studio, but at a mocap session, an artist is needed to make sure the data matches what is required and desired. If you're supposed to work with the data, and your producer won't allow you to go to the shoot, find another company to work for.

Video the sessions with time code. Most studios will have this covered, but it's crucial to have some sort of video reference to choose the motions you want. This makes selecting the *in* and *out times* (the beginning and end of a motion) easier and allows the clean-up process, which can be lengthy and somewhat painstaking, to happen more quickly. Also, keep notes during the mocap session; you will need to refer to them during the selection of animations to keep/cleanup, especially if many animations are captured.

Bring any appropriate character models to the session. While not mandatory, bringing models already rigged and weighted can't hurt. Even giving the Biped file that will be used with the data to be captured to the motion capture technician is helpful when going through the arduous cleanup process.

Be clear on the deliverable date. Before you leave the motion capture studio, make sure you have an understanding of when the data will be delivered to you in its final form. Plan on the process taking anywhere from one to four weeks, depending on the number of animations you've had captured.

While motion capture may not be for everyone, it behooves you as a character animator to not only learn more about it, but to actually give it a try and evaluate its usefulness before jumping in with the Purists and Luddites and refusing to even consider it. Of course, regardless of which approach you take, once you have your animations, you need to know what to do with them.

IMPLEMENTING THE CHARACTER

The last things to understand before animating are how real-time characters are implemented in the game, the relationship between art and code, and why characters are generally animated "in-place."

While in some ways, technology dictates the animation set, building a game is always a combination of art and code, vision and implementation. Art includes production design, models, textures, animation level design, and sound. Code is integral to the game engine, game tools, game functionality, and game design (which is definitely an art form, most of the time). Even the people who *work* on the game can be lumped into the two categories of artists or programmers. (Even though game designers generally straddle the line, individuals definitely weight toward either the artist or programmer.)

While a game may be your favorite due to nostalgia or to some other personal reason, most of the great games you've played over the years have had the perfect balance of art and code. Games that excel at one or the other are definitely memorable, too. Whether or not you'll like a game that is good at one and *bad* in another depends on the extremes, and of course, games that are terrible in both are not likely to remain in your possession. This idea that the combination of art and technology is important can also be carried down into the individual *components* of the game as well. The option menus, the game screen, the gameplay mechanics, and *especially* the implementation of the characters all benefit and work well when the ideal balance of art and code is attained.

Perpetual Windup Toy

So what is the actual mechanism by which a character is viewable and playable in the game world? The next time you play an FPS or action game, look at the characters' *feet* as they walk or run around. Undoubtedly, they're sliding a little bit, relative to the movement of the character. This is due to the fact that all your character animations are generally done *in place*. A good analogy of the relationship between the characters, their animations, and the code is that of a wind-up toy soldier: Pick the toy up, turn his key, and hold him off the ground slightly above the floor. His feet move, but no contact is made with the floor. You *simulate* him covering distance by moving him with your hand, instead of setting him down and letting him walk on his own. In the case of the real-time game character, the code becomes your hand, moving the character all over, triggering *this* animation when *that* happens, and *that* animation when *this* happens, making it *seem* like he's running, walking, strafing, and backpedaling (Figure 5.9).

This approach, while common, can't be realistic, because of two factors. First, the speed with which the code moves the character can't be in real time. Instead, the action has to be fast, furious, and frenetic. Thus, the characters tend to *move* faster than normal; given the usual vast scale of the game world, there's just no way you would want to *truly* travel in real-time over the vast distance that world represents.

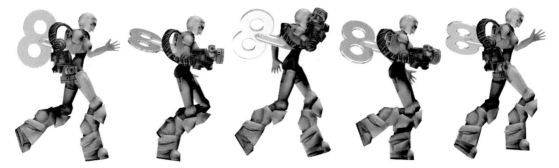

FIGURE 5.9 Introducing the "Action Betty" wind-up toy!

In Doom™, *it has been estimated that the player characters move about 90 miles per hour (mph) when running diagonally. In* Quake™, *the player characters slowed down to about 63 mph, and in* Quake II, *the player characters moved at a paltry 51 mph.*

The second reason why the characters move around in an unrealistic manner involves their *stride*. When a character is moved around programmatically, with its feet running to one speed and its displacement to another, the rate is uniform. There's no ramp-up or wind-down period found in any walk, run, or backpedal when they start or stop. Even the looping animation itself has slight discrepancies in the amount of distance that *should* be covered when moved, according to the motions of the loop. Look at Figure 5.10.

The distance from Point A to Point B is only 8.5 units, because Betty is just beginning her backpedal. The distance from Point B to Point C is 29.3 units, and she's almost into her stride. From Point C to Point D, she travels 33.7 units and is well into her stride, as she is from Point D to Point E, which is 39.8 units. From Point E to Point F is 34.1 units, but she is slowing down, hence her position bending a bit forward. While Points B through F could be a complete loop (look at the left leg), this still shows the variance in the distance covered with a series of strides. Unfortunately, some aspects of the animation have to take a backseat to reality and are at the mercy and uniform pace of the technology.

Fitting the Technology

In *Q3A*, John Carmack remedied the deficiencies of the character animation system by creating the three-piece player model's head, torso, and legs system. This is an example of technology supporting the animation system in a way that result in *fewer* animations.

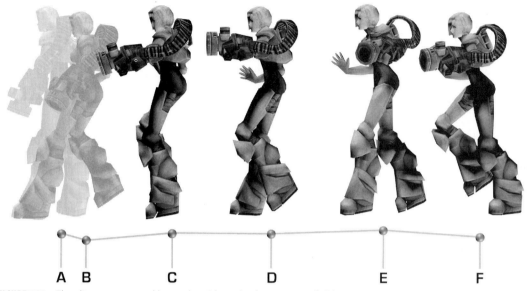

FIGURE 5.10   The distance covered by each stride varies from start to finish.

Betty Bad was not created using *Quake* technology, but WildTangent™ technology. Instead of a three-piece tag system, the character animations had to accommodate a *Quake II*-like *one-piece* system. Therefore, even though she isn't created for deathmatch, the Betty Bad character does accommodate many different circumstances, but at the cost of a much bigger animation set. The engine Betty was dropped into did have one helpful thing that most other game engines have as well: interpolation. That is, the engine can tell the character to go from one established pose to another established pose, at no cost in animation frames by the animator. Still, while helpful, it couldn't help the problem of having to double all the animations that Betty could also shoot from. So it's very crucial that you know and understand all the limitations and features of an animation technology, so that the character and its animations will fit properly in the game engine.

SUMMARY

Now that you have your character built, rigged, weighted, and ready to go, there are a few things to consider before you begin to animate. The first step is to *know* the character you're going to be working with. Bring it to life by assigning a personality to it based on its appearance, any written descriptions, and any additional traits you can imagine. Giving your characters an identity ensures that their animations are consistent with their perceived nature. Strive to apply at least one or two unique traits to a character that make it stand out from other characters in the game and from characters of *other* games. Determining the *animation set* is next on your pre-animation checklist. The animation set is the sum total of animations required for the character to be implemented in the game; it can be influenced by genre, game design, environment, file-size restrictions, game controls, and the overall game technology.

After an animation set is created, you need to ask yourself whether or not to use *motion capture* in addition to *keyframing* your animations. Mocap isn't for everyone, and the budget, time constraints, and complexity of the animation set will determine if it's right for you. If you do choose to use motion capture, be prepared. Shop around for the right motion capture studio or motion library. Use good talent, rehearse the motions beforehand, try to bring any models or Bipeds to the shoot, and when possible, have the animator destined to use the data direct the talent at the shoot. Videotape the session, and be clear on the delivery of the final data.

Finally, implementation of the characters, like all facets of a game, involves a combination of art and code. The programmer and animator need to come up with an animation system that fits the game and accommodates the required gameplay. Often, the success of the system relies on what's being closely focused on and who's in charge of the task. Yet, nearly all characters are manipulated and integrated into the game by programmatically moving them around, keying animations when events take place. The characters are oblivious to their surroundings and go through their animations diligently when told to by the code. Unfortunately, this approach to implementing the characters doesn't account for character motions like ramp-up and wind-down times, transitions, and other random changes in velocity. However, regardless of the system, it's crucial the animator knows and understands it completely, in order to make sure everything works properly when the character is dropped into the game.

KEYFRAME ANIMATION: PART I

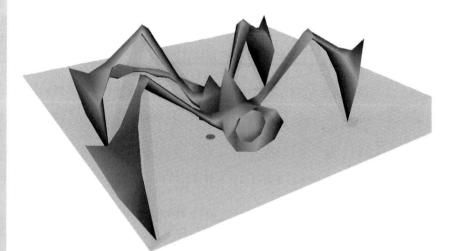

FIRST THINGS FIRST

Learning how to animate a character starts with mastering keyframes and the basic functionality of the tools (in this case, 3ds max 4 and character studio 3). You also need to develop a few procedural approaches specific to animating real-time characters. So, in order to introduce you to these methods and features, in this chapter you're going to create a simple *idle animation* for a relatively simple character: Widge.

Footsteps versus Freeform

In character studio, you can animate a Biped in Freeform mode, in Footstep mode, or using a combination of the two. *Freeform* simply means posing and animating a character the old-fashioned way, keyframe by keyframe. *Footstep* is a powerful tool in character studio that allows you to quickly generate walks, runs, or jumps with all the basic movements associated with them. Footstep parameters can be adjusted to suit different strides and gaits that are appropriate for whatever character you happen to be animating.

Footstep mode won't be covered in this book, but the tutorials that come with character studio are a great source of information if you want to learn how to utilize it. While powerful and comprehensive, the tool is complex and tends to cater to an approach to animating that is more technical than artistic. Animation is about posing and animating your characters, not pushing a button, drawing marks on the floor, and saying, "Go there." However, no malignment of Footstep mode is intended by omitting it from this book. It's just not the most ideal tool to animate *real-time* game characters if you're relatively new to character animation.

Think Animation Folder

Try to think of an individual 3ds max file as an animation *folder* and of the animations for your character as motion clips *within* that folder. The 3ds max file becomes a comprehensive, virtual dossier containing everything you need for your character, from mesh, texture maps, and rig, to the animations. The importance of taking this unified approach to your animations becomes painfully apparent when you have to make a structural change to the character or its Biped. If you have many separate animation files for the same character, you have to repeat the hypothetical structural changes for *all* those files. This just doesn't make good sense and the redundant work is a huge waste of time.

However, sometimes it's okay, and even necessary, to animate specific animations and save them as an individual file. This is more appropriate for creating a *Biped* file than a *character* file. It also applies mainly to motion capture or extremely long animation files (more on this later when you learn how to stream animations together using the *Motion Flow Editor*).

Preparing the Biped

The character on which you're going to cut your keyframing teeth is Widge. As stated earlier, he's one of the bad guys from the game *Betty Bad*. He's not a typical game character in the two-legged sense—he's a four-legged critter and must be animated using keyframes only. But Widge is an easy guy to animate, and more important, he illustrates the flexibility and utility of Biped.

ON THE CD

A Betty Bad demo can be found on the CD-ROM that came with this book. If you haven't installed and played it yet, you may want to, just to see how this animation will be implemented. It isn't mandatory, it's just a suggestion!

ON THE CD
Get started by loading Widge3.max from the Chapter6 directory on this book's CD-ROM (Figure 6.1).

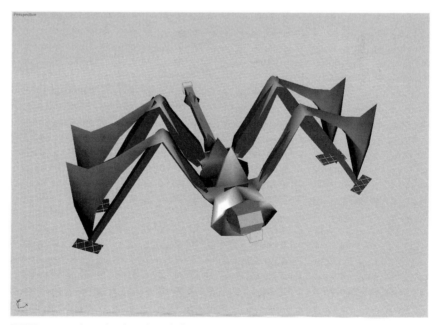

FIGURE 6.1   Widge is back and ready for you to make him a *baaad* guy.

As you can see, Widge is rigged, weighted, and ready to go. However, as with any character, there are a few things you need to do first to make your life a bit easier while animating. Begin by making the mesh easier to see in a shaded viewport by assigning a transparent material to all the Biped objects.

Click on the ⠿ Materials Library icon, and create a material called "invisio" that has an opacity setting of 0 (Figure 6.2).

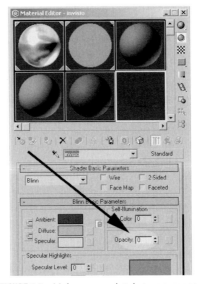

FIGURE 6.2 Make a completely transparent material to assign to the Biped objects.

Select all the Biped objects and assign this material to them. Next, click anywhere in your view to deselect the objects, and go to the Display panel. There's no need to keep the dummy objects in view, so check the box beside Helpers (under Hide By Category) to hide all of them (Figure 6.3).

It's always a good idea to think of your characters as groups of elements. In the simplest sense, any character can be divided into a mesh and Biped group. To quickly isolate them as one element of your scene, select all the Biped objects (without the dummies) and turn them into a *selection set*. Do this by typing the word "biped" into the blank Named Selection Sets box at the top of the screen, while the objects are selected (Figure 6.4).

Now when you want to select all the Biped objects at once, you simply need to click on the small arrow beside the Named Selection Sets box,

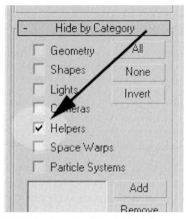

FIGURE 6.3   Keep the Biped 'Nub' dummy objects hidden to economize the object list.

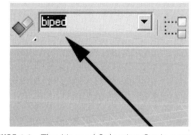

FIGURE 6.4   The Named Selection Set is a great way to select all the Biped objects at once.

and a list (there is only one item in your list so far) of assigned Selection Sets will pop up for you to choose from. This really speeds up your workflow.

Edit or delete your named selections by first going to Edit Named Selections under the Edit menu (1), and then selecting the Named Selections listed (2). Add or re-move objects in the Selection Set, or delete entire Selection Sets. You can even per-form a sort of text Boolean operation on multiple Selection Sets by combining, subtracting, or taking the intersection of them (Figure 6.5).

Finally, select and freeze the two Widge mesh objects, m_eye and m_widge, so they're not inadvertently selected while you animate the Biped.

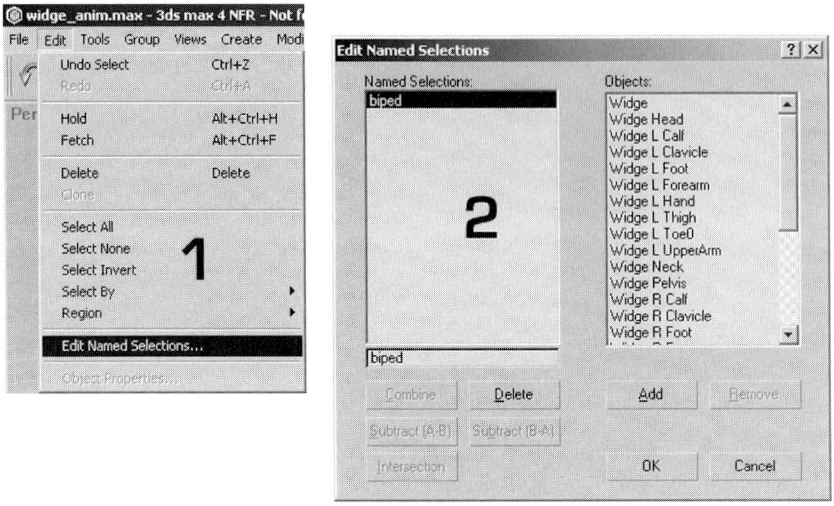

FIGURE 6.5   The only way to delete a Selection Set is through this dialog box.

KEYFRAME ANIMATION BASICS

Keyframing is the heart of animation. The act of animating by hand is rewarding, but can be frustrating, too. Experience and lots of practice will make your keyframing "skillz" improve, but there are also some shortcuts and suggestions that may help you along the way.

Frame Zero

It's a good idea to always leave Frame 0 alone when animating. If nothing else, it serves as a great starting point for any animation in the overall animation set. Yet in Widge's case, there's a very technical reason: Frame 0 has to be the default position in which the mesh was attached to the Biped, because of weighting values. WildTangent technology calculates the weighting parameters that are set with Physique for any character or "actor" based on sampling the *first frame* of an animation set. This is always Frame 0, so the character must be in the same pose for which the weighting was adjusted. If it's not, you'll get strange and undesirable results upon implementation.

Make sure Figure mode is turned off (you can't animate a Biped while in this mode). Pick the Biped Selection Set out of the Named Selection Sets you made earlier (or double-click the Widge COM Biped object) to select it and all its children. Click on the Select and Rotate button to make Rotate the current type of transform. In the Motion panel, click on the Set Key button (Figure 6.6).

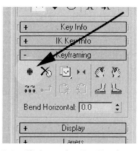

FIGURE 6.6   Click on the Set Key button to set a keyframe for selected Biped objects.

Now all selected objects have keyframes set for them. However, the COM root has three separate animation tracks compared to just one track for the other Biped objects. Set a keyframe for *each* animation track of the COM (Widge) by alternately clicking the Body Horizontal, Body Vertical, and Body Rotate buttons in the Track Selection rollout menu, *before* hitting Set Key (Figure 6.7).

FIGURE 6.7   Choose between Body Horizontal, Body Vertical, and Body Rotate animation tracks for the COM.

 The active axis of movement and selected animation track for the COM also affect the Type-In Transform menu when entering values to move objects. If, for some reason, typing in coordinates has no effect, double-check your current axis.

The Track View

Another way to add a keyframe for any animation track is by using the Add Key function in the Track View. Click on the ⊞ Open Track View icon to bring up the Track View window (Figure 6.8).

Track View is just a way to represent the keys being set for an animation as a series of points that can be manipulated. It is here that you can assign additional controllers, change the properties of keyframes, and even add sound to your animation.

 You can have up to 13 Track Views open and active in a single 3ds max scene. This is why you have the ability to name the Track View windows that are open. These individual Track Views will be saved along with the scene when you save the max file.

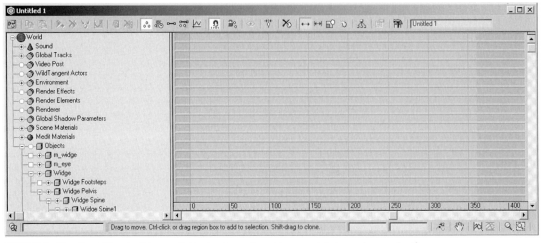

FIGURE 6.8   The Track View in 3ds max is the best way to add, copy, delete, and move keyframes.

The sheer amount of information that can be displayed in the Track View is so great that the designers of 3ds max gave you a way to *filter* things you're not interested in seeing displayed. Click on the 🖳 Filters icon in the upper left-hand corner of the Track View window. This brings up the Filters option window, where you can customize what's displayed in the Track View. Check the Animated Tracks box under the Show Only sub-menu to display the tracks for just those objects that are animated or have a keyframe set for them (Figure 6.9).

Click OK, and the Track View only displays those tracks that have keyframes. Next, left-click on Objects—just under Sound in the track list to the left—to select it (it turns yellow). Holding your cursor over Objects, right-click to bring up another list of menu options. Slide your mouse down to Expand All and click again (left- or right-click, it doesn't matter). This expands all the children under the Objects tree. You can also limit the expansion to individual sub-objects or tracks under Objects (Figure 6.10).

Now re-size what's displayed in Track View by clicking on the 🔍 Zoom icon at the bottom of the Track View window and zooming in so you can clearly make out Frame 0.

If you have a three-button mouse and a spinner on the middle button, spinning it will zoom in and out while in the Track View. The Zoom icon also has the functionality to limit the zoom vertically or horizontally. Just hold down the icon, and select either option from the fly-out menu (Figure 6.11).

Hit the H key to bring up the "hit list" of selectable objects in your scene, and select the COM (Widge) Biped object from the list. Go back to the Track View, and you'll notice that the yellow box beside "Widge" in

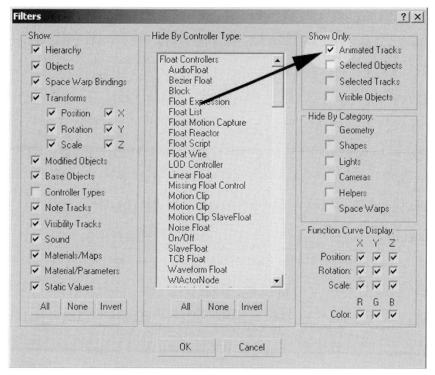

FIGURE 6.9   Check the Animated Tracks box to *only* show animated tracks in Track View.

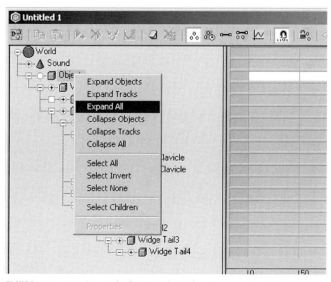

FIGURE 6.10   Use Expand All on tracks to have access to all their keyframes at once.

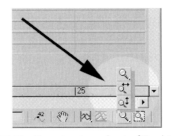

FIGURE 6.11   Zooming in and out of Track View can be limited to the vertical or horizontal.

the list of tracks has a yellow highlight to it. This is a quick way to tell from looking at the Track View whether or not an object is selected. If you had the Select and Rotate button active when you enabled Set Key for the COM, then there would only be a keyframe set in the Widge/Transform/Turning track. If the Select and Move button had been active and the X-, Y-, or XY-axis were current, a key would have been set for the Widge/Transform/Horizontal animation track. With the Select and Move button active and the Z-axis current, a key would have been set for the Widge/Transform/Vertical track.

Regardless of which key is set, you need a key for each animation track of the COM. Do this by using the 💍 Add Keys button at the top of the Track View. Simply click it to make it active (1), and then click in the empty space where you want a keyframe in any of the three Vertical, Horizontal, and Turning tracks (2). Fill in the blanks, and now you have keys for all Biped objects at Frame 0 (Figure 6.12).

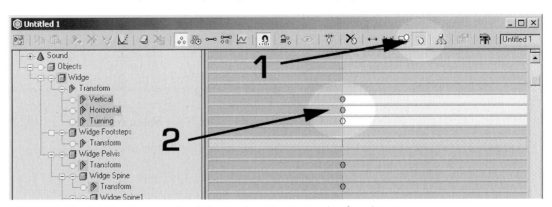

FIGURE 6.12   Use Add Keys to manually add keys in the animation tracks of an object.

Configuring Time

With that done, you need to prevent yourself from accidentally overwriting Frame 0, which is accomplished by changing your Time Configuration. Close the Track View and click on the 🖃 Time Configuration icon at the lower right-hand part of your screen. When the menu pops up, enter 0 for Start Time and 60 for End Time. Leave everything else set to default, but remember your playback frame rate is 30 frames per second (fps) (Figure 6.13).

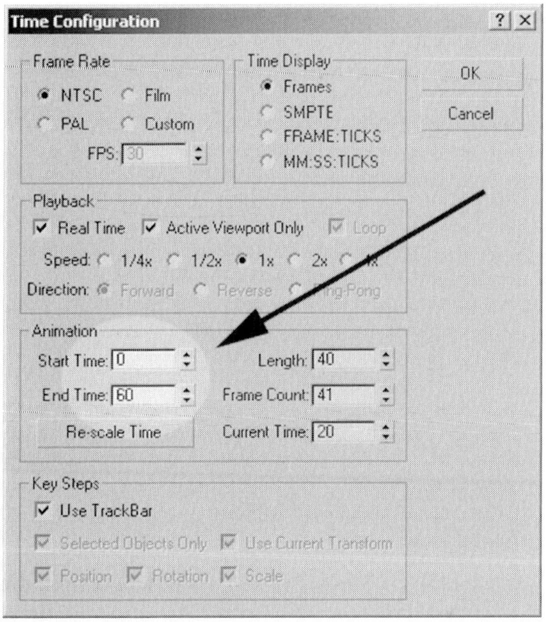

FIGURE 6.13   The Time Configuration menu lets you specify a range within which to animate.

You can change your frame rate and playback speed in Time Configuration, or you can even *scale* an active animation range, if you want. However, the range you set in Time Configuration can have an impact on your access to the keys displayed in Track View. This will make more sense in a few moments. Meanwhile, you need to learn about copying keyframes.

Copying Keyframes

Now you will copy some keyframes. Go down to the Current Frame box, just to the left of the Time Configuration button, type in 20, and hit Enter (Figure 6.14).

This jumps you to Frame 20. This is a nice tool to have when working with a huge animation made up of hundreds or thousands of frames. Now, open Track View again, and apply Expand All if you have to. Click on the 🖾 Zoom Horizontal Extents icon to center the active time range

FIGURE 6.14 The Current Frame box allows you to jump to a frame by simply typing it in.

in the view at the lower right of your Track View window. Zoom in so that Frames 0–30 are in view, using the Pan icon to move the view left or right, if necessary.

If you use a three-button mouse (and you should be), the middle mouse button will usually include a built-in spinner. Like in the regular 3ds max viewport, dialing this up and down while in Track View will let you zoom in and out, expanding and contracting the number of keys displayed. You can also pan left and right by holding down the middle button and moving your mouse left and right.

Next, select all the keyframes at Frame 0 by simply dragging a selection fence around them. Then, make sure the ↔ Move Keys icon is active (it should be, by default), hold the Shift key down with one hand, and while holding the left mouse button down, drag the keys to the right until they are over Frame 20. This results in copied or "cloned" frames, just like when you copy or clone objects or sub-objects.

 An alternate way to copy keyframes from one frame to another is to right-click on the Time Slider. This is the movable bar at the bottom of your viewport that reflects the size of the animation range and the current frame. If you right-click on it (1), it brings up the Create Key menu (2), and gives you the option to copy all transforms or just some. However, you still need to bring up the Track View if you want to set keys for all tracks of the COM (Figure 6.15).

Notice that there is a pink line running through the keys just copied to Frame 20. This color-coded reminder of which frame you're on is very useful. As you move the Time Slider, of course, the pink line moves with it.

Animation Space Buffer

When using the "animation folder" approach with your 3ds max character files, you need to keep some space between the animations so that

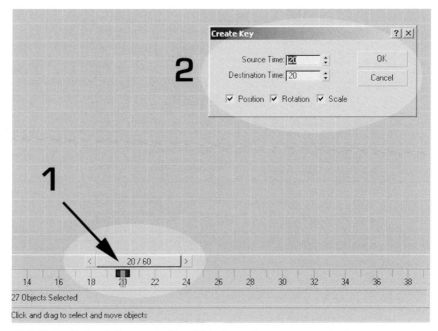

FIGURE 6.15   Right-clicking on the Time Slider is another way to copy keyframes.

they're easy to find and edit in Track View. Leaving noticeable gaps between the animations also means you have to set complete columns of keys for all the Biped tracks at the beginning and end of each animation. This keeps the motions separate and distinct, making it visually easy to see where they start and stop in the Track View.

Go back to Time Configuration, and set the Start Time to 20 instead of 0. Open up Track View again, and hit the Zoom Horizontal Extents icon to center the range of keys displayed.

Instead of closing the Track View each time you're through with it, you can simply minimize it.

The idle animation you're about to create will be 41 frames long, from Frame 20 to Frame 60. However, because the 3ds max file is your animation folder, it really doesn't matter where the idle animation is. Starting it on a tenth frame between each animation is just an issue of convenience more than anything else; always try to give yourself *at least* a 20-frame buffer between animations. Anything less, and the gap dissolves when looking at the entire animation set in Track View—especially when dealing with motion capture, which typically has a key set for *every* track at *every* frame of the animation.

Track View and Active Animation Range

If you're wondering why you didn't just set the active time range to 20 and 60 from the beginning, it's due to a limitation of Track View which makes viewing keys dependent upon the active animation range. Try zooming in or out and panning left and right in Track View, now that the range is from 20 to 60. In 3ds max, when navigating in Track View, the program decides that when you set an active animation range, you really don't want to view any keyframes *before* that range (and sometimes after, as well). While you may occasionally get it to work and see those keys at Frame 0, save yourself the frustration of even trying, and simply expand the Start and End frames when you need to access frames before or after the current animation range. This is why you included Frame 0 when configuring time, earlier. It was the only way you could get to the keys there.

Posing the COM and Limbs

The first step in any keyframe animation is posing your character while the Animate button is red and active. The idle animation is no exception. In Widge's case, he's always on the move, and he should look as if he's ready to pounce even when standing still. His idle animation should convey a pent-up, nervous energy. His idle pose also needs to be generic enough so that when he begins to walk or attack, it seems like a natural transition.

When posing any character, begin with the root object of the Biped hierarchy, and move your way down. For Widge, you're going to select his COM (Widge), position it, and then move the arms and legs into position. Once those five Biped objects are in place, you can lock down the hands and feet and adjust the rest of the character. The coordinates shown in Table 6.1 have been provided to help you position Widge for his idle animation, but feel free to just approximate the pose.

TABLE 6.1   Widge's Idle Animation Coordinates

OBJECT	X-AXIS	Y-AXIS	Z-AXIS
Widge (COM)	−22	−12	66
Widge R Foot	−168	24	0
Widge R Hand	−191	−175	0
Widge L Hand	192	−98	0
Widge L Foot	165	99	0

Make sure your Animate button is on and red, and move the COM, hands, and feet into position (Figure 6.16).

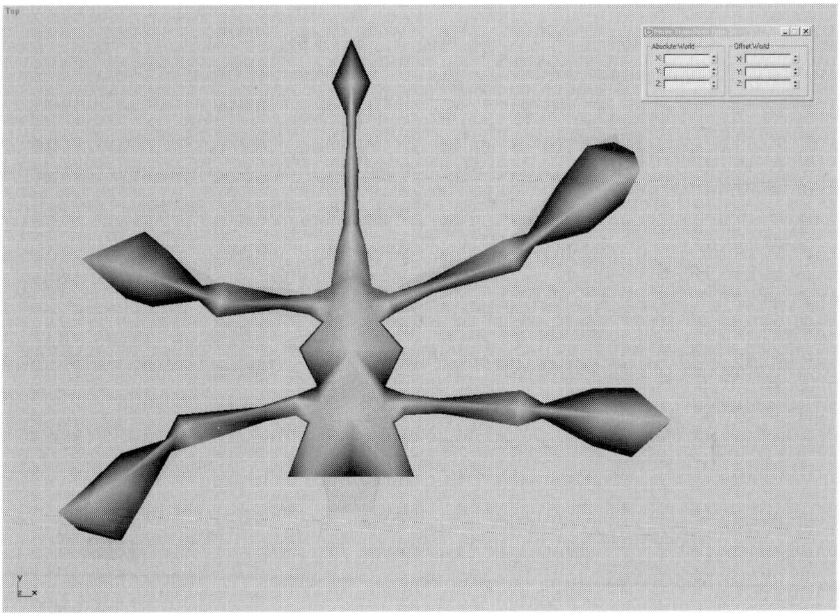

FIGURE 6.16   Posing the COM and the limbs is the first step for Widge's idle pose.

With the basic pose established, you need to further refine it by adjusting the Pelvis, Spine, Head, and Tail objects. But before you can do that, you need to lock down the hands and feet. Doing this means you don't have to reposition the hands and feet each time you move or rotate objects that are above the limbs in the hierarchical chain.

Locking Down the Feet and Hands

In character studio, locking down the hands and feet is as easy as clicking on a special Set Key that's available in the IK Key Info rollout menu. Still at Frame 20, select Widge R Hand, and open the IK Key Info rollout menu on the Motions panel (Figure 6.17).

In this menu, in addition to the normal Set Key red dot, you have three other Set Key buttons: Set Planted Key, Set Sliding Key, and Set Free Key. With Widge R Hand still selected, click on the Set Planted Key button. Uncheck Join to Prev IK Key, and look at the changes that have occurred with the keyframe (Figure 6.18).

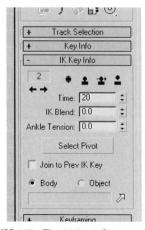

FIGURE 6.17   The IK Key Info menu has everything you need for locking the feet and hands.

FIGURE 6.18   Using Set Planted Key results in different IK Blend and world space settings.

 To access the special Set Keys, like Set Planted, you have to select one limb at a time. You can't select multiple limbs and use these IK-specific keys.

Achieving this "planted" limb is a result of two things: *IK Blend* and *Object space*. IK Blend determines whether or not you will have a more forward or inverse kinematic solution for the limb selected. Zero is the default IK Blend setting, and in combination with *Body* being checked, it means the limb is in normal Biped space and using a forward kinematic solution for its motion. By clicking on the Set Planted Key button, the IK Blend changes to 1, and the limb is now in Object space. When in Object space, you can further choose one of two options; you can choose an object in your scene for the selected limb to follow, or you can choose for the limb to be in that object's coordinate space. By *not* choosing an object in your scene for the selected limb to follow, character studio concludes you want to lock it in place, residing in World coordinate space instead of the Biped's space. *Join to Prev IK Key* is just a way to link keys between each other; it puts the selected limb in the coordinate space of the previous key.

This may seem a bit confusing; it may help to remember that when setting a key for a foot or hand that has to stay *planted*, make sure the IK Blend for that key is 1, with Object selected (instead of Body) for the coordinate system.

Refining the Idle Pose

Next, you need to refine the pose further by rotating the Pelvis, Spine, and Head objects. Use the coordinates in Table 6.2, or simply estimate their rotations.

TABLE 6.2   Coordinates for Rotating Widge's Pelvis, Spine, and Head Objects

OBJECT	X-AXIS	Y-AXIS	Z-AXIS
Widge Pelvis		6 degrees	
Widge Spine1	6 degrees		4 degrees
Widge Head		−2 degrees	

By rotating the torso objects, you take the character away from the stiff default pose. Next, refine the limbs further by rotating the forearms and calves along the X-axis. This pivots the whole arm and leg, rotating them forward and back, using the hand and foot as pivot points. Table 6.3 provides some coordinates if you need them.

TABLE 6.3   Coordinates for Pivoting Widge's Arm and Leg

OBJECT	X-AXIS	Y-AXIS	Z-AXIS
Widge R Calf	18 degrees		
Widge R Forearm	15 degrees		
Widge L Forearm	−1 degree		
Widge L Calf	16 degrees		

Finish your refinements of the first frame of the idle by posing the Tail objects. Again, this kind of tweaking takes the character out of a stiff, default pose and gives it an organic and more *animated* stance. Use the coordinates shown in Table 6.4.

TABLE 6.4   Coordinates for Posing Widge's Tail

OBJECT	X-AXIS	Y-AXIS	Z-AXIS
Widge Tail		33 degrees	–22 degrees
Widge Tail1		5 degrees	
Widge Tail2		23 degrees	4 degrees
Widge Tail3		18 degrees	
Widge Tail4		10 degrees	6 degrees

The pose is complete once you have made the refinements (Figure 6.19).

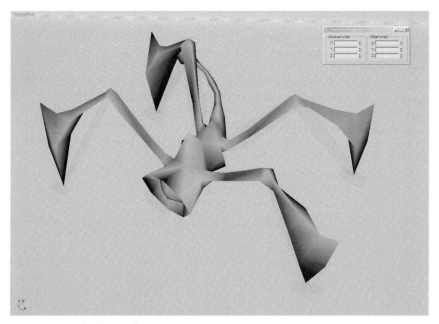

FIGURE 6.19   Widge has his first pose.

With the base pose fully established and refined, you can copy those keyframes to the end of the animation range to establish a loop. Somewhere in the middle, of course, you need to make Widge *do* something. It also needs to be subtle enough so that it doesn't distract you with its repetitive irregularity. Open the Track View, make sure that the 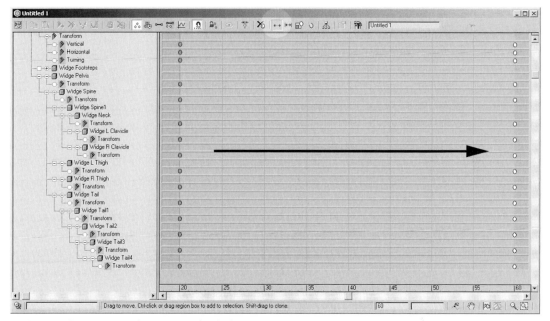 Move Keys icon at the top of your screen is active, select the keys at Frame 20, and Shift-drag them over to Frame 60. This gives you a duplicate start-and-stop point for the animation—the first step in creating a loop (Figure 6.20).

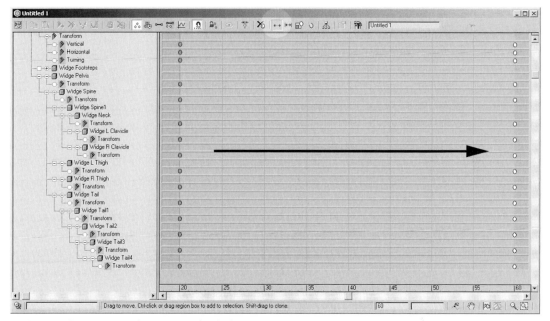

FIGURE 6.20   Create start and stop points for the loop.

Move the Time Slider back and forth, and you'll see some light movement of the character. This is because of the default animation controller that is assigned to the Biped animation tracks whenever you set a keyframe. It's called a TCB controller, which stands for . . .

Tension, Continuity, and Bias

There shouldn't be any movement at all if the keyframes are identical at Frame 20 and Frame 60 and if no other keyframes exist in between. However, because you have keys set at 0, 3ds max thinks you want to apply an animation curve from key to key. Because there are at least three keys with intervening space between each key, you get the subtle motion caused by the application of an animation curve. The curve that's been applied to the keys is determined by the C in TCB: *Continuity*.

Continuity controls how smooth an animation is by giving the keyframe a tangential property to the animation curve; this helps the animation be smooth and natural-looking. *Tension* controls the amount of curvature in the animation curve and can be used to create a slight "ease to" and "ease from" effect. *Bias* controls where the animation curve occurs in respect to the key set. To view the TCB parameters, select the COM (Widge) Biped object, and go over to the Motion panel. Click open the Key Info rollout menu, and look over the TCB settings for the selected object (Figure 6.21).

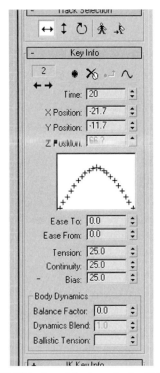

FIGURE 6.21   As a default controller, TCB works fine, most of the time.

The Key Info for a selected object will only appear if the active Transform button matches the animation track for which the key was set. For example, if an object has a keyframe set for the rotation track, and the Select and Move button is active, the rotation key information won't appear in the Motion panel.

The default TCB settings are shown in Figure 6.21. They're designed to produce a smooth transition from keyframe to keyframe. To see the effect of a Continuity setting of 0, make sure the current frame is still Frame 20, double-click in the number field for Continuity, and enter 0. Click on the Next Key button (the small burgundy arrow pointing to the right) at the top of the Key Info rollout, advance to the next keyframe for the COM at Frame 60, and change that key's Continuity setting to 0, too. Now, where there was a curve in the window above the setting values, there's an inverted V shape. This means there is no curvature to the interpolation between keys, just a straight line from key to key (Figure 6.22).

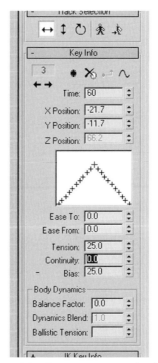

FIGURE 6.22 With a Continuity setting of 0, the motion will reflect the linear interpolation between keyframes and *not* add any extra motion.

If you were to select each limb, Spine, Head, and Tail object, change their Continuity to 0 for all their keys set, and scrub the Time Slider back and forth, all extra motion would be gone, and the character would remain in place. However, if you did have to do that (instead of going object-by-object, key-by-key, using the Motion panel's Biped rollout menu), use Track View instead.

Open Track View, if it isn't already open, and select both keys at Frame 20 and Frame 60 for Widge L Clavicle. Right-click on either selected keyframe, and a small menu (similar to the TCB sub-menu on the Motions panel) will appear. Through Track View, you have access to TCB settings *and* IK settings for the limbs (Figure 6.23).

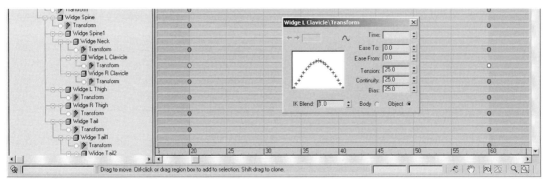

FIGURE 6.23   You can access and change the TCB and IK Blend settings from Track View, as well as from the Motions Panel.

While this is a great way to affect multiple keys, it only works on one animation track at a time. You can't affect all keys at once or more than one track of a single object like the COM.

 The tracks for the limbs are compressed for easier keyframing; they are compressed into one track each for the clavicle to the fingers and for the thighs to the toes, but they can be expanded to show keys set for each limb sub-object. With a Biped object selected, simply go to the Animation Properties sub-menu on the Motion Panel, and check Arms and/or Legs under Separate Tracks (Figure 6.24).

Adjusting your Continuity settings can help add or subtract minor motions that affect the integrity of the loop. There exists yet another couple of parts of the TCB controller that you can use to your advantage when animating a loop like the idle, and those are the *Ease To* and *Ease From* options.

Ease To and Ease From

Widge is tensed, ready to attack, and has the pose copied to the first and last frame of the animation, but he still needs to *do* something. How about swaying back and forth in anticipation? It's simple enough and shouldn't be a noticeably repetitive motion. Advance to Frame 38, and click on the

FIGURE 6.24   With Separate Tracks boxes checked, the Track View will display animation tracks for the rest of the limb parts, such as hands, fingers, and toes.

Animate button, making it red and active. Select the COM, and move it over to the right (about 55 units) along the X-axis. Use Zoom Extents so you can see the character clearly, go over to the Motion panel, and click on the 🖼 Biped Playback button. A "no-poly" version of the Biped plays the animation back, which is great if your machine is processor-challenged (Figure 6.25)!

As you can tell, the effect of changing Continuity for the COM (Widge) to 0 for the first and last frame of the animation gives the loop a jarring effect when it reaches the repeat point. This is easy enough to fix. Go back into Track View, select the three keys set in the Horizontal animation track for the COM, and right-click on one of them. Change the Continuity back to 25 (Figure 6.26).

 When a keyframe is set in between two keyframes with identical settings, it will have those same settings—even if the default is different.

This changes all three keys back to a curve instead of a pointed V shape. Next, go down to Time Configuration, and change the End Time to 59 instead of 60 (Figure 6.27).

This removes the repetition of the first and last frame and should result in an even smoother loop. Go back to the Top Viewport, apply Zoom Extents, and play the animation back again. Hmmm . . . there's still some

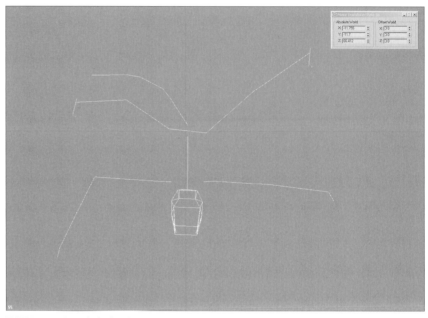

FIGURE 6.25 Biped Playback is a way to see your motions in a simple stick-figure mode.

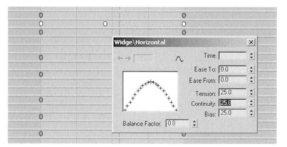

FIGURE 6.26 Changing the Continuity settings back to 25 ensures smoother animation.

sort of hitch when the animation begins to loop, going from the last frame back to the first. The first thing to check is whether the first and last keyframes for all tracks are the same, by copying them again from Frame 20 to Frame 60. Try playing the animation back. Drat! There's still a hitch. Well, here's where you dig deeper into the keyframe controls by adjusting *Ease To*. This extra setting in the TCB controller allows you to "ease to" (slow down) the position of a particular keyframe, by exponentially decreasing the amount of change from the previous keyframe position as it approaches the keyframe.

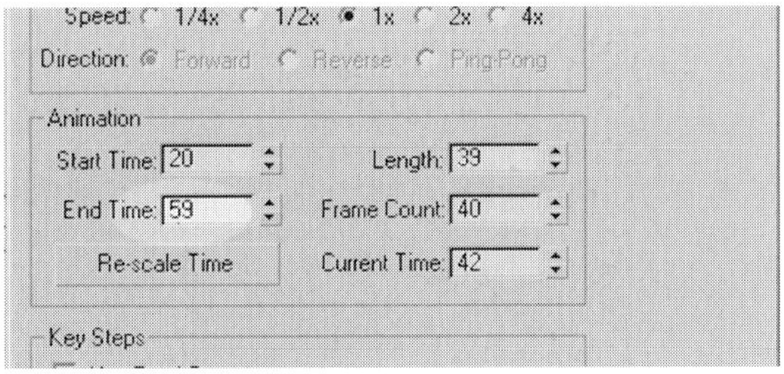

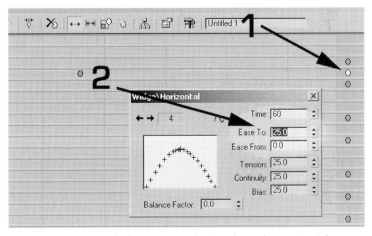

FIGURE 6.27   Change the End Time to one frame less, so the frames don't "stick" during playback.

Bring Track View back up, and select the last Horizontal key for the COM. Right-click on it (1), and enter a value of 25 in the Ease To box at the top of the small menu (2) (Figure 6.28).

FIGURE 6.28   "Easing to" a frame means slowing down the motion right before the key.

Close the box, close Track View, and try playing the animation. *Muu-uuch* better. But now it seems that at the start of the animation, Widge is almost lurching out of the animation to the middle keyframe position. What would it look like if you added an *Ease From* value to the first key, so that Widge didn't leave that position so quickly? As you can guess, Ease From causes an animation to *accelerate* as it leaves one key for another.

Bring up the Track View again, select and right-click the keyframe at Frame 20 for Horizontal, and enter a value of 25 in the Ease From box. However, instead of closing the animation track menu and the Track

View this time, move the Track View out of the way and hit the Biped Playback button (Figure 6.29).

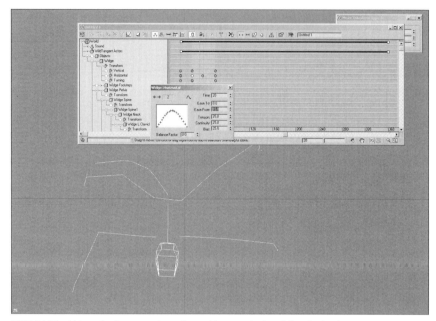

FIGURE 6.29 Values for keys can be adjusted interactively while playback occurs.

It looks okay, but maybe a value of 25 is too much. Without stopping the playback, go up to Ease From, and type in 15. The animation changes accordingly. Feel free to experiment more with the values of any of the keys while the animation plays, to see the effects of your changes.

 Instead of tweaking the values using Track View, you can always go to the Motion panel and adjust the setting there. Make sure you select the object whose values you want to adjust before *you play back the animations.*

Keyframes and the Time Slider Bar

When you're ready, go to the Front viewport, hit Zoom Extents, and play back the animation. Widge moves from side to side, but what about adding some sort of *bobbing* motion? He seems like he should be going up and down just a little bit. Select the COM (Widge) again, make sure the Animate button is red and active, go to Frame 40, and lower the COM by 2 units along the Z-axis, setting a new keyframe in the Vertical animation track of Widge. Now go to Frame 30, and *raise* the COM about 8 units along the Z-axis.

Next, you should notice that the keyframes you've been setting are displayed on the Time Slider bar, showing red blocks for unselected keys and white blocks for selected keys (Figure 6.30).

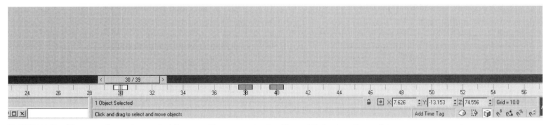

FIGURE 6.30 Keys set for selected objects will appear in the Time Slider bar for editing.

  Keyframes will only appear in the Time Slider bar when the object selected has keys set in that time range.

These keyframes aren't just for show. You can move, delete, and copy these keyframes just like you can in Track View. Select the keyframe you just created at Frame 30, hold your Shift key down, and drag it to the right over to Frame 50. Let go, and you've just cloned a keyframe in the Time Slider bar. Now play back the animation and see how it's shaping up (Figure 6.31).

Now *that's* got more character to it. Go to the Right view, and further refine the animation by getting the head involved.

Keyboard Shortcut Override Toggle

Since you're learning all kinds of things while working hard to make Widge do virtually nothing in an interesting way, why not add a few more useful tools to what you've learned so far? Click Zoom Extents in the Right viewport and then click on the Keyboard Shortcut Override Toggle button, located just beneath the Z-coordinates readout box, at the lower right-hand part of your screen (Figure 6.32).

With this button active, any hotkey assignments that come with plug-ins like character studio will take precedence over the default or custom 3ds max hotkeys assigned. Some of the more useful character studio hotkeys are as follows:

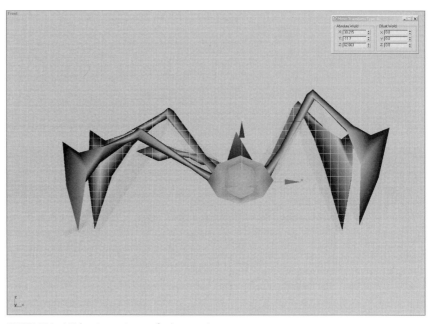

FIGURE 6.31 Widge is starting to feel creepy!

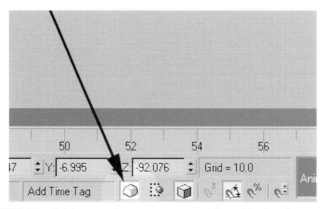

FIGURE 6.32 This button gives you access to additional hotkey shortcuts.

0 Sets a Biped key
V Toggles Biped Playback
ALT-C Copies posture of selected Biped object to clipboard
ALT-V Pastes posture from Clipboard to selected Biped object

Try out at least two of these as you give the head a little bit of *secondary* motion.

Secondary Motion

One of the most important aspects of an animation (and the most time-consuming to create) is *secondary motion*. This is a term applied to small, almost insignificant motions that augment or accent the main motions of the animation. Secondary motion is something like a foot tapping during an idle, or a slight flexing of the fingers, or anything else that's barely noticeable yet crucial to making the character come alive.

In the Right viewport, select Widge Head, select the Rotate transform, and make the Z-axis the active axis of rotation. Left-click on the Angle Snap icon to make it active. Then, right-click on it to bring up the Grid and Snap Settings menu. Change the default of 5 degrees for Angle to 3 degrees, and close the dialog box. Now when you rotate an object, it will be restricted to increments of 3 degrees (Figure 6.33).

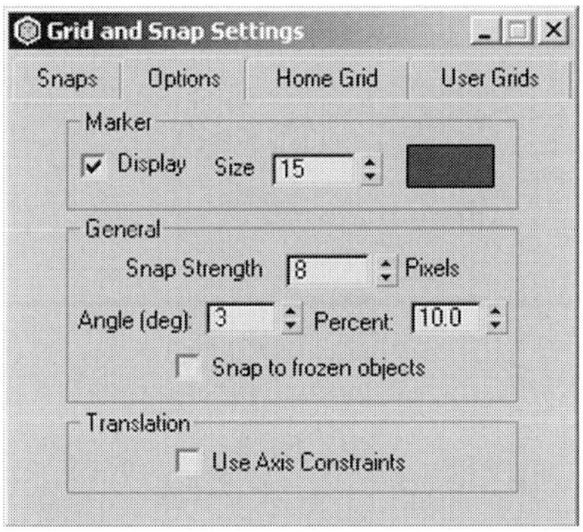

FIGURE 6.33 Easily and quickly change your Snap Settings to fit the situation.

To add this secondary (or *ancillary*) motion to the head, first set some keyframes *without* doing any rotations. With Widge Head selected, go to Frames 30, 40, and 50, hitting the 0 key at each frame to set a key for the head as it is posed by default. Next, go to Frame 25, and rotate the head *down* along the Z-axis (the blue axis) by 3 degrees, or one "tick" of rotation. Go to Frame 35, and rotate the head *up* by 3 degrees along the Z-axis; go to Frame 45, and rotate the head *down again* by 3 degrees (or simply Shift-drag the key from Frame 25 over, via the Time Slider bar), and, finally, go to Frame 55, and rotate the head *up* 3 degrees along the Z-axis (or clone the frame at 35).

Now play back the animation by hitting the V key or the slash (/) key (if you have a fast machine), and check the animation (Figure 6.34).

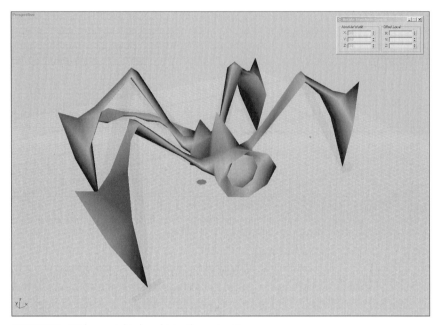

FIGURE 6.34 Widge gets his head into the animation.

This very slight head motion is designed to give the head geometry a more flexible, natural feel. You want to make it appear as if the head motion has somewhat of a lag, though, so this is why you have set keys at 30, 40, and 50—to provide *anchors* to the position the head would be in without the bob. By rotating the head *between* these anchor keys, you make the movement feel more attached to the act of going up or going down. That is, as Widge *raises* his body (Frames 20–30), the weight of the head would bring it *down* slightly (Frame 25) before assuming its forward-facing pose (Frame 30). Setting these anchor keys takes a little bit of thought when animating, but always keep the approach in mind when adding secondary motion.

Animating the Tail

The next step in Widge's idle animation is to do something with the tail. In order to add to his nervous energy and impatient urge to attack something, making his tail swish from side to side like a cat's seems the thing to do. The first calculation to work out is the timing. While complex formulas can be applied to any animation to determine what the correct timing should be, just go with what looks right, given the range of frames you're dealing with. In other words, try it, see if it works, and try something else if it doesn't. Since doing keyframes every five frames worked for the head motion earlier, and resulted in the timing supporting a loop, use this base of five for the tail motion, too. However, the main motion of swinging side-to-side needs to be every 10 frames, to give enough time to insert the secondary motion that achieves a cat-like look instead of a dog-like wagging look.

Go to the Top viewport, go to Wireframe mode, and look at the first tail bone, Widge Tail (Figure 6.35).

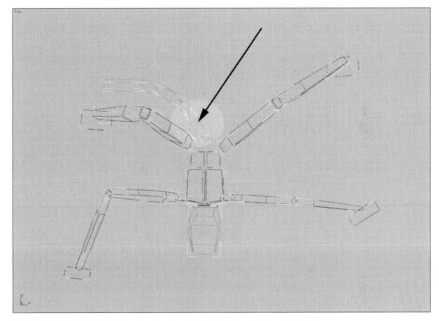

FIGURE 6.35   Widge Tail is already bent to the left with the initial idle pose.

Since the first tail object is already bent to the left throughout all the frames, select Widge Tail and set an anchor key at Frame 40. Do this by keeping the Time Slider at Frame 20 and right-clicking on it. Enter 40 in the Destination Time box and *uncheck* Position and Scale (Figure 6.36).

Always remember the default setting for Create Key is for all three animation tracks. Try to specify which track you are targeting, even if it doesn't seem necessary, as with most Biped objects. This prevents problems when dealing with additional bones that do have all three tracks available.

Now, right-click on Angle Snap again, and change the Snap setting back to 5 degrees (Figure 6.37).

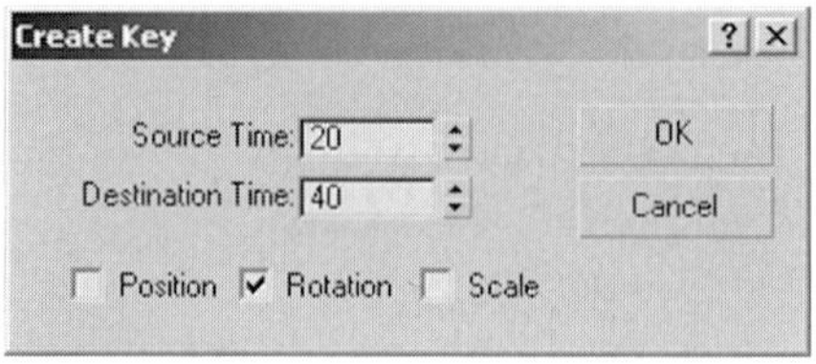

FIGURE 6.36   The Create Key menu is always useful in cloning keys.

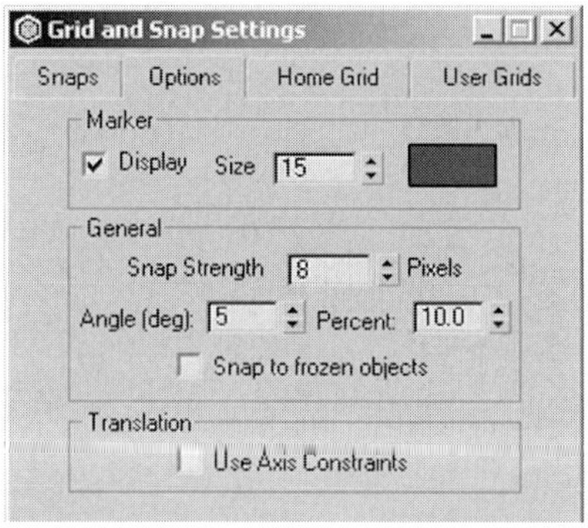

FIGURE 6.37   Change the Snap setting for Angle Snap back to 5 degrees.

Close the menu, make sure the Animate button is on, move to Frame 30, and rotate the tail over to the right about 70 degrees, either by clicking on the yellow part of the Y-axis indicator icon, or by hitting the F6 key to make it the axis of rotation. Pose the rest of the tail as well, so that it looks like Frame 20, but in reverse (Figure 6.38).

Now, with all the tail links selected, Shift-drag the *single* key visible in the Time Slider bar to Frame 50. This is the quickest way to copy a key for multiple objects. Slide the Time Slider back and forth to see how it looks. You'll notice on Frame 40 that the tail doesn't reflect the position from Frame 20 (Figure 6.39).

This is due to the fact you set a key only for Widge Tail, instead of for all the tail bones. No problem. With all the tail bones selected, simply Shift-drag Frame 20 over to Frame 40, and re-key Widge Tail and all its children bones. Now, scrubbing the Time Slider, the motions are as they should be, interpolating the transition between the two poses you've set.

While the motion is smooth, the tail seems stiff, still more like a dog's tail than a cat's more prehensile appendage. This is an easy problem to fix using secondary motion again. Go to Frame 25, keep all the tail bones

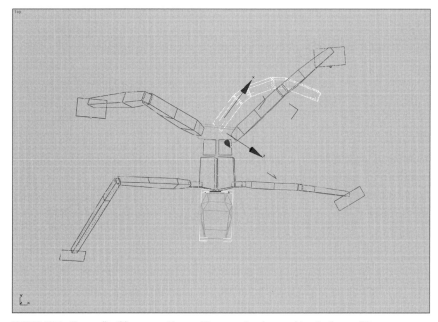

FIGURE 6.38   Pose *all* tail bones at Frame 30, opposite the position in Frame 20.

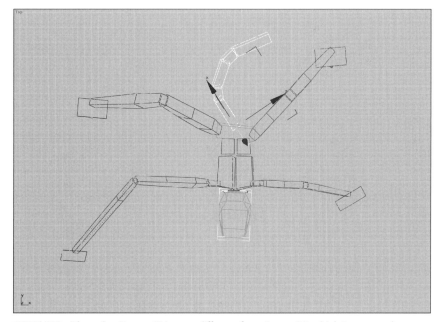

FIGURE 6.39   The tail at Frame 40 is now different from Frame 20, which is *not* good.

except for the main Widge Tail, and bend them all back simultaneously toward the direction they just came from (Figure 6.40).

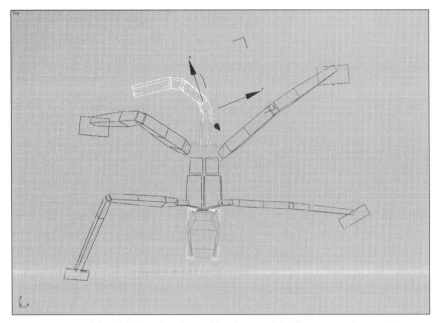

FIGURE 6.40   Bend the children of Widge Tail back toward the first pose at Frame 20.

Copy the new pose to Frame 45, and advance to Frame 35. Now bend the selected bones back toward the pose at Frame 30, and copy the new key to Frame 55. Play the animation back and check the results. Definitely more catlike!

 You can also use the Time Slider bar to access controller properties like Continuity for a key, even if multiple objects are selected. Simply right-click on the bar itself at the desired key—not on the Time Slider itself—(1) and select the bone whose key you want to tweak (2) to bring up the keyframe attributes menu (3) (Figure 6.41).

Even though you've basically completed the idle animation for Widge, there's one more tool in character studio that you need to be aware of: *Layers.*

Using Layers

Layers are used in character studio as a way to add animations *on top of* animations for your Biped. This is basically an ideal way to affect a global

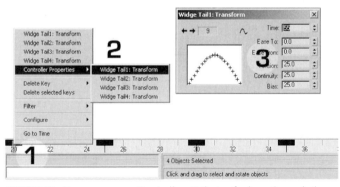

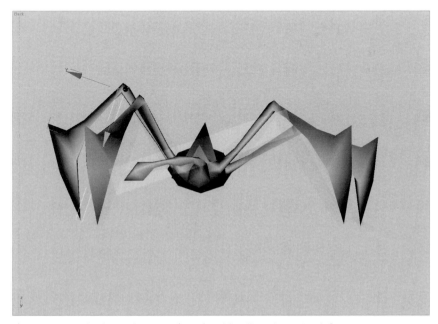

FIGURE 6.41   You can access Controller attributes for keys through the Time Slider bar, too.

change to a character's animation set. Layers can be viewed individually or collapsed into a new animation. In Widge's case, you're going to add yet *more* secondary motion using this powerful tool.

Hit the K key to bring up the rear view (the Back view) of Widge, and scrub the Time Slider back and forth. Notice how, from Frame 20 to Frame 35, the tail goes *down* as it goes to the left. You're going to use Layers to give that same downward motion to the tail as it goes to the *right* (Figure 6.42).

FIGURE 6.42   Widge has a downward *swish* to his tail motion going left.

Hide all Biped Objects except for the Widge Tail objects. By default, character studio assumes you want access to all these tail bones. Since you won't need access to the keys of the children of Widge Tail, compress the display when working in Track View by collapsing the hierarchy tree for the tail (uncheck the box beside Tail under Separate Tracks) (Figure 6.43).

FIGURE 6.43 Uncheck Tail under Separate Tracks to compress its hierarchy tree

Keep in mind that whenever you want to, you can always separate the tracks for those animation tracks available, and can close them just as conveniently. Now, select just Widge Tail, open up the Layers sub-menu on the Motion panel, and click on the 🔲 Create Layer button. This applies a new layer to your animation and makes the other Layers buttons active (Figure 6.44).

FIGURE 6.44 Nearly all the buttons in the Layers sub-menu are available now.

Begin this added layer of animation tweaking by going first to Frame 20, then rotating the tail root along the X-axis about 60 degrees so that the curve of the tail is pointing downward (Figure 6.45).

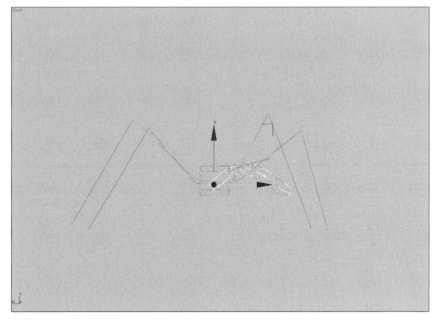

FIGURE 6.45   Rotating the tail at Frame 20 will make the *swish* more pronounced.

Setting a key at the first frame of the animation range for the layer affects the rest of the animation. Go to Frame 30 and rotate Widge Tail about 95 degrees along the X-axis, so that it's also pointing further downward than it was before Frame 20 was set (Figure 6.46).

A red stick figure that represents the original position of the bones before the layer was added shows you just how much of a change you're making as you animate in the layer.

Bring up the Track View so you can copy the two keys that you just set to their respective positions in the rest of the animation. Copy the key at Frame 20 to Frame 40 and to Frame 60. Copy the key at Frame 30 to Frame 50 (Figure 6.47).

Upon opening Track View, you should immediately notice that Widge Tail has all its children displayed, with keyframes set as well, even though you just unchecked the box under Separate Tracks. This is due to a bug in character studio 3 concerning Separate Tracks, Tail, and adding layers. If you add a new layer to the animation, the program still keeps the Separate Tracks box in its default state: *checked*.

Close Track View and play back the animation to see how the new layer looks (Figure 6.48).

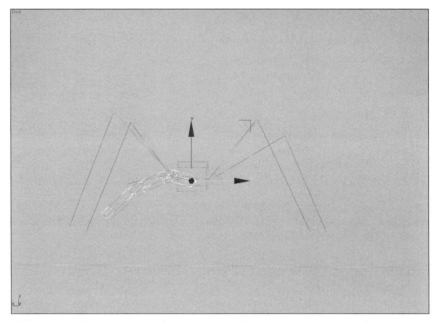

FIGURE 6.48 At Frame 30, rotate the tail along the X-axis so it's also pointing down.

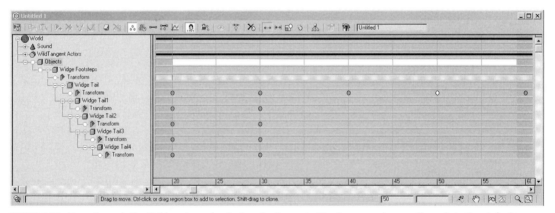

FIGURE 6.47 Even though the Tail box is *unchecked* under Separate Tracks, a new layer will result in the default checked box.

The last step in using Layers is to collapse them back down, once the appropriate tweaks are satisfactory. Do this by clicking on the Collapse button (Figure 6.49).

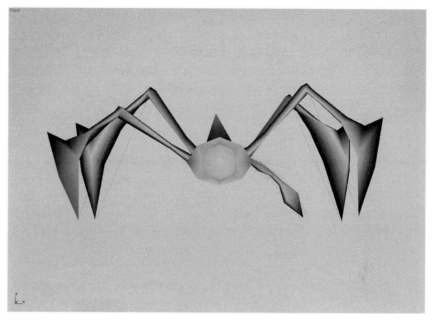

FIGURE 6.48   The new animation layer gives more "swishiness" to the swish.

FIGURE 6.49   Once the layer is done, collapse it down to a normal, layerless animation.

Using Time Tags

Now that the idle animation is complete, you can help yourself easily pinpoint it for future reference with a neat feature of 3ds max called *Time Tag*. Go to Frame 20 and click on the area next to the Keyboard Shortcut Override Toggle that reads Add Time Tag (1). Then select Add Tag (2), and enter Idle for Tag Name (3). Now, whenever your Time Slider is at Frame 20, Idle will appear in the Time Tag box (4) (Figure 6.50).

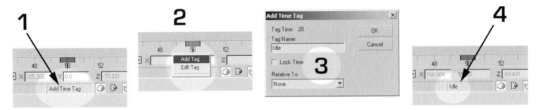

FIGURE 6.50 Adding a Time Tag gives you a nice shortcut to an animation clip.

Move your Time Slider to Frame 50. Click on the Add Time Tag box, and a new option is there for you to click on: 20 Idle. Click on it, and the Time Slider automatically goes to the first frame of the idle (Figure 6.51).

FIGURE 6.51 Time Tags will appear when clicking on the Add Time Tag message box.

Since Widge will be used for a WildTangent export, you will need to know the start and end time of the animation when you export the animations later. Bring up Time Configuration again, and change your End Time to 60 instead of 59. Then go to the Time Tag menu and select Edit Tag (Figure 6.52).

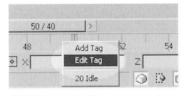

FIGURE 6.52 Edit Time Tags to change the name or delete a time tag.

When the Edit Time Tag menu pops up, select 20 Idle from the list and rename it in the Tag Name field to Idle Start. Hit OK, and then go to Frame 60. Click on Add Time Tag again, and create a new time tag called Idle End (Figure 6.53).

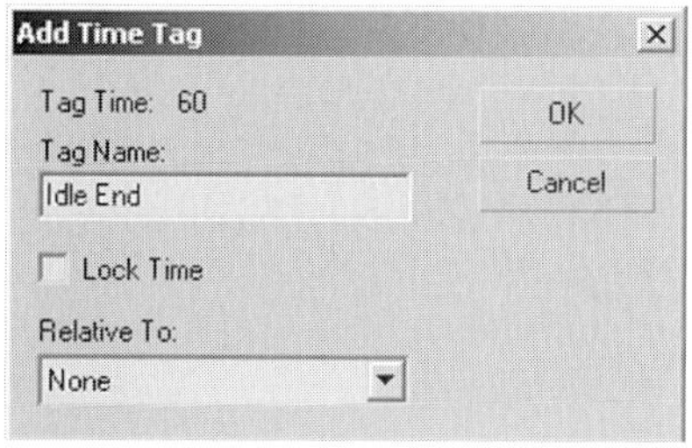

Add Time Tag

Tag Time: 60

Tag Name:

Idle End

☐ Lock Time

Relative To:

None

OK

Cancel

FIGURE 6.53   Add the end of the idle motion to the Time Tag list.

The benefit of using time tags should be obvious. They are definitely most useful when a character has a substantially *large* number of animations. With the animation complete, save your max file, skip ahead 20 frames, and you're ready to move on to any other animations required. If you want or need to, load Widge4.max from the Chapter6 directory on this book's CD-ROM (Figure 6.54).

ON THE CD

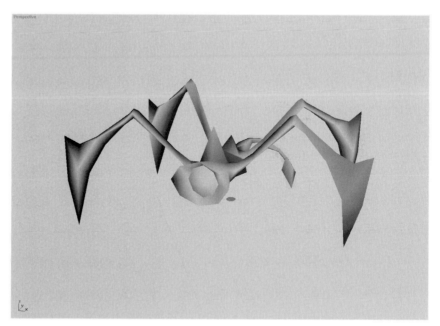

FIGURE 6.54   Load Widge4.max to see how the alien psycho's supposed to look.

SUMMARY

Before animating, decide whether or not to use keyframes, motion capture, or a combination of the two. Whichever method you choose, think of your 3ds max file as an animation folder that holds all your character's moves. Prior to setting any keyframes, make sure you prepare your Biped for animation by assigning a transparent material to it and/or creating a Named Selection Set out of it for quick selection.

Once you're ready to begin animating, start by saving Frame 0 in the Biped's default position, exactly as it was when attached to the mesh. Do this using either the Track View or Set Key buttons in the Motion panel. When working on an animation, define its range in the Time Configuration menu. You can also define frame rate and playback speed there. Copy keyframes either in the Track View or via the Time Slider bar, but always keep a buffer between animation clips for easy identification. Learn the effects of the tension, continuity, and bias settings of the default TCB animation controller. Use them to create smooth loops for your animation clips. Always strive for secondary motion to add that extra bit of detail to your animation. Use Layers to add this sort of additional motion *over* the rest of an animation.

Finally, make navigation through your collected animations (your animation folder) easier by adding time tags to the start and end points of your various motion clips.

KEYFRAME ANIMATION: PART II

Y
ou now have the fundamentals mastered for using 3ds max and character studio to create keyframe animations, but Widge was just your appetizer. As an enemy character for a game, he has a relatively less demanding animation set and mainly plays the role of *target*. He sits idle, runs, walks, attacks, reacts to being attacked, and dies (Figure 7.1).

This isn't such a lengthy list; the *player* character, on the other hand, is a much more demanding type of real-time game entity.

FIGURE 7.1   Widge only has the most basic animation set because it's all he *needs*.

Betty's Animations

Betty Bad is and isn't a "typical" real-time character. At 2,000 polygons and with WildTangent's dynamic LOD code, she has a medium to low poly-count, yet she's in a third-person, online-only action game, using an atypical game engine: WildTangent's Web Driver technology. She could just as easily have been implemented in a *Quake*, *Unreal*, or LithTech game engine as well. Another of Betty's non-typical features is her lack of access to a multitude of different weapons that magically appear and disappear on command. She only has one weapon, which processes energy into different forms of ammo.

One Chick, One Gun

Despite not having to change an arsenal of weapons, Betty still has a shotgun, grenade launcher, machine gun, rocket launcher, and railgun; they're represented more by their *effects* than by a different physical weapon. The decision to use this approach addresses two issues common to action shooter games: the magic backpack and the cumbersome task of holding a weapon that obscures most of the character. Taking away her ability to carry around artillery consisting of a dozen different weapons doesn't hurt the gameplay mechanics. It actually saves polygons while introducing the aforementioned alternate theory to the magical backpack: a weapons-manufacturing backpack. Whenever Betty kills an enemy, it leaves behind energy for her to pick up and add to her weapons system backpack. Along with this variant of a popular paradigm for the weapons, Betty also serves as a guinea pig for animation ideas that the game's designers wanted to try (but never did) in special move animations for *Quake III Arena (Q3A)*.

Special Moves

Like fighting games, action games in which characters have to run around and shoot things can be spiced up a bit with combination moves, or *special moves*. These animations are triggered by the player hitting a couple of keys simultaneously or by a condition met during the game, such as a character changing direction quickly. So, in addition to the standard animation set that a typical game character of this genre will have, Betty has a few extras to support this special-move functionality. She also has extra animations due to the environment and the constraints of the game technology. Yet she still has the following standard animations: Idle, Run, Backpedal, Walk, Jump, Strafe, Shoot, Melee, Pain, and Death.

She also has the use of Special Moves, Use Moves, Swimming, Recovery, and Angled animations.

As mentioned before, Betty has almost 3,000 frames of animations and that's *definitely* not your average animation count. It's due primarily to the way her character had to be implemented and fit within the game technology. It's also because the player sees her in the third-person perspective. Being on the screen all the time in a typical shorter animation set would get repetitive and uninteresting very quickly, but Betty has a wide range of animations. Betty also provides an excellent opportunity for you to learn about animations similar to those you may be faced with when animating a game character of your own. You'll create parts of her animation set in this chapter by first concentrating on those motions that are completely keyframed. In the next chapter, you'll use motion capture to create the remaining animations. Let's begin by creating a couple of idle animations.

IDLES

ON THE CD

Betty needs three idle animations: left foot forward, right foot forward, and both feet even. The reason for this is for variety, and so that her transition from one animation to another is properly supported. Creating these idles will also give you some idle pose ideas for animating your own character. Load Betty08.max from the Chapter7 directory on this book's CD-ROM (Figure 7.2).

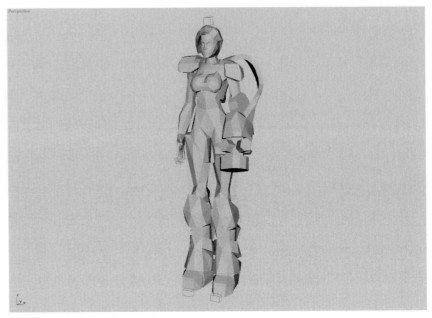

FIGURE 7.2   Betty needs some idle moves.

It's All in the Pose

Since idle animations have to be relatively short loops that can't be *too* involved because of their receptiveness, they are mainly all about the *pose*. Change your Time Configuration settings to a Start Time of 20 and an End Time of 50. Then, using your Rotate and Move transforms, pose Betty at Frame 20 so she looks like she does in Figure 7.3. Use the main construction plane as a ground reference to keep her feet right on their line.

With her body turned slightly, her gun at the ready, her right hand poised for balance, and a lower center of gravity, Betty is alert and ready to go. Now you need to lock her feet and copy all the keyframes at Frame 20 to Frame 50. Do this by alternately selecting each foot and hitting the Set Planted Key button on the IK Key Info rollout menu. Make sure to *uncheck* the Join to Prev IK Key button (Figure 7.4).

 Set Planted Key cannot be used on multiple limbs at the same time. Select and set a key for one limb, and then repeat the process for any others.

In character studio, setting a planted key will automatically cause a red dot to appear on the selected limb, which indicates the active IK pivot point. These points on the hands and feet not only give you better use of

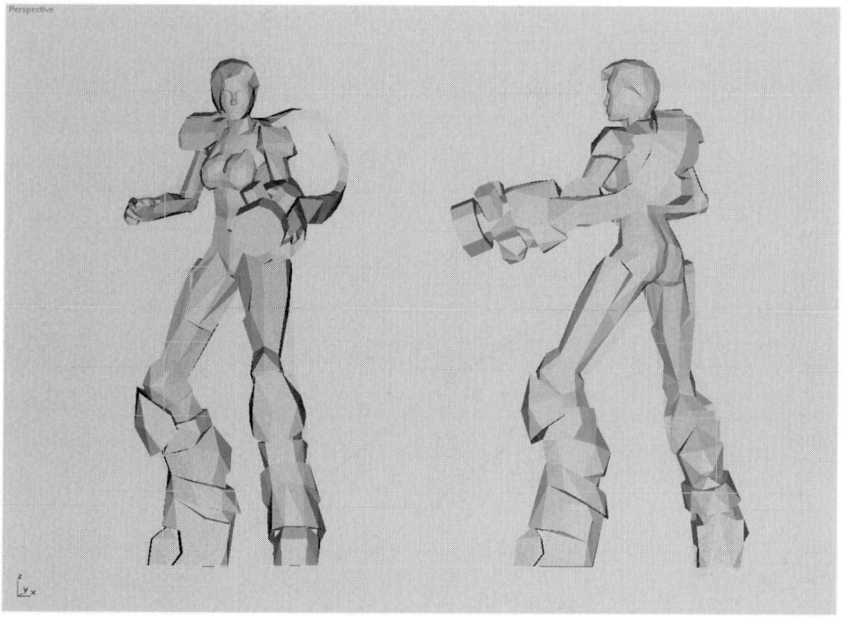

FIGURE 7.3   Make the idle pose interesting.

FIGURE 7.4   As soon as the pose is established, lock the feet with the Set Planted Key button.

the IK chain that's established for the arms and legs, but can result in some interesting animations. Select Betty L Foot and hit the Select Pivot button in the IK Key Info rollout menu to see all the available pivots for the foot. Change the active pivot by clicking on any of the dots that appear on the foot with Select Pivot active.

While you can change the pivot of an object at any time by using the Select Pivot button, the hand or foot only rotates around that point if the limb has a Planted Key set. Otherwise, it rotates from the normal forward kinematic pivot point.

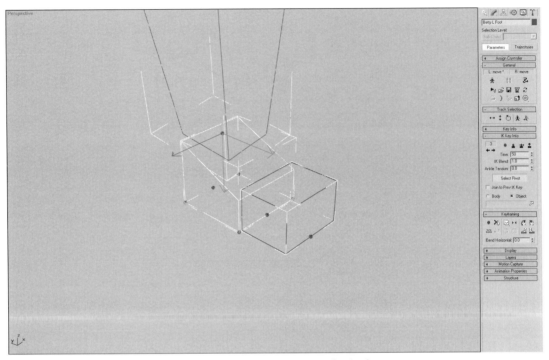

FIGURE 7.5   With the Select Pivot button active, pick a new pivot point for the foot.

Turn Select Pivot off, open Track View, and copy all the keys at Frame 20 to Frame 50. Close or minimize Track View, and scrub the Time Slider back and forth. You will see a subtle motion because of the Continuity setting of 25 for all keys, and the keys set at Frame 0.

Anchor Keys

It's crucial that you lock down the feet at the beginning and end of the animation so that you can animate Betty by having her perform a small motion in the middle of the animation segment. While using Set Planted Key is one great way to lock the feet, another way is to use Anchor Keys in the Keyframing rollout menu (Figure 7.6).

To see how this method for locking the feet works, go back into Track View and delete the key for Betty R Thigh at Frame 50. Close or minimize Track View, select the right foot, go to Frame 20, and hit the Set Free Key button in the IK Key Info rollout menu. This turns the IK Blend to 0 and puts the foot back in Body coordinate space, effectively *unlocking* the foot (Figure 7.7).

FIGURE 7.6 You can also lock the feet down using the Anchor Key buttons.

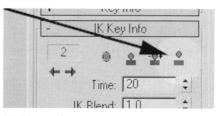

FIGURE 7.7 The Set Free Key button changes the keyframe back to an unlocked key.

The red dot that was the pivot will go away; when scrubbing the Time Slider, you will see that the foot isn't planted. Now, go to Frame 20 and click the Anchor Right Leg button to make it active to lock the right leg in place (Figure 7.8).

Click again on the Anchor Right Leg button to toggle it off, and Frame 20 becomes a planted key again for the right foot, changing the IK Blend to 1 and putting it back into Object space (Figure 7.9).

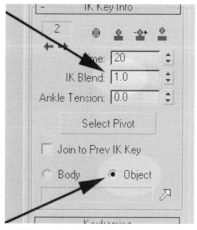

FIGURE 7.8 With Anchor Right Leg active, the right foot is locked in place.

FIGURE 7.9 Keyframes for limbs are automatically converted to a planted key just by clicking on the Anchor button.

Regardless of the method you use, planting the feet is necessary when adding a small motion in the middle of the animation segment. But first, strip out the extra motion caused by the Continuity setting by going into the Track View, selecting a row of keys, right-clicking on one of the keys, and entering 0 for the Continuity value. Repeat this for all animation tracks except Betty L Clavicle and Betty R Clavicle—change their Continuity settings to 15 (Figure 7.10).

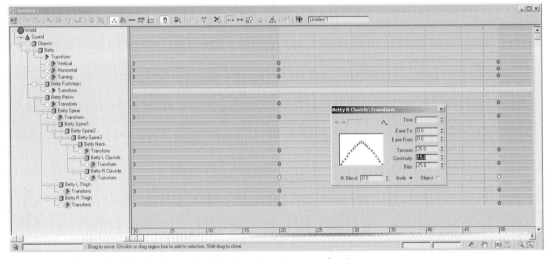

FIGURE 7.10   Change the Continuity settings for all tracks to 0, except for the arms.

Close the Track View, then scrub the Time Slider to see the change in the movement of all the Biped objects. Next, make sure your Animate button is still active, select the COM (Betty), advance to Frame 35, and drag it down about 0.6 units along the Z-axis. Hit the slash (/) key or the V key to play the animation and check how it looks (Figure 7.11).

Change your Time Configuration to have an End Time of 50, and create Time Tags for the animation. Call the first frame Idle1 Start and the last frame Idle1 End (Figure 7.12).

Doubling Keys

While it's extremely useful to use your 3ds max file as an animation folder to store the animation set of your character, the TCB controller can cause you some problems with all the extra motion that results from the default Continuity setting. Instead of manually changing the Continuity to 0 to get rid of this motion "drift," you can achieve the same results by *doubling* the keys. Use this technique, also called *bracketing*, for Betty's

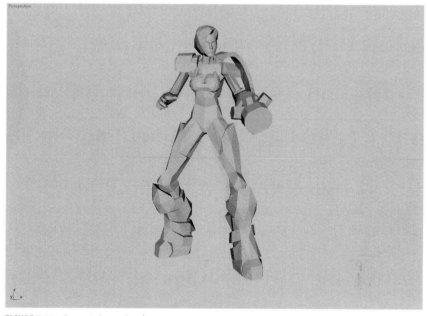

FIGURE 7.11   Betty is happily idling away.

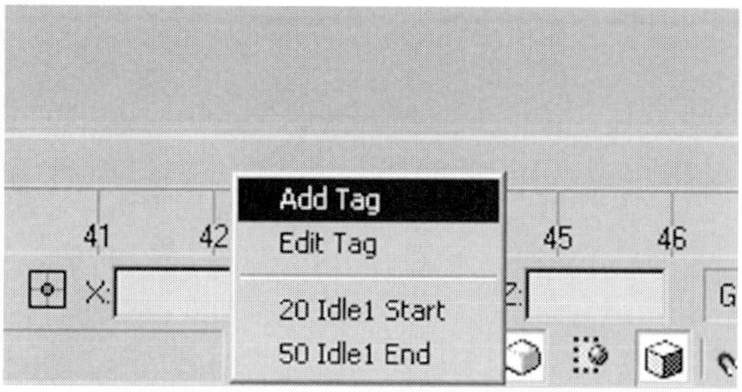

FIGURE 7.12   Add Time Tags to the beginning and end of
the animation.

next idle animation. First, change your animation range to have a Start
Time of 70 and an End Time of 99. At Frame 70, pose Betty so she looks
like she does in Figure 7.13, with her right foot forward.

Lock down the feet again, but this time use Track View to manually
enter the IK Blend and to make the change to Object space. Open Track
View, select the key at Frame 70 for Betty L Thigh, and right-click on it so
the keyframe parameters open; change IK Blend from 0 to 1 and change
Body to Object (Figure 7.14).

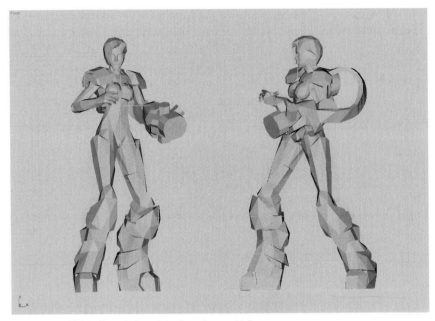

FIGURE 7.13   This is Betty in her right-foot-forward idle pose.

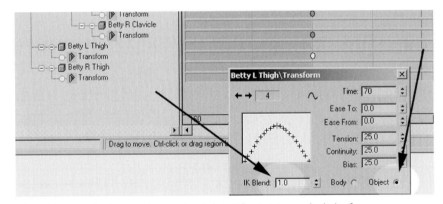

FIGURE 7.14   Set the IK Blend to 1 and switch to Object space to lock the feet.

Do the same thing for Betty R Thigh, and then copy all the keys at Frame 70 to Frame 100. Minimize Track View and scrub the Time Slider back and forth. The excess animation is there. Go back into Track View and copy the column of keys at Frame 70 to Frame 69 and to Frame 101 (Figure 7.15).

Close Track View and scrub the Time Slider back and forth again— now there's no extra movement. This "double-tap" bracketing tech-

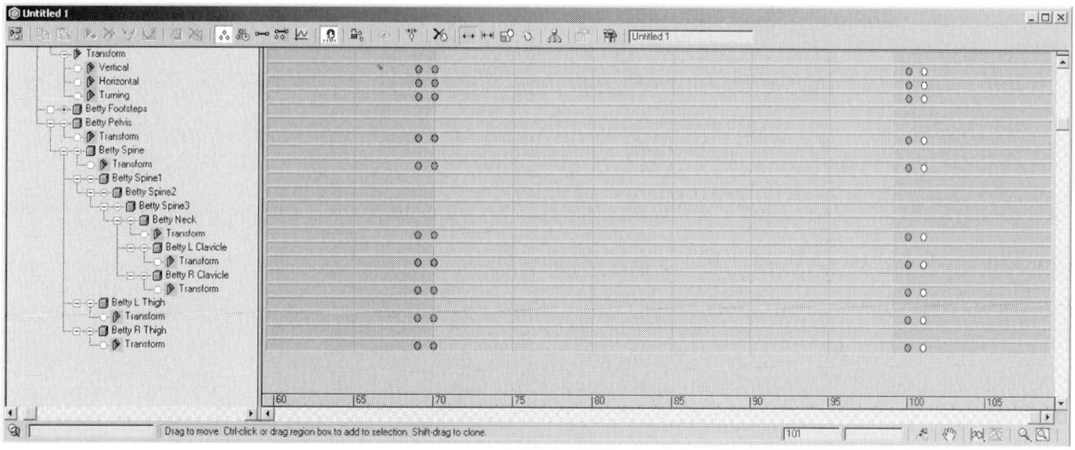

FIGURE 7.15   Doubling keys has the same effect as changing Continuity to 0.

nique strips out the effect of the animation curve of the Continuity setting, even though it's still set at 25. Without a space between keys, the animation curve becomes non-existent and affects Continuity as if it were set to 0.

Now you need to give the character a slight animation like you did for the first idle, just a subtle bouncing motion. Do this by going to Frame 85, selecting COM (Betty), making sure Animate is active, and lowering the Biped root object by 0.7 units along the Z-axis (Figure 7.16).

Secondary Motion

At Frame 85, select all the fingers of the right hand (but not the thumb), and rotate them along the Z-axis, to look as if Betty were slightly flexing her hand. Curl the thumb downward and in slightly (Figure 7.17).

The quickest way to select only the fingers is to double-click on the Biped hand. Then, holding down the Alt key, click on the Hand and Thumb objects to deselect them.

Next, while still at Frame 85, select Betty L UpperArm and rotate it down just 2 degrees along the Z-axis. Now hit the Page Down key to select the left forearm, advance to Frame 90, and rotate it about 3 degrees downward, also along the Z-axis (Figure 7.18).

While at Frame 90, rotate Betty's head 3 degrees downward to give her a slight head nod (Figure 7.19).

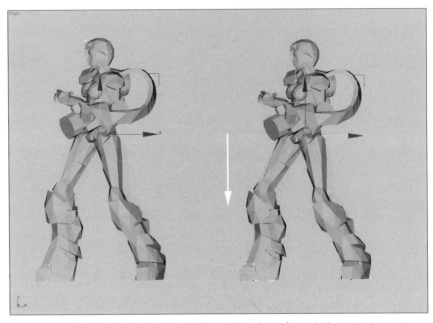

FIGURE 7.16 Shifting the body down slightly while midway through the animation will result in a motion that suggests impatient readiness.

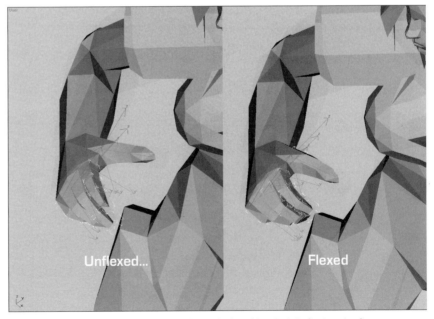

FIGURE 7.17 Add secondary motion to the right hand by slightly flexing the fingers.

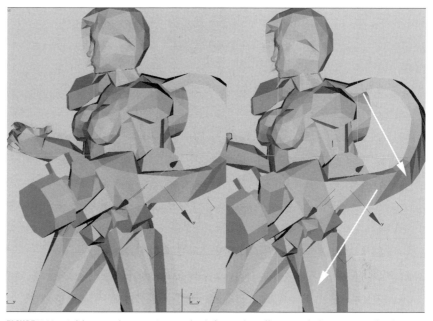

FIGURE 7.18   Add secondary motion to the left arm by offsetting slight rotations for the upper arm and forearm.

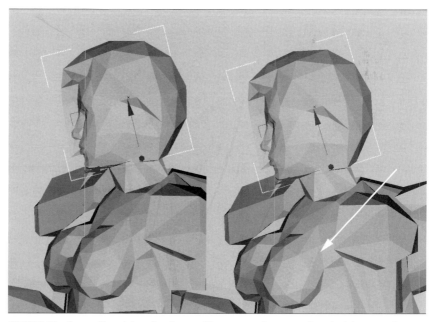

FIGURE 7.19   Rotate Betty's head at Frame 90 to create the sense that she's loose and ready.

Complete the secondary motions by giving the keys at Frame 100 for Betty Head, Betty L Clavicle, and Betty R Clavicle an Ease To value of 25; this will make the loop smoother (Figure 7.20).

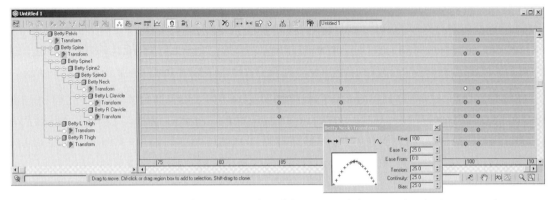

FIGURE 7.20   Adding an Ease To value of 25 to the last key of the animated objects makes the loop smoother.

The reason for putting the head nod and forearm rotation at Frame 90 is because of the lag it creates. With the head nodding slightly, but off-set with the main body motion, it gives Betty a limber, loose, ready-to-go look. The forearm lag creates the impression that the huge gun is little bit heavy. Add time tags at the start and end frame of the second idle, and it's finished.

Join To Previous IK Key

Before you animate Betty's third and last idle, there's something you need to fix. Unless you've been tricky and thinking on your own, you didn't set a keyframe at Frame 50 for Betty R Thigh. Creating the second idle animation, specifically the key set at Frame 70 for Betty R Thigh, ob-viously has an adverse effect on the first idle animation. Change the ani-mation range in Time Configuration to a Start Time of 21 and an End Time of 50 (Figure 7.21).

In the process of adding the missing keyframe, you're going to give something new a try—seeing just what Join to Prev IK Key does. Go to Frame 50, select the right foot, and hit the Set Planted Key button (1), making sure the Join to Previous IK Key box is checked (2) (Fig-ure 7.22).

Betty R Foot snaps to the position it was in for the previous key set for Betty R Thigh (Frame 20). However, there's still a problem. Scrub your Time Slider back and forth. The foot rotates—severely (Figure 7.23).

FIGURE 7.21   Change the Time Configuration to revisit the first idle and fix the missing keyframe.

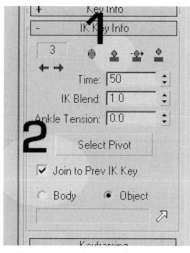

FIGURE 7.22   Finally, a use for this setting!

Sometimes a combination of tools is necessary to fix a particular problem. Go to Frame 21 and turn on Anchor Right Leg (Figure 7.24).

Now go to Frame 50 and hit Set Key—with the foot anchored, just to be sure. Scrub the Time Slider and you can see the foot is now locked. However, the act of hitting the Anchor Right Leg button will set a key for Betty R Thigh at whatever frame you happen to be in. Thus, a key was set at Frame 21. It's perfectly fine to either leave the key there or delete it. Either way, as long as the keys are in place at Frame 20 and Frame 50, the animation is complete. Scrub the Time Slider and you'll see the foot is still locked.

Of course, you're probably wondering why you didn't just go into Track View in the first place, and simply copy the keyframe from Frame

FIGURE 7.23   The foot is in the same position as the Prev IK Key, but it rotates incorrectly.

FIGURE 7.24   Anchor Key is in use once again, but this time to assist Join Prev IK Key.

20 to Frame 50. Well, that works just fine, too. But if you had done that, you still would have seen the excess motion caused by Continuity being set at 25. You would have to change it to 0 (Figure 7.25).

The Third Idle

Betty's third idle is somewhat more static and less action-oriented, because it's mainly a transition animation. It was added to her animation set as an afterthought in order to accommodate other animations and the

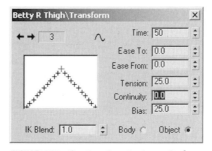

FIGURE 7.25 Setting Continuity to 0 after copying the first key fixes the problem, too.

need for her to be facing forward. The other reason is just for variety. By having three idles (left, right, and both feet), the rest of the animations will not snap back to just one idle animation. The code's ability to choose from the closest idle pose at the end of an animation loop gives a much more diverse and interesting flow to Betty's animation.

Again, here are the steps to creating a short, repetitive idle:

1. Set the animation range.
2. Pose the character.
3. Lock the feet.
4. Copy the key from the start frame to the end frame.
5. Create a slight movement in the middle of the animation.
6. Adjust the TCB settings or *double* the frames to ensure a smooth loop.
7. Add time tags to the start and end frames of the animation.

In the case of this idle, create a pose where the character faces forward, her right foot *slightly* leading the left. Lock her feet. Then, for movement, have her sway a little bit side-to-side, flexing and unflexing her fingers. Change your Time Configuration to 120 and 149, go to Frame 20, make sure Animate is on, and pose the character to look like she does in Figure 7.26.

At Frame 135, shift her from one side to the other, adding some secondary motion to the left arm and head like you did for the previous idle animation. Curl the fingers slightly at Frame 135 as well, to get that clenching/unclenching motion. When you're through, change the Time Configuration settings so you can see Frame 150, add time tags for the beginning and end of the animation, and you're done with the idle animations.

ON THE CD

Save your work, or load Betty09.max from the Chapter7 directory on this book's CD-ROM to see how the three idles should look. Now you can move on to the Shooting animation!

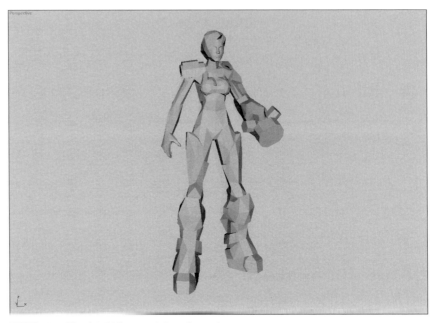

FIGURE 7.26   The third idle pose is less dynamic.

Shooting

What's an action game without someone shooting stuff? Most real-time game characters run around holding large guns and they shoot things aplenty. Unfortunately, posing a character with a gun and accommodating the positioning of many weapons can be a real hassle.

 During the development of Q3A, *the design of the weapons had to be such that they all fit in the character's hands for* one *firing pose. Although a different pose per weapon would have been nice, the idea was dropped because it added too many additional animations to the animation set. Using the same pose for all weapons also affected the weapon design, because even though the weapons had to look substantially different, they all had to be held the same way by the character.*

The first shooting, or firing, animation that needs to be created for any character is "Shooting while idle." Of course, the first step is the firing pose.

The Firing Pose

The firing pose for a typical game character sometime depends on the weapon, but it's generally a two-handed rifle grip. In Betty's case, it's a little different (Figure 7.27).

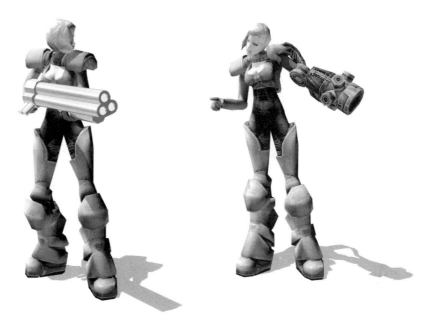

FIGURE 7.27   What if Betty had to carry a *big* gun like regular characters?

Betty has one weapon strapped to her arm, with a weapon's plant strapped to her back. While holding a weapon with both hands often obscures the front of most characters, Betty doesn't have to worry about that. This also makes the firing animations easy to create, the only caveat being that multiple firing animations are required to fit the different poses she can fire *from*.

ON THE CD

Load Betty09.max from the Chapter7 directory on this book's CD-ROM, if you haven't already, and change your Time Configuration settings to an End Time of 200. Open Track View and copy the keys from Frame 20 to Frame 165 and 170 to give you a starting point for the firing pose.

When you are copying keyframes in Track View, looking at the destination frame window that indicates where the keys are being copied to can help you make sure you're copying to the right frame (Figure 7.28).

Once you copy the keys, go to Frame 170, turn on your Animate button, and pose Betty to be in a *firing-ready* position. Do this by lowering her COM slightly so she looks like she's getting ready by centering her weight. Rotate all four Spine objects so she turns her gun arm toward the target. Raise her gun arm, rotating it along the X-, Y-, and Z-axis so that

FIGURE 7.28   Watch at the bottom of your Track View to confirm that the frame to which keys are moved or copied is the correct one.

the front of her weapon is *perpendicular* to the target. (Don't forget to rotate the Clavicle along the Y-axis to raise her shoulder, too.) Rotate her right arm down and slightly back, as if she's using it for a counter-balance, with her fingers straightened. Finally, rotate her right leg slightly, so that the foot and shin are pointing more to her right, giving the viewer the feeling that—again—she's bracing herself for the shot. Once you have the pose, use Arc Rotate to look around her, making sure she doesn't appear off-balance in any way.

With the automatic constraints built into Biped, it's impossible to turn the Calf objects along the Y-axis. However, you can rotate them along the X-axis with interesting results. You can't move the foot, either, even if it hasn't been locked. Try it when posing legs to see the effects.

When you're through posing Betty, she should look something like she does in Figure 7.29.

Once you've created the pose, scrub the Time Slider back and forth to see the transition from the first idle pose to the firing pose. This is the only reason you copied the keys from Frame 120 to Frame 165: so you could see the effect. This won't be a part of the animation set when exported, because of the way the animations will be implemented. Basically, when the character is in Idle1 and starts firing her weapon, she will immediately jump to the pose at Frame 170. The programmer will specify

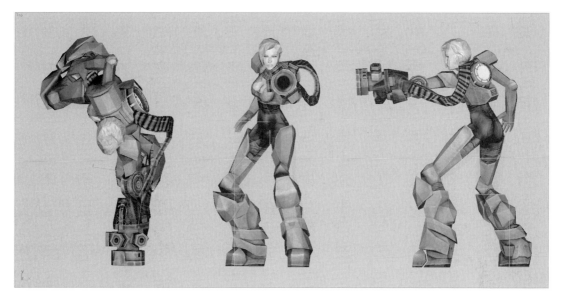

FIGURE 7.29   Betty is ready to do some damage.

the amount of time it takes to go from the last frame of the idle to the pose you just created. The game engine will then "lerp" (short for *interpolate*) to the pose, making it almost appear animated.

 The characters in Quake II *were animated at 15 fps with linear interpolation. Instead of being bone-based, the animation system relied on vertex deformation to simulate animation, which is called a* morph-target *approach. Each frame of an animation was exported to what became a* vertex keyframe. *If you watch the characters move in slow motion, their shapes tend to do strange things as their vertices just go from frame to frame, taking the straightest route to the next pose.*

In *Betty Bad*, the interpolation between frames affects the *bones* that drive the mesh. Being able to rely on this approach, going from one pose to another without actually animating the movement, reduces the total number of animation frames. In other words, a bone-based animation system works better than a vertex deformation system. This is because the bones rotate or move the vertices they influence, instead of just squishing them from pose to pose. Without the lerping, the poses would just snap to one another, looking jerky and unnatural.

With Betty now posed, copy the "firing-ready" keys to Frame 177 in order to go to the next step in her firing animation, which is adding recoil.

Adding Recoil

Seeing the transition from Frame 165 to Frame 170 gives you an idea what the lerp to the firing pose will look like in the game, but there still needs to be some sort of firing animation. In most games, players need and want instant results from hitting the Fire button. They don't want the character getting ready, charging the weapon, and *then* firing. Therefore, Betty's firing animation, like a typical character's firing animation, has to be short and sweet. The purpose of the weapon-ready pose you just created is so that after the character fires, she's in a position to do so again in a short time with relatively little noticeable lerping.

Since you don't need them now, delete the keys you copied to Frame 165. With keyframes set at Frames 170 and 177, go to Frame 172 and add the effect of the gun firing. It can't be too severe, because it has to accommodate several ammo types. Just move the COM back a little, and rotate the Spine objects along the X-axis as if the gun fires and drives the shoulder back. Rotate the head down slightly and you're finished. The often annoying IK solution for the hands, which keeps them in the same relative place when the Spine objects are rotated, actually works in your favor this time (Figure 7.30)!

The animation is subtle because it needs to accommodate the effect of a rapid-fire weapon as well as a single-shot weapon. Giving more time to

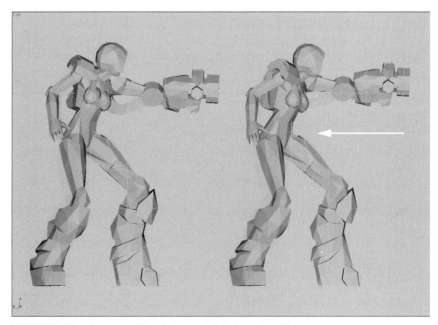

FIGURE 7.30   The firing recoil is subtle yet definitely noticeable.

get back to the default firing stance makes the shot/recoil seem more abrupt and more realistic. However, concentrate on the pose at which she gets into the firing-ready stance. As you'll see in the next chapter, sometimes recoil isn't even necessary if the gun is simply pointed in the right direction. Add time tags for this firing animation, and move on to the next two firing sequences.

Before advancing to the next animation, avoid any unwanted drift due to the Continuity settings. Make sure to double the keys at the beginning and end of the motion clip you just finished.

The Other Two Idle Attacks

Repeat the following steps for the other two idle animations:

1. Copy the first or last frame of the desired idle animation.
2. Set the animation range for the firing animation.
3. Pose the first frame of the firing-ready stance.
4. Copy the keys to a point eight frames later.
5. Advance two keys after the first key and add a recoil.
6. Double the keys at the front and back of the motion clip.
7. Add time tags.

The second shooting-when-idle animation should take place from Frames 200–207. Here are some suggestions for creating it and the recoil: Lower and rotate the COM slightly; rotate the Spine objects slightly; thrust the arm out so the gun muzzle is perpendicular to the ground and pointing at the target; and tilt the head down slightly and double-check the overall posture, so the character doesn't appear off-balance in any way. When she fires, start by moving the COM back a little, and rotate all Spine objects along the X-axis to pull the left arm back. Rotate the left clavicle along the Z-axis a little bit to emphasis the "kick," but leave the right arm as is (Figure 7.31).

The third animation should take place from Frames 230–237. Try something a little different with this one and give her a gunslinger look. Lower her COM and get her in a ready stance. Then place her right hand on top of her weapon, like Clint Eastwood slapping the hammer back with his opposite hand in some spaghetti Western (Figure 7.32).

When you make the firing motion, be sure to keep the right hand in the same position for all three frames (Frames 230–232). Moving and rotating it so it appears it's bucking with the gun will solidify the motion, because it makes the viewer's brain link the two shapes and he'll believe

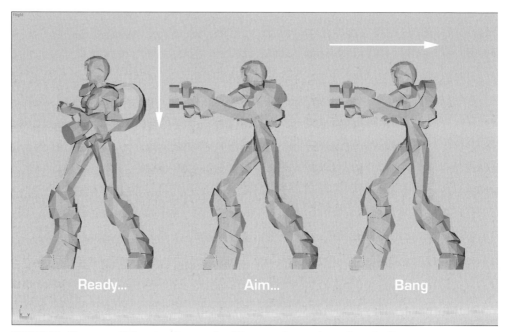

Ready...   Aim...   Bang

FIGURE 7.31 The second idle animation needs a firing pose just as dynamic as the first.

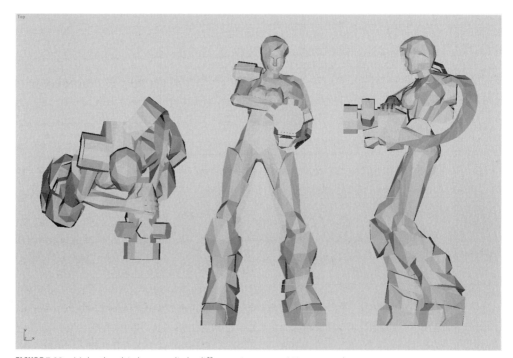

FIGURE 7.32 Make the third pose a little different, in a more Western style.

that Betty has a hand on her gun. Make sure it stays on top of the gun while returning to the ready stance, too (Figure 7.33).

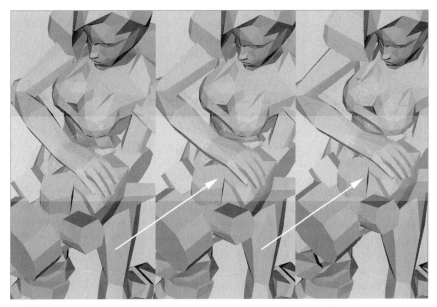

FIGURE 7.33   Make sure the right hand stays in place through the recoil.

Complete the animations by doubling the keys at either end of their ranges, and add time tags for the start and end frames. Then you need to do one more step for the shooting animations. You need to give Betty some sort of aiming mechanism.

Aiming Mechanism

When real-time game characters shoot their weapons, the programmer needs to know where the shot comes from. The only way he can tell the game engine to make it look like the shots are coming from the end of the weapon is for you to identify it for him. In *Q3A*, the same tag system that allowed for a three-part animation scheme provided the mechanism to determine the origin of the shots on the weapon: a tag. In Betty's animation system, you need to add a bone that can be *promoted* during the export process (this will be covered in Chapter 9), letting the programmer know where the firing will come from. Since any object can be a bone in 3ds max, you're going to link a dummy object to Betty L Forearm to serve as this bone. That way, no additional polygonal geometry is added or rendered.

Click the Helpers icon to make it active in the Helpers panel, and click the Dummy button to make it active. Create and position a dummy object so it lines up with the front of the gun muzzle at Frame 230 (Figure 7.34).

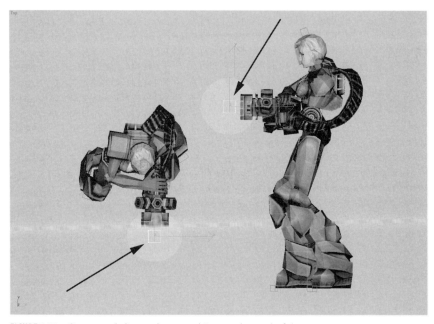

FIGURE 7.34   Create and align a dummy object to the end of the weapon.

Rename the dummy object Weapon Pointer, and link it to Betty L Forearm. Do this by selecting the dummy object and turning on the Select and Link button (1). Then hit the H key to bring up your scene's "hit list" and select Betty L Forearm from the list (2). Complete the operation by clicking on the Link button at the bottom of the menu (3) (Figure 7.35).

Linking the Weapon Pointer object to Betty's forearm makes more sense than linking it to the hand, because the hand isn't used or animated. This frame of reference for the source of the shots coming from the weapon also provides a point for attaching *muzzle flash* geometry and effects. Wrap up the shooting animations by adding time tags, and save your work. If you want to, load Betty10.max from the Chapter7 directory on this book's CD-ROM to see the way the firing animations look. Then crouch down, swing your arms, and get ready for some jumps!

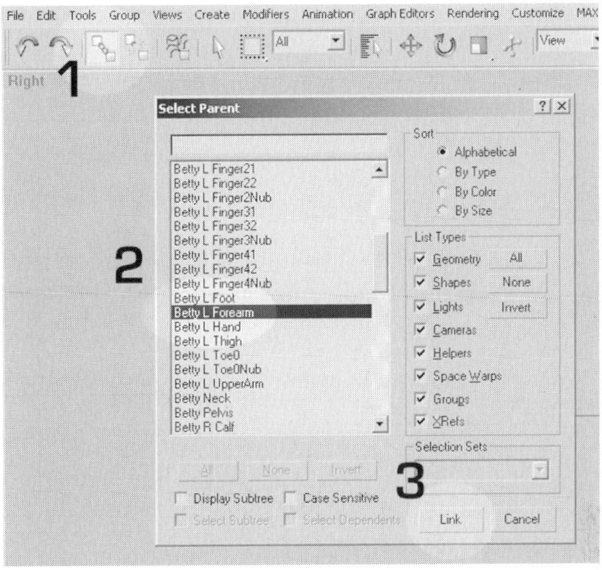

FIGURE 7.35 Linking the Weapon Pointer object to Betty provides a place from which gunfire originates.

JUMPS

If you've played *Quake II* or *Q3A* online, you're probably familiar with the sound that every character of either game makes while they're jumping. An endless barrage of "Huh, Huh, Huh" assails you as experienced players impersonate Mexican jumping beans doing their best to avoid being "fragged."

Standing and Running Jumps

The jump animation itself is an important part of the overall animation set, but it is a tricky motion to create because of its implementation. A normal *standing* jump has four parts to it: anticipation (1), launch (2), hang-time (3), and landing (4) (Figure 7.36).

As you can see, the landing is slightly more complex than the other parts, because it includes both the impact with the ground and recovery. A *running* jump is even more complex, because it has the added effect of momentum, which influences the anticipation and landing motions (Figure 7.37).

In most real-time games, distance is taken into account and can even be a part of the game play, requiring you to do something special to get that *super-jump* to work right. Also, most of the time when you find your character jumping while running, the motion generally doesn't reflect

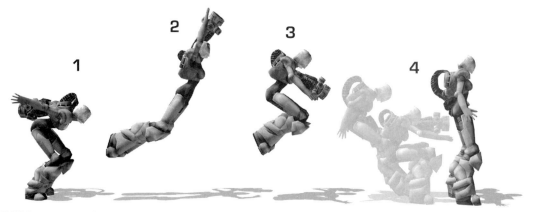

FIGURE 7.36 A standing jump can be divided into four distinct parts.

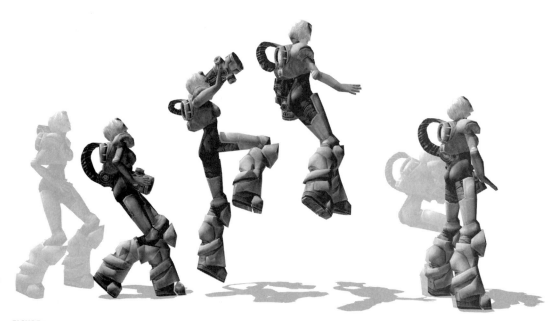

FIGURE 7.37 A running jump needs longer beginning and end phases than a standing jump.

the longer anticipation and landing recovery that should be there. The only thing that most game engines take into consideration when characters jump is their relative velocity while in the air. They can cover that extra distance when required.

Implementing the Real-Time Jump

To make a character jump in the game, the motion has to be broken up into pieces or segments that a programmer can trigger, based on how high the character needs to go, how far, and when he hits the ground. To be implemented, the jump can't be one long motion, because it's impossible to tell how long a character would be in the air after the launch, and how far it would go, since velocity changes all the time. The only way a jump can work in a game is if it's thought through a bit differently and is divided into three parts: jump (1), idle (2), and landing (3) (Figure 7.38).

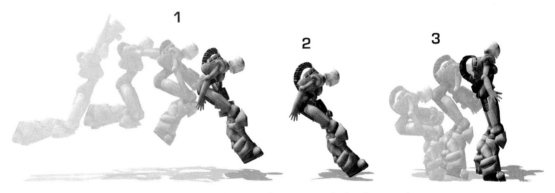

FIGURE 7.38   The jump sequence has to be broken into three parts to be implemented.

Anticipation for a jump isn't even considered, because of the requirement that a character react *instantly* to input from the player. The launch is expanded to include the hang-time up to the point *just before* the character lands, so it's really launch and hang-time combined (hence the new name of *jump*). The frame just before making contact with the ground becomes an idle pose that the programmer can hold for as long as it takes to make contact with the ground—then the landing animation can play. Put differently, the jump animation has to accommodate three things: input to jump, waiting to re-establish contact with a surface, and contact with the surface once again.

Another stipulation for the implementation of a jump is that it's animated *in place*. This means the characters don't attain any height during the animation, because they need to be translated vertically and horizontally by the code, based on input from the player. This is also due to bounding box restraints and other collision-based considerations. When creating a jump animation, take this last fact into consideration *after* you've made the animation look right. Then just take out the vertical keys for the COM, and let the code do the work when the character's in the game.

ON THE CD *Most real-time characters have what's known as a* bounding box *around them, which is based on a pre-determined size and/or by the extreme boundaries of the vertices of the character. Bounding boxes can also be generated in zones (high, medium, and low) or can be generated per bone in a skeletal animation system. Of the three approaches to bounding boxes, the first solution is the least expensive, while the last is the most expensive.*

See Betty Jump

As with the idle animations, Betty has more than one jump—she has *eight*. She has so many because of the third-person perspective and because having just one or two jumps would quickly become repetitive. However, you're only going to come up with five. This will give you ideas for making your own character jump.

ON THE CD If you haven't already, load Betty10.max from the Chapter7 directory on this book's CD-ROM (Figure 7.39).

Change your Time Configuration Start and End settings to 250 and 300, respectively (Figure 7.40).

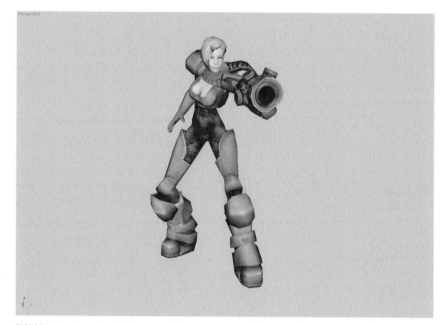

FIGURE 7.39 Now that Betty's ready to shoot something, it's time to make her *jump*.

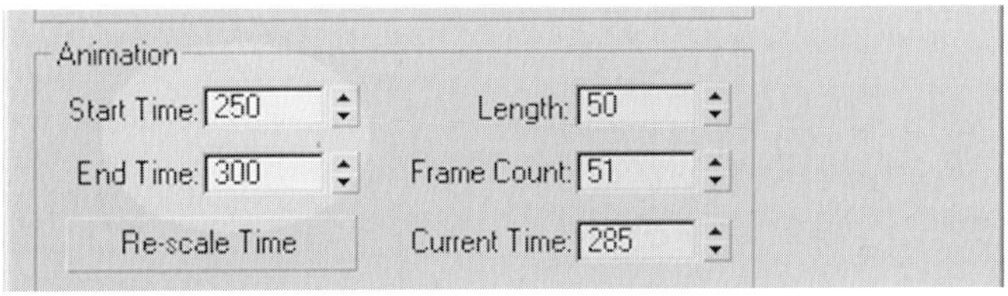

FIGURE 7.40   Change the Time Configuration—again.

Copy the keyframes for the idle pose at Frame 150 to Frame 250 in order to have a default pose to check against the jump animation. It won't look perfect, but you have to imagine it in the game assisted by the interpolation code and the displacement of lifting the character up and out when the input to jump is received. The timing for any jump varies based on the game and the game engine, but for Betty, 11 frames are enough for the jump duration. Go to Frame 155 to pose the first jump frame. Pose Betty in a jump-split pose like something a cheerleader would perform at a pep rally. Keep her back relatively straight, and lift her left arm slightly. Keep the arm pointed somewhat forward so that the lerping isn't as noticeable when she shoots from the position. As you rotate her upper and lower legs, notice how the toes of the feet point outward, giving an auto-assist with the pose. Don't rotate the legs completely in the split, but save some room for the second pose, in which the legs will be fully extended. Finish the pose by straightening her right arm, and selecting and pulling the hand down along the Z-axis (Figure 7.41).

When cheerleaders do the sort of move Betty's trying to pull off, they go up, and then as they go down, their body bends noticeably forward as they stretch their legs even further apart. Go to Frame 165 and bend the Spine objects a little more and rotate the legs further upward. Straighten the fingers on her right hand so she seems tensed while in the air (Figure 7.42).

Before you set the pose for Hang-time2, copy the Idle3 pose from Frame 250 to Frames 278 and 285. This will allow you to establish the foot position for the landing part of the animation. While any of the three idles could have been chosen for the landing, Idle3 is the most generic. Whenever the character jumps, it will land and automatically go into this idle.

Now go to Frame 278, lock the feet, and pose Betty as if she's just hit the ground after having been dropped from a height. Picture jumping and landing and what *your* body would be doing. Add little details, like the head looking slightly down and the hand tilted up (Figure 7.43).

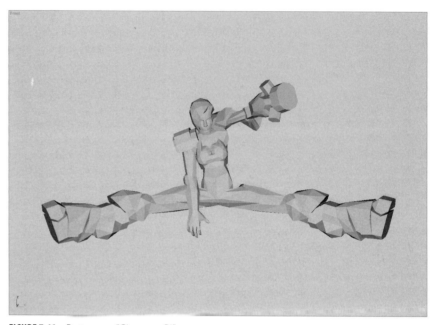

FIGURE 7.41 Betty says, "Gimme a B!"

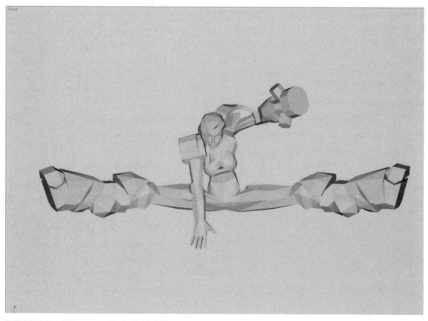

FIGURE 7.42 "Gimme a B–E–T–T–Y!"

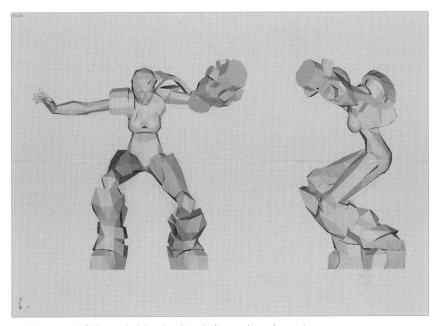

FIGURE 7.43   *Oof!* She *nailed* that landing, ladies and gentlemen!

Advance two frames and then add some secondary motion, such as her head bend down, her arms coming down, and her waist bending forward. This provides cues that suggest *impact* (Figure 7.44).

Now you can go back to Frame 275 and create the pose for Hang-time2 *just before* the landing part of the animation. This animation is important; for really big jumps in any game, this is the pose that the engine will hold the character in while waiting for her to make contact with something to land on. When you pose her, think of the hang-time you would experience while falling from a height. Make sure her feet are poised just above the ground, ready to assume the landed-feet positions (Figure 7.45).

Betty's arms can't be raised too high because of her shoulder pads, but having them outward gives the sense she is striving to keep her balance as she falls. Hang-time2 is all about the pose of landing "readiness," so no animation for it is required. However, WildTangent's technology is such that all animations must be at least three frames in length. Therefore, once you're happy with the pose, copy it to Frames 273 and 274. Scrub the Time Slider to see the whole jump animation.

Next, you need to spread out the jump components, treating them like individual animations complete with time tags and frame buffers. Open Track View, and start by deleting the idle pose at Frame 250, and

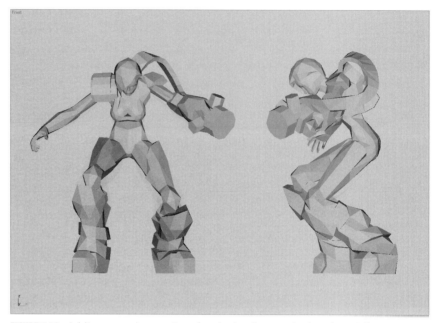

FIGURE 7.44 Adding secondary motion after the landing emphasizes the motion.

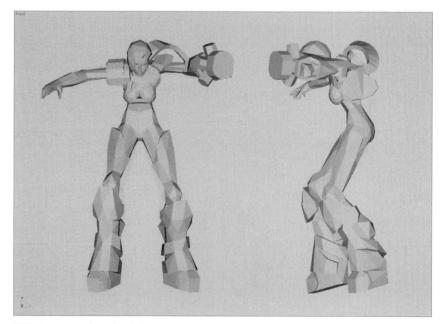

FIGURE 7.45 Ready to land, the character still needs to look as if she is airborne.

then slide the two jump-split keys over. Double-tap or "bracket" the keys at the front and end of the motion to keep Continuity sway out of the animation. Then, slide over the column of three keys that make up the Hang-time2 pose so that they begin at Frame 280. Finally, slide the landing sequence over to start on Frame 300, doubling the keys at either end of that animation as well (Figure 7.46).

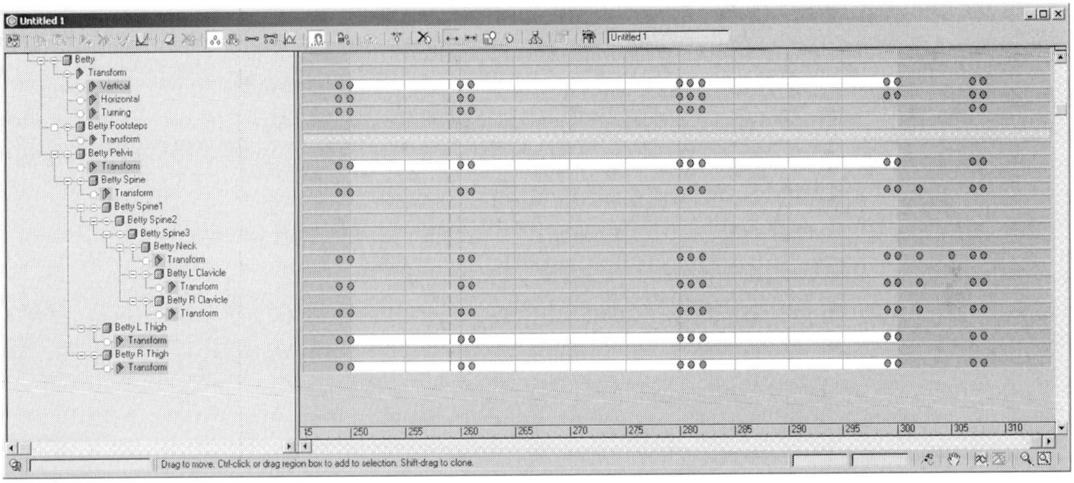

FIGURE 7.46   Shift the keys around so there is a buffer between the jump components.

Add time tags so that the animations are easy to find. This should make quite a long list of time tags so far, so don't enter Start and End tags for all the animations. All three idles are the same length, all the firing animations are the same, and all the jumps will be the same length. By only entering the Start and End tags for the first in a series of animation clips, you'll find that your list of time tags will be more manageable (Figure 7.47).

Now, you can create some alternate jumps for Betty, keeping in mind the need for variety when staring at the same character for the whole game!

See Betty Jump . . .Again

One of the great comic book artists of the 1980s and early 1990s was Frank Miller. He still does great work today, but his early work (*Daredevil*™, *Spider-Man*™, and, of course, *Batman*™) defined a style of storytelling that is crucial to the character animator: *dynamic action*. Every

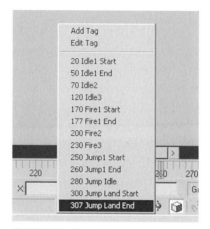

FIGURE 7.47   Keep time tags manageable by limiting the Start and End entries.

panel featuring a Frank Miller character in motion is pure kinetic magic. Staring at them, you feel like any of these 2D characters could leap off the page at any moment. This is due to Miller's ability to capture an animation in the most powerful and interesting snapshot of a pose: hands out, legs tucked, perfect balance, and with total awareness of their environment. His character rendering is amazing.

When posing your character in any animation, think of it as a panel in a comic book. Go out and buy any Jim Lee compilation, like *X-Men*™ or *Divine Right*™. He, too, is a master at the interesting, eye-catching *action* pose. As you look over the following poses for two of Betty's other jumps, try to come up with some poses yourself that would look good in any Jim Lee or Frank Miller comic book (Figure 7.48).

As you create the first pose of the 11-frame animation, don't forget to change it slightly at the back end as well; picture the slight movements as the character sails through the air. Try to make each pose unique. For example, the pose in Figure 7.49 shows Betty leaning to her right with her right leg up. Figure 7.49 shows Betty with her left leg up, leaning forward instead of backward. Even in silhouette, the two poses should be easy enough to recognize.

Turnaround Jumper

For the fourth jump, try for something from the repertoire of a basketball player or skater: a turn-around jump shot. First, change your Time Configuration to have a Start Time of 390 and an End Time of 410. Then, pose Betty at Frame 390 by lifting her knees, dipping her right shoulder,

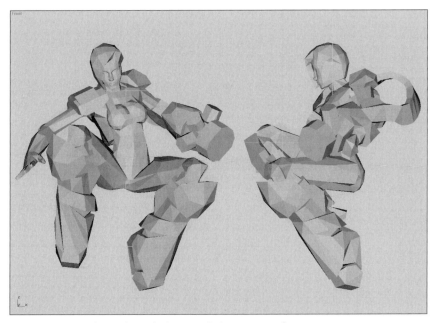

FIGURE 7.48   Betty leaps through the air with the greatest of ease.

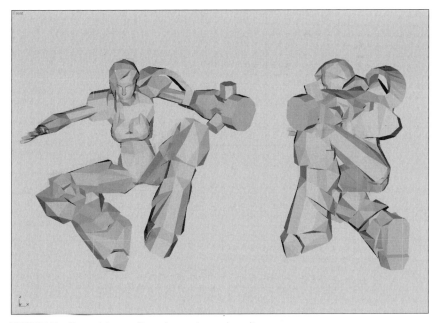

FIGURE 7.49   Even airborne, Betty has poise and readiness.

putting her right hand behind her and down, and lowering her gun arm so it almost seems like it rests on her hip. It's important that her arms are down, so that they can come up as she spins, imparting the sense of centrifugal force. She's going to spin counter-clockwise, so lean her body slightly toward that direction (Figure 7.50).

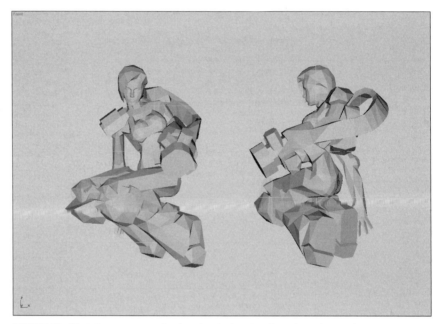

FIGURE 7.50 Start the turnaround animation by leaning Betty into the motion.

This animation needs to last a little bit longer than the other jumps, about 13 frames in total. But instead of going to the end of the animation and rotating the COM one complete rotation, you're going to divide it into three separate rotations. So, to start, advance four frames, select just the COM, and rotate it 120 degrees along the Z-axis (1). Don't animate anything else yet. Advance another four frames, rotate the COM another 120 degrees (2), then advance another four frames and rotate another 120 degrees. Youwill have a complete turn at Frame 402 (3) (Figure 7.51).

Test the turn to see how it looks. Now set the end pose; raise Betty's arms and bend her forward, as if she's using her body to increase the speed of the spin. Rotate her Spine objects and her right arm a little more to the right than in the first frame. Adjust her legs so that they're facing more forward (Figure 7.52).

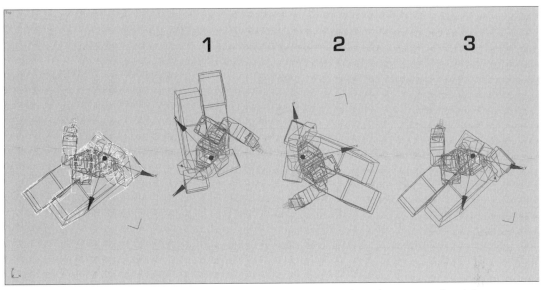

FIGURE 7.51   Complete a 360-degree turn by turning in three increments of 120 degrees every fourth frame.

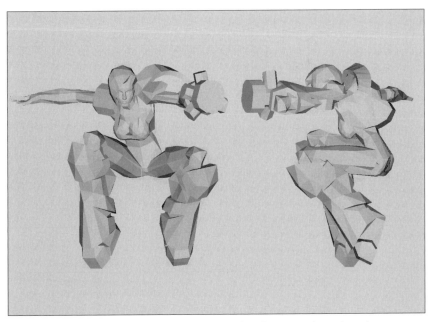

FIGURE 7.52   The end of the turnaround jump needs to be just as dynamic as the beginning.

Whenever you see a competitive diver or figure skater execute a series of high-speed spins or flips, you'll see them lead the motion with their head. This is for the practical purpose of allowing them to see where they're going to land, or to find some sort of mark to keep their bearings. Refine this animation by adding some of that kind of secondary motion to Betty's spine, head, and arms. Go back to Frame 396. Arch her back and rotate her Spine objects along the X-axis so that she's twisting *into* the spin. Turn her head along the X-axis as well, and tilt it slightly along the Y-axis. Straighten her left arm to again emphasize the centrifugal force of spinning. Bend her right arm so it seems like she's in the middle of throwing her leading arm into the spin (Figure 7.53).

FIGURE 7.53   Add a secondary motion pose midway through the animation.

At Frames 393 and 399, rotate the head and tilt it into the turn to add to the impression she is searching for her bearings. At Frame 400, bring the right arm up and slightly back, extending to look like a whip motion, further imparting the sense of spin and speed (Figure 7.54).

Scrub the Time Slider to see how the animation looks. If it's effective, double the keys at the beginning and end of the motion clip, time tag it,

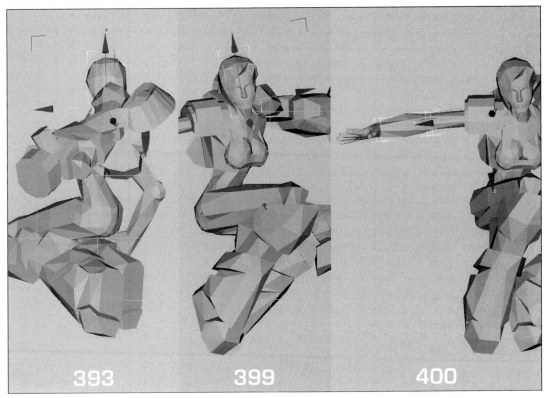

FIGURE 7.54   Complete the animation with final secondary-move tweaking.

and you're done with the fourth jump. The fifth jump animation is created in case the character needs to shoot while jumping and/or landing.

Jumping while Shooting

To create this version of the jump, you'll start with animations that have already been done. You're going to copy the keyframes that make up Jump2, Hang-time2, and the landing, but don't bother changing your Time Configuration to get to them. You're about to find out one of the benefits of using the Time Tags feature. Click on Add Time Tag and then click on Jump2 (Figure 7.55).

If you haven't been adding time tags then, yes, you will *have to change your Time Configuration to get to the keys in Track View.*

Time Configuration changes automatically as the Time Slider "jumps" to Jump2. Open Track View and copy all the keys from Frame

FIGURE 7.55 Clicking on Jump2 takes you to that point regardless of the Time Configuration settings.

329 to Frame 341 to *start* at Frame 419. Of course, the Time Tag trick doesn't help you with Time Configuration if it needs to go *further* in time. Change the Time Configuration to a Start Time of 280 and an End Time of 480; this gives you access to Hang-time2 and the landing, as well as pushing the animation range out to create the new jump animation. Once you copy all the keys from Frames 280–308 to Frames 450–478, change your Time Configuration again to a Start Time of 420 and an End Time of 480. The keys should look something like this in Track View: Jump2 (1), Hang-time2 (2), and Landing (3) (Figure 7.56).

Now that you've copied the keys, delete all of them from the following frames: 419, 430, 431, 451, 452, 469, and 478. (Because you're going to be creating new versions of the existing keyframes, you're going to recopy the new poses anyway.) Then, go to Frame 420 and pose Betty so she's in a shooting-ready position. Rotate the COM, Spine objects, arms, and head to get something poised-looking and *deadly* (Figure 7.57).

Using Snapshot for Reference Objects

With the pose established, you'll need some way to keep the gun in a steady position throughout the 11-frame jump animation. The best way to do this is to make a *snapshot* of the end of the gun and use it as a guide. Unfreeze All, select m_gun (1), go to Snapshot under the Tools menu,

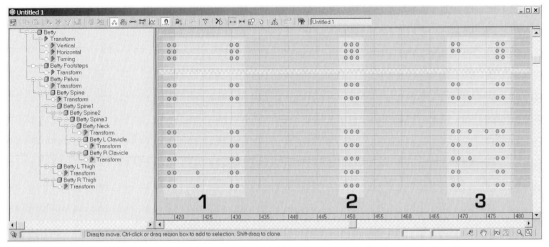

FIGURE 7.56   Copy the keys of previous animations to provide a starting point for the new animations.

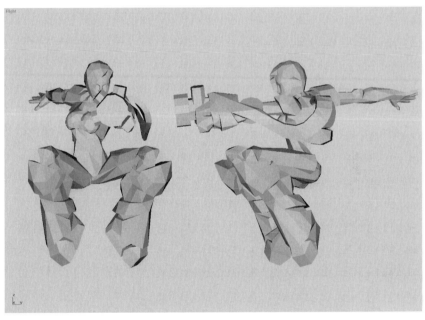

FIGURE 7.57   Betty is jumping again, but ready to rock and roll this time.

and click on it (2). Then make sure Single is selected in the Snapshot dialog menu, and hit OK (3) (Figure 7.58).

Change the mesh color of the new object so it stands out against the current color. Then copy the keys you just set at Frame 420 to Frame 430, and make a few changes to the pose, just for the sake of interest.

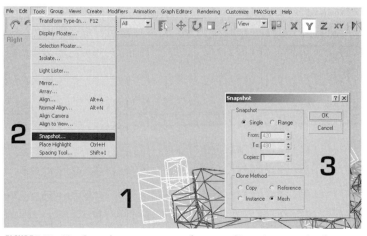

FIGURE 7.58 Use Snapshot to create a reference of Betty's gun in the firing position.

Rotate her COM and torso in the direction opposite to the one they're now facing, aligning the gun arm with the reference object you just created. When you align the gun, concentrate on the front edge of the weapon so you ensure it's parallel to the reference (Figure 7.59).

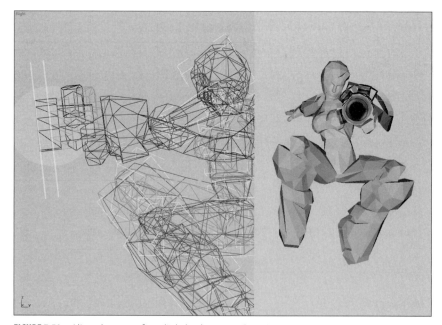

FIGURE 7.59 Align the gun after slightly changing Betty's pose.

Double the keys to get rid of Continuity drift, and check to see if the gun arm needs to be adjusted at any other frame of the animation. It should be fine, so delete the reference gun object, and add a time tag.

 Because a jump is such a relatively short animation, and one that involves gross *movement, there's no need to really animate a kickback part to the animation. This applies to Betty's integrated gun and to a traditional game weapon as well.*

Now go to the Hang-time2 key at Frame 450. Have Betty point the weapon downrange and give her trademark "come hither and get shot" look (Figure 7.60)!

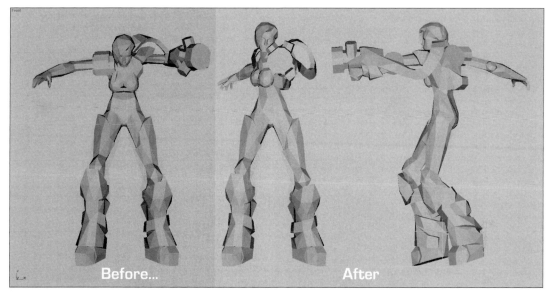

FIGURE 7.60   Betty, waiting to touch down, still wants something to shoot.

There's no need to snapshot a reference to which to align the gun arm, because there's no animation for this part. Just copy they keyframes to Frames 451 and 452, time tag Frame 450, and give the same sort of pointing-weapon treatment to the landing phase of the jump. Advance token to Frame 470 to finish this last part of the jump.

Hitting the Ground Shooting

Again, the key to this sort of pose is to balance it with the reasoning be-hind the current pose: landing. In a jump landing, even Clint Eastwood would find it difficult to steady a gun like the cannon that Betty's carrying. While suspending your disbelief is part of the allure and demands of an action game, adding just enough heroic realism to make it believable is required. Keep this in mind as you set the first pose of the landing (Figure 7.61).

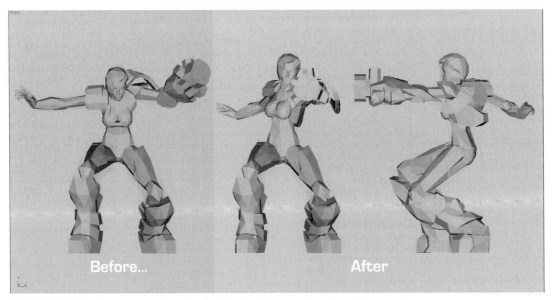

FIGURE 7.61   With the weapon pointed during landing, it's bound to take a dip soon after.

Now, add a twist to the animation by borrowing from the Fire3 animation. Since the feet position is taken from the landing, which in turn is taken from Idle3, it makes sense to end up in the Fire3 pose. So, bring up your Time Tags and click on the Fire3 animation at Frame 230 to use it as the end pose for *this* animation. Copy the keyframes at Frame 230 to Frame 480, lengthening the landing by a few frames.

Next, add evidence of an impact by advancing to Frame 273, bending Betty at the waist, bringing her arms down a little, and bending her head and hand down, too. Adding these secondary motions as Betty rises from her post-impact crouch reinforces the feeling she has just landed (Figure 7.62).

Advance to Frame 275 and add the last bit of secondary motion, reinforcing Betty's *recovery* from the impact by rotating her head, gun arm, and right hand slightly upward before she moves into the pose from Frame 230. This will make it seem as if her reflexes are quick and she's ready to go (Figure 7.63).

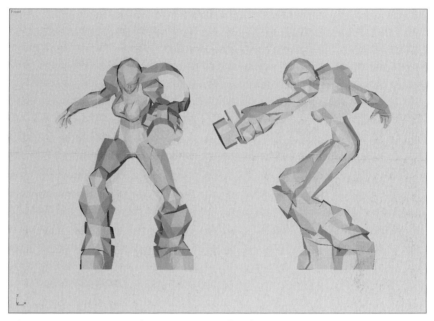

FIGURE 7.62   Betty reacts to the jarring impact of landing.

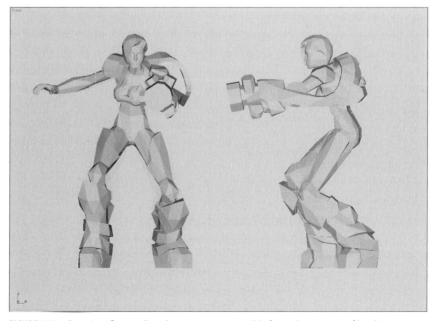

FIGURE 7.63   Betty's reflexes allow her to recover quickly from the impact of landing.

Finally, make one more refinement to the animation. Go into Track View and slide the keys for Betty Spine, Betty Pelvis, and Betty Head at Frame 480 to Frame 478. This makes the hands that are assuming their positions (at-ready and atop the weapon) more noticeable, because the torso attains the pose before them (Figure 7.64).

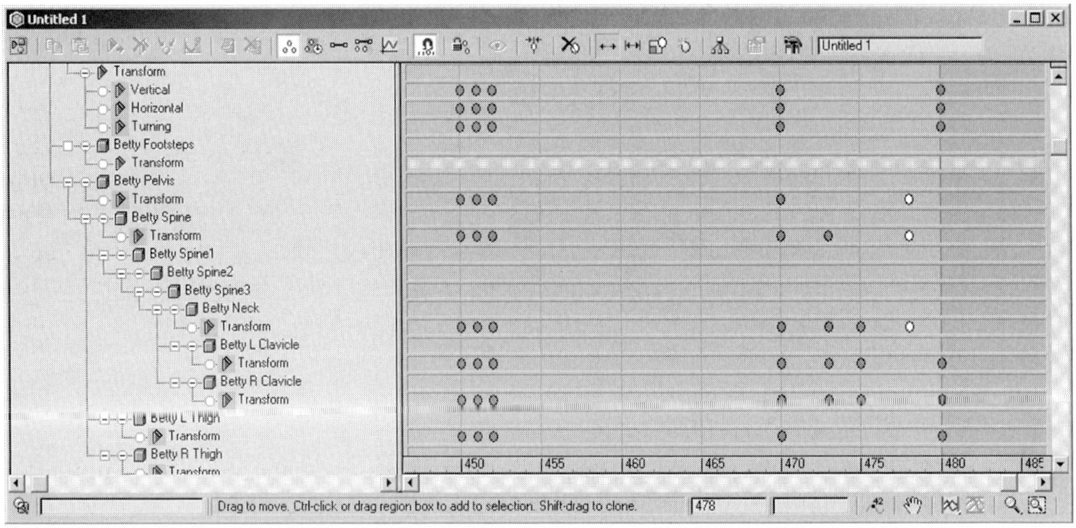

FIGURE 7.64   Slide the keys for the Pelvis, Spine, and Head tracks to focus on the hands.

Add keys for the missing spots at Frame 480 and double-tap the animation, front and back. Last, time tag the start and end, and you're done.

Animation Ideology

You may be wondering why so much information has been thrown at you for a relatively minor and often ignored animation (*Q3A* didn't have this type of jumping-and-shooting motion). Well, this book is as much about the *ideology* of character animation as it is about real-time animation, 3ds max, and character studio. The importance of simulating effects such as momentum, centrifugal force, and impact on a character cannot be overstated. These sorts of real-world phenomena imposed upon fantastic creations and motions add up to superior real-time character animation. Small details make big impressions on the mind of the viewer. Constantly reevaluate your animations and ask yourself if can they be better. Should the head be tilted left—or right? Should the foot be turned in—or out? To be a master of character animation, you have to be a student of *life* first.

SWIMMING

Not all games feature characters that swim. In *Q3A*, characters swim, but there's only water in a few levels. *Betty Bad* features water as an integral part of the game, forcing you to flood a level and then drain it. Correspondingly, while *Q3A* just had the characters doing a simple frog kick or scissors kick, Betty has an extensive set of animations to support her while swimming, including swimming forward, swimming forward while shooting, swimming backward, swimming backward while shooting, swimming idle, swimming idle while shooting, swimming pain, swimming death—you get the picture. She is shown completely submerged, utilizing the same sort of breathing apparatus that Qui-Gon Jinn and Obi-Wan Kenobi used in *Star Wars: Episode I*. This requires all her animations to look as if she is realistically moving underwater. To give you the general idea for aquatic animation, you're going to make Betty tread water and swim forward.

Treading Water

The illusion of being underwater in a game is pulled off by making the "air" of the level murky and/or increasing the amount of "fog" present. Add in some random bubbles, a few objects floating serenely, and an imaginary current, and you have a fairly realistic watery world—but what really pulls off the feeling of being in the water is the animation of the characters that are submerged in it. Betty is a little handicapped when it comes to getting wet, because she really only has the use of one hand (in addition to her legs, of course). The first step is to get her idle animation going by having her float or hover convincingly. Then it's a simple matter of having her slowly tread water, waiting for some action.

ON THE CD Continue with the file you've been working with, or load Betty11.max from the Chapter7 directory on this book's CD-ROM. Change your Time Configuration to a Start Time of 500 and an End Time of 100 (swimming idles take a *long* time to look properly languid and fluid). As in any major animation, the first step in the idle is to "block it out" first, and then add refinement and secondary motion with each pass. This just means that an efficient workflow establishes the main poses at the beginning, middle, and end; you then add poses between the beginning and the middle, and between the middle and the end. This gives you a chance to play the animation back, getting a feeling for the timing, and think about the next pass you're going to make.

Betty's underwater idle motion will feature a slow cycling of her legs, and movement in her arms that suggests treading water. Go to Frame

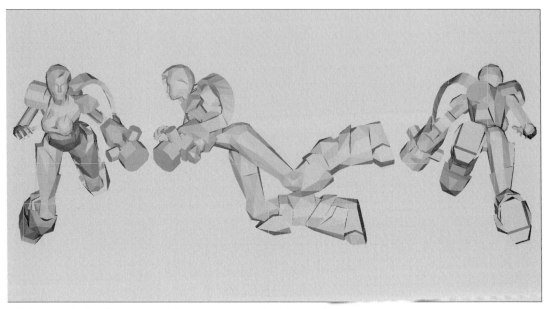

FIGURE 7.65   The first frame of the swim animation is mid-stride, treading water.

500 and pose Betty like she appears in Figure 7.65. Be sure to twist her waist and pelvis in opposite directions by first rotating the COM and then the Spine objects (Figure 7.66).

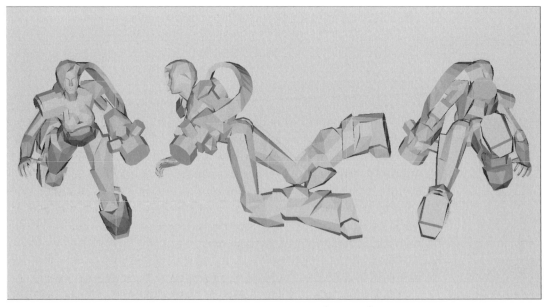

FIGURE 7.66   This is the halfway point in the swim idle, the opposite of the first frame.

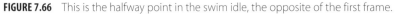

Copy the keyframes you just set to Frame 600 and go to Frame 550 to set the next pose. This time, pose Betty the way you did before, but mirrored: the left arm is in the right arm position, the left arm is in the right arm position, and the Spine objects are rotated in the opposite direction of her pose at Frame 500. Start by rotating her COM and Spine, then do the arms and legs. Don't bend her feet too much, because they'll have to bend on the downward stroke in later passes (Figure 7.66).

The quickest way to copy one limb pose and transfer it to the opposite limb at a different frame is to follow these steps: Go to the frame where the pose is, double-click on the limb root, and hit the Copy Posture button (1). Advance to the frame where you want the pose to be transferred, make sure Animate is active, double-click the target limb, and hit the Paste Posture/Pose/Track Opposite button (2) (Figure 7.67).

FIGURE 7.67   Paste Posture/Pose/Track Opposite is a great way to keep both side arm and leg poses consistent.

Now, double the keys at the start and end frames of the animation to get rid of any Continuity-based motion, and play back the animation to see how it looks. It should be a smooth, looping animation of Betty doing a basic, lazy, kicking motion. To impart a sense of floating, go to Frame 525, then, in the Right viewport, select the COM, and lower it by about 1 unit along the Z-axis. Copy the key to Frame 575 and play the animation back. Betty now has a little bit of a bobbing motion to reinforce the illusion of being underwater.

Whenever animating a Biped, try to have the Motion panel always active. This keeps all the coordinate axes correct relative to the Biped (that is, Z is up instead of Y).

The next type of secondary motion you need to add is some extra leg motion. This will also emphasize weightlessness and the look of floating in water. Go to Frame 525 again, and adjust the left leg: Rotate Betty L Thigh −20 degrees along the Z-axis, Betty L Calf −20 degrees along the Z-axis, and Betty L Foot 60 degrees along the Z-axis. Pose the right leg by just rotating Betty R Calf 50 degrees along the Z-axis. The default IK will pose the foot for you automatically (Figure 7.68).

FIGURE 7.68 Bending the legs in anticipation of the downward kick adds to the illusion of being underwater.

Double-click on Betty L Thigh and hit the Copy Posture button to copy the pose for the left leg. Advance to Frame 575 and click Paste Posture/Pose/Track Opposite to paste the pose to the right leg. Go back to Frame 525, click on Betty R Calf, and hit Copy Posture; advance to Frame 575 and paste it onto the *left* calf in the same way (Figure 7.69).

Creating a Smooth Loop

Sometimes it's very difficult to achieve a perfectly smooth loop in 3ds max. No matter what you adjust or tweak, there's always some sort of a slight twitch or snap. In most cases this goes unnoticed, and/or the game engine helps by using interpolation. However, it's crucial during swimming motions that the loop be absolutely smooth. Remember that the

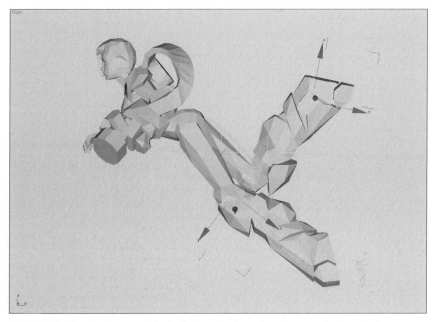

FIGURE 7.69   Use the Copy and Paste Posture tool to mirror the pose just created.

3ds max file is really an animation folder, so you're free to create as many keys wherever you want during the animation, since most game engines allow you to specify the beginning and end times of animations at the time of export (more on exports later). This is why time tags are so useful. Keeping all that in mind, there's a very simple way to create a nearly perfect loop by using a few extra frames.

Change your Time Configuration to have a Start Time of 500 and an End Time of 700. Delete the keys you doubled at Frames 499 and 601. Then, copy all the keyframes at Frame 525 to Frame 625, and all the keys at Frame 550 to Frame 650. Change your Time Configuration settings to 525 and 624, and play back the animation (Figure 7.70).

The animation should be completely smooth now. Copying keys like this is really just a variation of the key-doubling trick that forces 3ds max to either recognize or ignore keys before and after the animation you're working on. This is why the animation folder approach should make you think of your animations within the 3ds max file more as motion clips than distinct animations. The analogy will help you later on as you work in Flow Mode (which we'll discuss in the next chapter).

You can experiment with secondary motion for the arms and head, but with the leg tweaks, the swimming idle animation is fine as is. Now you can move on to the animations for swimming forward.

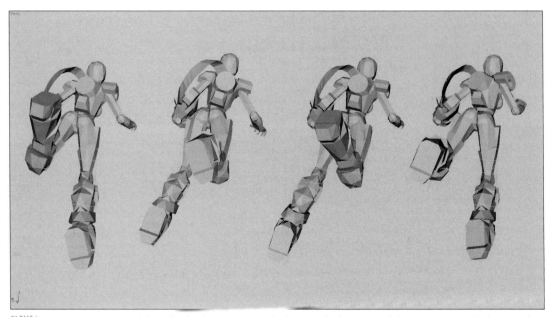

FIGURE 7.70 Create a smooth loop by duplicating keys, which extends the range of the animation and changes the range itself to fall *within* the larger set.

Swimming Forward

While any character carrying a weapon needs to rely on their legs to propel them through the water, scissor kicks and frog kicks are about all you can get away with. You can take the mermaid-style approach like in *The Man from Atlantis*, in which the whole body gets into the motion, but the carried weapon makes it very difficult to transition into other animations.

The first frame of the animation is important because it's the pose the character moves into from the idle. With the help of interpolation, it's not a huge issue, but it is something to think about. In Betty's case, her first frame shows her flat out, in a prone position, with her right hand back as she knifes through the water. The idea here is that interpolation will almost make it seem as if she *pushes off* into the swim from the idle. Change your Time Configuration to a Start Time of 410 and an End Time of 670. Pose Betty at Frame 470 so that she looks like she does in Figure 7.71.

Copy the keys at Frame 670 to Frame 710, and advance to Frame 690 to create the next pose. This is the halfway point at which Betty is drifting and then reaching up for another stroke, getting ready to push off with a powerful kick. However, the most important thing here is the movement of the COM. As you create the pose in Figure 7.72, pull the COM *back* along the Y-axis by four units, and *down* along the Z-axis by eight units.

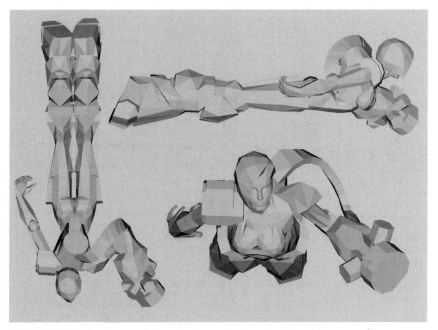

FIGURE 7.71   The first frame of the swim-forward animation takes advantage of lerping.

Even though Betty will be moved through the water programmatically, moving her like this will make it look like her pause between strokes results in her losing a little momentum, even sinking a bit. This helps with the general impression of moving underwater (Figure 7.72).

With the COM taken care of, you next need to adjust the legs. This is an example of the process of adjusting the parent object before the child object. Whenever you find yourself preparing to animate a limb, make sure the parent doesn't need animating first. For the legs, it's the COM and Pelvis, while for the arms, it's the Spine objects. There are sometimes exceptions, however, especially for the arms, as you'll see in a few minutes.

The legs need to perform the frog-kick motion that will propel Betty through the water. With the legs drawn up at Frame 690, they then need to flex outward a little, just before flicking back at Frame 695. Finally, they'll kick straight out at Frame 702, before going back to the default start/end position (Figure 7.73).

With the main leg poses in place, refine the feet positions so that they roll a little with the force of the leg movements. At Frame 695 and Frame 698, exaggerate the amount the feet roll inward along the Y- and X-axes as the legs flex outward. Then, at Frame 702, rotate the feet *outward* as

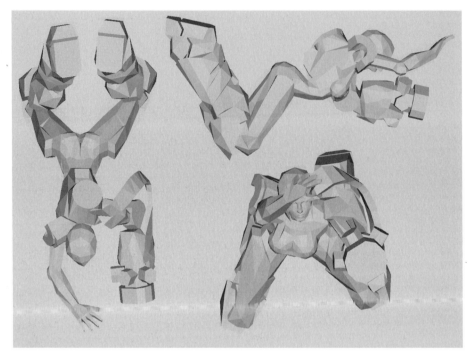

FIGURE 7.72   At the midway point in the animation, Betty is ready to stroke and kick.

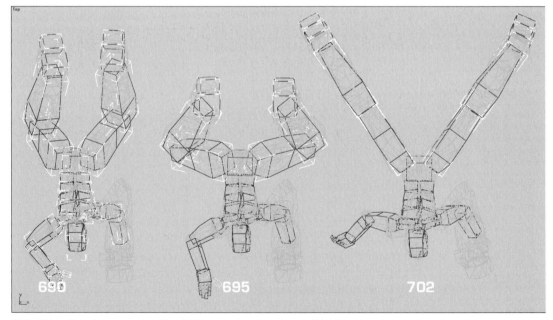

FIGURE 7.73   The three steps to a frog kick are to draw up, flex, and kick back.

the legs push toward each other, simulating the effects of the water volume being displaced between Betty's legs. By forcing the slightly flimsier feet to roll with this pressure, the illusion of the swimming motion is complete (Figure 7.74).

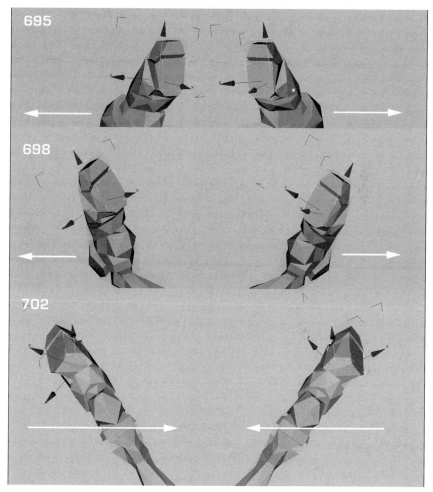

FIGURE 7.74   The feet react to the legs displacing water.

With the legs set, you need to tweak the right arm so it looks more like it's taking a stroke. However, keep in mind that Betty doesn't have great mobility in her right arm because of her huge shoulder pad. Go to Frame 680, hide the Spine and left arm Biped objects, and rotate the right arm up so the hand is near the position it's in at Frame 690. Close the fingers so they look like they want to push through the water. Close the finger at Frame 690, as well. At Frame 696, keep the hand where it is, but rotate the elbow down as the arm tenses to push down and back. Then, go to Frame 706, open Track View, and copy the key at Frame 710 for Betty L Clavicle to Frame 706. Close Track View and straighten the fingers. Finally, go back up to Frame 702, and rotate the hand and fingers slightly along the Z-axis so that it appears they're flexing back from pushing through the water (Figure 7.75).

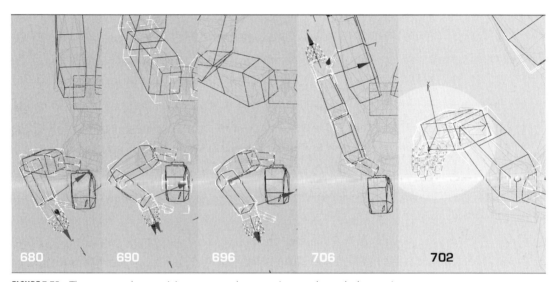

FIGURE 7.75 The arm needs to anticipate, act, and react as it goes through the motion.

The last thing to adjust is the waist. Go to Frame 684, apply Unhide All, and select all four Spine objects. Open Track View, and delete the key you had set for Betty Spine at Frame 690. Rotate all four Spine objects to Betty's left along the Y-axis as the right hand reaches up and out to take the stroke. Then, go to Frame 705, and rotate the Spine objects along the Y-axis back toward the motion of the stroke (Figure 7.76).

Animating the Spine objects (the parent) after animating the arm (the child) is one of those special cases that is normally performed the other way around. With Biped, you can get away with it because of the unique IK arrangement of the Biped hand. With the animation complete, there's only the matter of that smooth, fluid loop. However, the start time of the swim is more important than was the start time for the idle. Therefore, you need to move the entire motion clip and add keyframes in front and back to get Continuity to work in your favor.

Open Track View, and Add Keys to all tracks at Frames 680 and 702 (Figure 7.77).

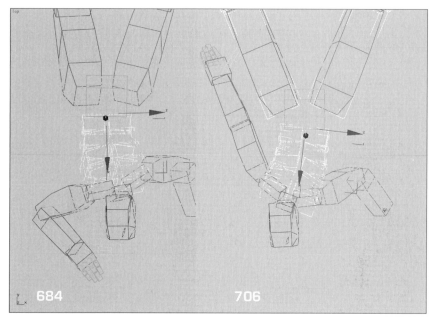

FIGURE 7.76   Complete the stroke with some subtle Spine object rotations.

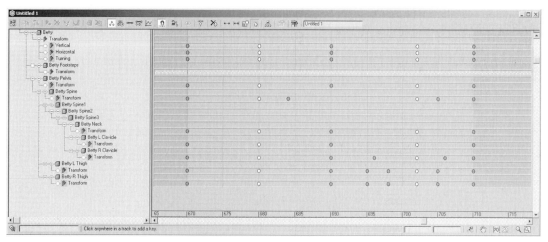

FIGURE 7.77   Add keyframes at Frames 680 and 702 so they can be copied elsewhere.

Next, change your Time Configuration to a Start Time of 670 and an End Time of 720. Go back to Track View, select the keys you added at Frame 680, and copy them to Frame 720. Then click the ⊢⊣ Slide Keys button to make it active, select all keys at Frame 670, and *slide* the entire animation 20 frames to the right. Click the Move Key button active again, select the keys at Frame 712, and copy them over to Frame 670.

Change Time Configuration again, to a Start Time of 680 and an End Time of 720. Play the animation back and see how it looks (Figure 7.78).

FIGURE 7.78 Betty is now on her way to being a certified swimmer.

Of course, Betty has a bunch of other swimming animations. She has to swim backwards, shoot while idling, swim forward and backward, and she has to feel pain and die a couple of times. The point of this chapter, though, has been to cover just *some* of the animations you'll need to create for a real-time game character using solely a keyframe approach. Load Betty12.max from the Chapter7 directory on this book's CD-ROM to see the completed swimming animations. Then get ready for the next chapter, where you'll find out a bit more about mocap.

ON THE CD

SUMMARY

A typical real-time game character can have anywhere from a couple hundred to a couple thousand frames of animation. How small or how great the number of animations will be will depend on the role of the character in the game, as well as the way in which the character will be implemented. Player characters definitely have the biggest share of animation frames in a game because they have to do so much, especially if the game is in the third-person perspective.

Generally, the first motion you want to create in the animation "folder" (the character's 3ds max file) is some sort of idle animation. Whether the character has one or several idles, the motion is mainly about taking an interesting pose and changing it slightly as it loops continuously. After the first pose is set, lock the feet using Set Planted Key, and copy the pose to the end of the animation range. Change the Continuity settings to get rid of any excess animation, or use *key doubling* as a way to quickly get rid of this sort of extra motion. Secondary motion is crucial to the quality of any animation. Always find ways to add extra detail to the animation.

When creating shooting or firing animations, start by establishing the character's pose while he is holding the weapon. Then add a "knockback" effect that simulates the weapon firing. As with the idle animation, concentrate on creating an interesting pose that fits the requirements of the animation set. Don't be afraid to experiment with different ideas. Once the weapon is posed, attach some sort of bone or dummy object to the Biped Forearm; this will act as an aiming mechanism for a programmer so that he can determine the point where a weapon's round will originate.

While using motion capture is a great way to create jump animations, jumps are so specific to the real-time implementation of the character that they're just as easy to keyframe. In the physical world, jumps have four parts: anticipation, launch, hang-time, and landing. In the world of real-time game characters, the jump animations are divided into three distinct parts: jump, idle, and landing. Animate one complete jump sequence, *then* divide it up into these parts to suit the game engine and the character. Some characters may have to shoot while jumping, which requires a different animation—one that relies on the weapon always being pointed at an imaginary target. Use the Snapshot function to create a reference guide by which you can line up the weapon as the character goes through the jump motion.

Finally, while there are many animations required for the player character for which motion capture would be effective, the swimming action calls for particularly *keyframe-intensive* animation, because of the difficulty in getting accurate underwater motions with motion capture. In order to get that languid, fluid motion looping correctly, it's sometimes necessary to duplicate keyframes beyond just the "double-tap" practice, copying whole segments of keyframes before and after the animation range.

CHAPTER

8

USING MOTION CAPTURE

M otion capture, or *mocap*, is the character animator's best friend. It adds realism and detail to any motion and subtracts from the amount of time it takes to create it. Movies, television, advertisements, and even scientific research benefit from the use of motion capture, and 3ds max makes it easy and quick to use.

MOTION CAPTURE FILES

There are three different types of motion capture files you can work with in 3ds max and character studio: BIP, CSM, and BVH. While BIP files are the proprietary Biped motion file, CSM and BVH are raw data ASCII files that are the usual forms of output from the motion capture process. As an animator, you should only really be working with the finished BIP files that have been cleaned by the service that either did the capture or that sells the data to you from a library. Although character studio does have the ability to tweak the mocap data to suit your characters, the companies that specialize in delivering motion capture are better equipped to alter the data. Still, knowing a little bit about CSM and BVH is always helpful, because character studio 3 gives you the ability to convert these file types to the standard BIP file format.

CSM Format

The CSM format is used to import positional marker data from optical motion capture systems onto a Biped. The acronym stands for *Character Studio Motion* Capture file. The CSM format is a little limiting, because to be compatible with character studio, it must use names that match the character studio setup. It also has to have an appropriate number of markers in the specified locations on the actor (although character studio 3 does allow a few extra bone "props" now). The CSM format itself is capable of holding any kind of marker data, but it's assumed it adheres to the name and marker configuration required by character studio.

BVH Format

The BVH file format is also generated from optical motion capture systems. It was originally developed by a motion capture services company called BioVision as a way to provide motion capture data to their customers. The name BVH stands for BioVision Hierarchical data. This format primarily replaced an earlier format that the company developed (the BVA format) as a way to provide skeleton hierarchy information in addition to the motion data. The BVH format is an excellent all-around format, but its drawback is its lack of a full definition of the basis pose. While still seen from time to time, it's no longer a prominent motion capture file format.

Converting CSM and BVH Files

Start or reset 3ds max and create a Biped. The new Biped's COM is automatically selected, so go to the Motion Panel, open the Motion Capture rollout menu, and click on the Load Motion Capture File button (Figure 8.1).

FIGURE 8.1 Click the Load Motion Capture File button to import CSM or BVH files.

ON THE CD

When the Open file menu appears, select BVH from the three available file types in the *Files of type* drop-down menu. Then go to the Chapter8 directory on the CD-ROM that came with this book, and load Walky.bvh by selecting it and hitting the Open button (Figure 8.2).

When the Motion Capture Conversion Parameters menu appears, make sure the Footstep Extraction selection is set to None: Freeform, and that Conversion is set to No Key Reduction. Hit the OK button (Figure 8.3).

After 3ds max processes the conversion, the motion is loaded into the Biped. Immediately, you'll notice the configuration and proportions of the Biped change. This is because of the marker placement during capture and the export to the BVH format (Figure 8.4).

Always use a generic, default Biped to convert any BVH or CSM files, instead of using your actual character. The Marker configuration and Biped configuration at the time of capture and export to the BVH or CSM file format will alter the shape and configuration of the Biped they're loaded into, thus severely distorting or ruining your mesh.

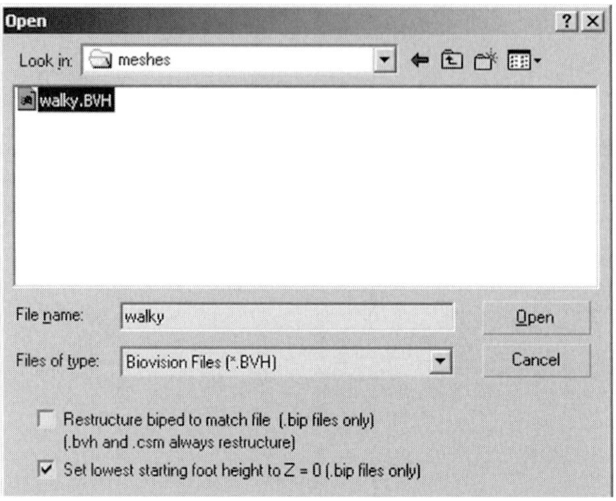

FIGURE 8.2   In order to load a BVH file, that format needs to be selected under the *Files of type* menu.

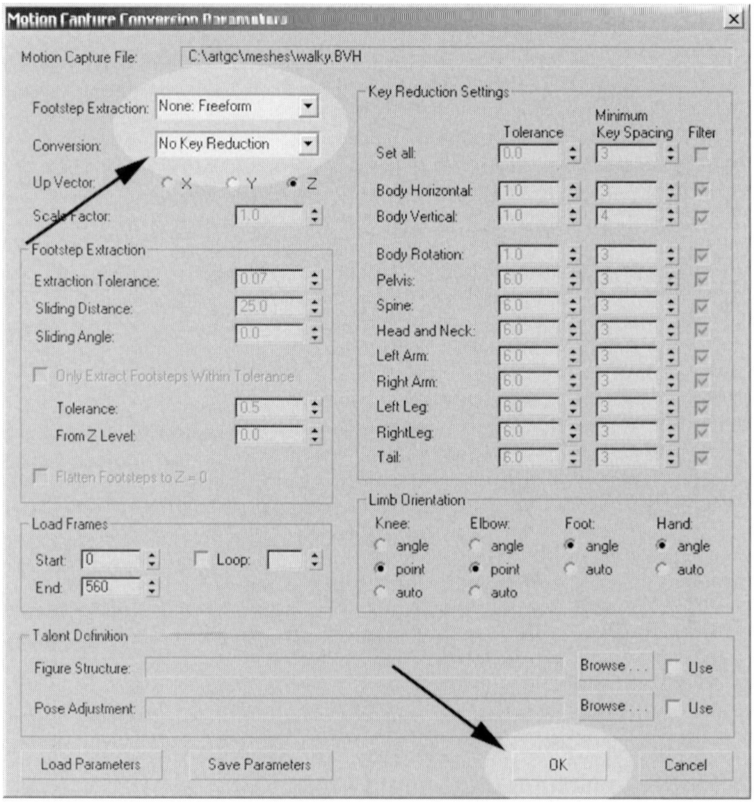

FIGURE 8.3   The Motion Capture Conversion Parameters menu is a great tool for quickly converting BVH and CSM files.

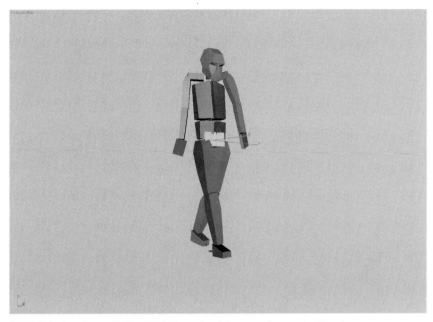

FIGURE 8.4   Loading a BVH or CSM file noticeably re-configures the Biped.

Move your Time Slider to Frame 0 if it isn't already there. Notice that the bottom row of buttons on the Motion Capture rollout menu is now available. This is because whenever a BVH or CSM file is loaded, these buttons allow you to recalibrate marker data. However, you rarely need to access them, and it's best to leave that sort of tweaking to the mocap service that gives you the data.

Using Key Reduction

One of the most useful features in the Motion Capture Conversion Parameters menu is the ability it gives you to reduce the number of keyframes in the motion capture file. Since mocap files typically have a key set for every animation track at every frame, filtering the data to reduce keys makes it easier to edit the data when you want to customize it to fit your character. However, it's usually best to keep at least one version of the mocap file with all the keys intact as a source of reference.

With the Biped still selected, click on the Load Motion Capture File button again, and this time load a CSM file called Shotdrop.csm from the Chapter8 directory found on the CD-ROM that came with this book (Figure 8.5).

FIGURE 8.5 Converting a CSM file is just a matter of choosing that file type and loading it.

Leave the settings as they were before in the Motion Capture Conversion Parameters menu. Once it's been converted and loaded into your Biped, save it as a BIP file by clicking on the Save File button under the General rollout menu (Figure 8.6).

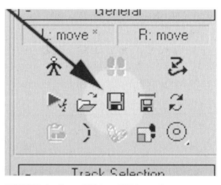

FIGURE 8.6 Save BVH or CSM motion capture files as *un-reduced* BIP files first.

Save the file as Shotdrop.bip, and click on the Load Motion Capture File button once again. This time, choose Biped Files as the file type and load the file you just saved (Figure 8.7).

Notice at the bottom of the Open menu that there are always two checkboxes. Loading a BIP for conversion like this gives you the extra

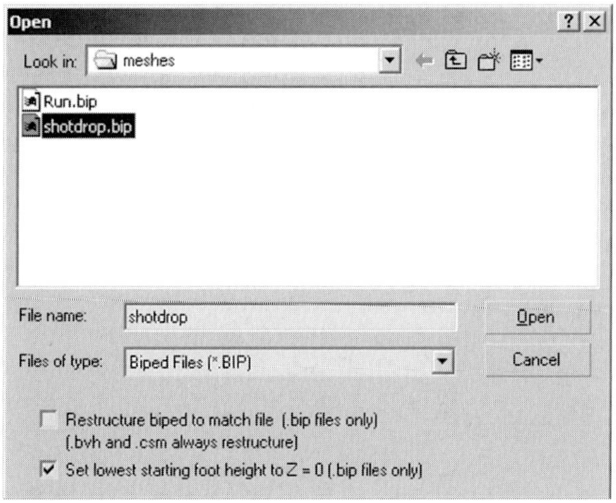

FIGURE 8.7 This time load a BIP file into the Motion Capture Conversion Parameters menu.

ability to choose whether or not you want to re-structure the Biped you're going to load the data into. This is one of the benefits of saving BVH or CSM files as BIP files and then tweaking them afterward. However, by doing so, you do lose access to the marker data at Frame 0.

When the Motion Capture Conversion Parameters menu pops up, select Use Key Reduction from the Conversion drop-down menu (Figure 8.8).

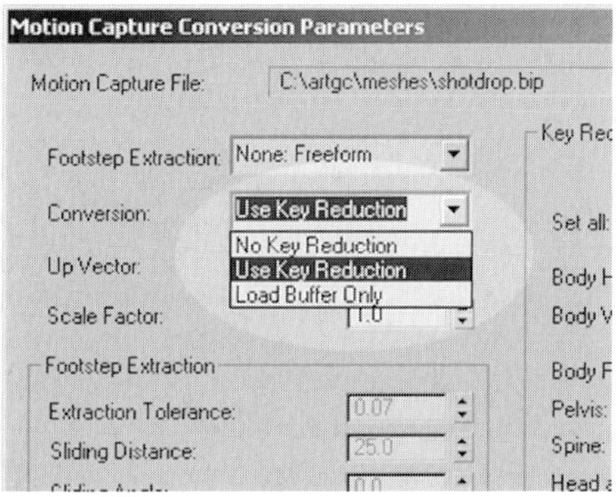

FIGURE 8.8 Choose Use Key Reduction to reduce the number of keys in the mocap data.

Hit the OK button; the same motion has now been optimized with many fewer keyframes. Character studio makes it easy to see the difference of the reduction of keys by storing the original un-reduced data in a motion capture buffer. To compare the effect of the reduction you just did, first go to the Display rollout menu, turn on Bones (the first button), and turn off Objects (the second button) (Figure 8.9).

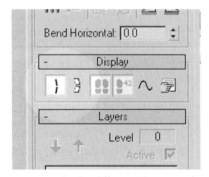

FIGURE 8.9 Make the difference between the reduced and un-reduced keys easier to see by viewing only the Biped's *bones*.

Finally, to see the original motion capture data with all keyframes in place, click the Show Buffer button to make it active (Figure 8.10).

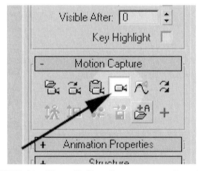

FIGURE 8.10 Show Buffer allows you to view the original motion before the keys were reduced.

Scrub the Time Slider back and forth to see the differences between the purely red stick figure and the regularly colored stick figure. The differences between the two are negligible except for where the motion is most extreme, like when the Biped hits the ground (Figure 8.11).

To try for an even more extreme reduction, you can increase the tolerance under the Key Reduction settings. Instead of re-loading the mocap file using the Load Motion Capture File button, click on the Convert from

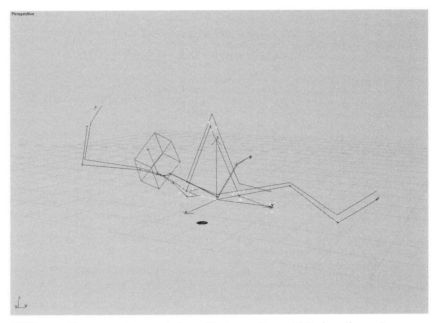

FIGURE 8.11   There are only several places (like here at Frame 164) where the motion differs.

Buffer button to bring the Motion Capture Conversion Parameters menu back (Figure 8.12).

FIGURE 8.12   The Convert from Buffer button is a shortcut to the Motion Capture Conversion Parameters menu.

When the conversion menu comes up, increase the Tolerance value to 10 for all the tracks except for Body Horizontal, Body Vertical, and Body Rotation. Leave their Tolerance value at 1. Change the Minimum

Key Spacing value to 6 for everything except those same three tracks, keeping them at 3, 4, and 3 respectively (Figure 8.13).

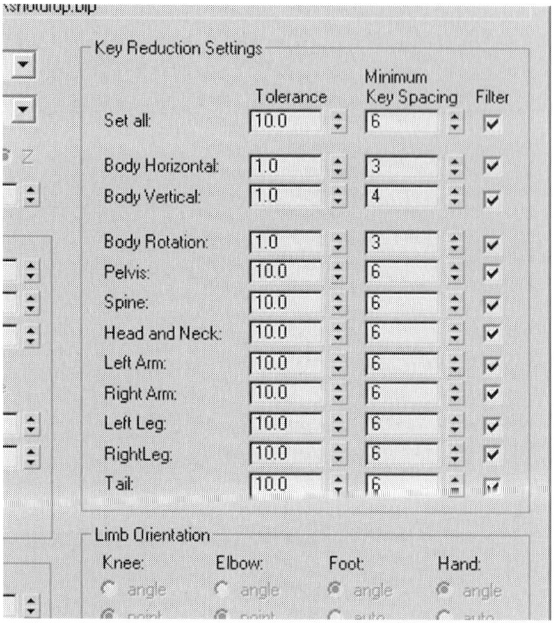

FIGURE 8.13 Increasing Tolerance and Minimum Key Spacing values increases the amount of key reduction.

If most of the tracks have the same settings, use the Set All line at the top of the Key Reduction Settings menu to change all tracks at once for one or both Tolerance and Minimum Key Spacing values. Then go back and adjust individual settings that need to be different.

Hit OK, and you can see the difference that the higher values produce. Tolerance sets the maximum amount of units (or degrees) a positional or rotational track will deviate from the original position. Once character studio calculates the Tolerance setting, it then reduces the keys further using the Minimum Distance between Keys setting. This value basically tries to put a bottom limit on the space between each key, but even after reduction the space can be less than that, based on the results of the Tolerance setting.

Most of the time, you don't have to worry about key reduction. If you have to make adjustments to the motion capture data, layers are a great way to do it. However, one benefit of reducing the keys on an animation is removing any "jitter" that sometimes occurs when a keyframe is set for every frame of every track.

DECIDING WHICH MOCAP FILES TO USE

Of course, you can't always afford to record a new motion capture session every time you have to animate a character. Sometimes you need to make do with what you have or what you can find that's free and clear to use. House of Moves supplies a wide range of CSM files for male and female characters both on spec and via their online Diva™ system. Modern Uprising has BVH files for male and female characters that are available upon request.

When deciding whether or not the mocap file will work for you, consider these two factors: *quality* and *ability to implement*. Quality starts at the time of the shoot; you are relying on the actor, the director, then on the company's finished result after the files have been cleaned and fixed. Having had nothing to do with any of those, the best thing you can do is to just load the data into a Biped and observe it. It's either good enough to suit your purposes or it's not. Ability to implement relies on the duration and *loopability* of the data, since real-time game characters have to run, jump, swim, and shoot in endless repetitive loops. To achieve a loop, there has to be a segment within the motion that has a similar beginning and end pose (or poses close enough that they can be created).

A run animation is one of the best examples for illustrating the difference between good and bad mocap data.

A Bad Run Animation

For real-time game characters, most if not all animations occur "in place." Therefore, the motions you need to use have to be generic enough to support the motions of the character in the game properly. A run animation can't bias towards one direction or another. There can be no "lean" or traces of acceleration or deceleration.

Unless otherwise directed, the frame rate for all animations is the default 3ds max setting of NTSC or 30 fps.

ON THE CD

Go to the General rollout menu for Biped and click on the Load File button. Navigate to the Chapter8 directory on the CD-ROM that came with this book and load Badrun.bip into your Biped (Figure 8.14).

Turn Show Buffer off and switch back to Object display instead of Bones. Go to the Left viewport and scrub your Time Slider to see the animation. The angle of the body during the animation goes from being slanted to the right in the beginning to being slanted to the left toward the end. This indicates acceleration and deceleration in the motion (Figure 8.15).

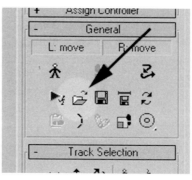

FIGURE 8.14 Load a BIP file into your Biped by clicking on the Load File button and finding the file.

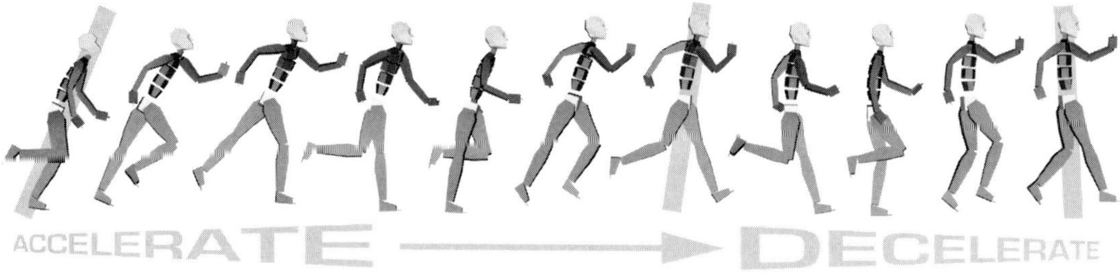

ACCELERATE ——————➤ DECELERATE

FIGURE 8.15 An example of a bad run animation.

Velocity (or the lack of velocity) is crucial. When deciding whether or not you can use a run animation, the first things you should look for are the looping points. Looping points are the two nearest poses in the animation that can be joined based on consistent body angle, foot placement, and arm swing. In the case of the mocap file you loaded, the closest place you could call a start and stop looping point is Frame 0 and Frame 23 (Figure 8.16).

However, as you can tell from Figure 8.16, even though the left foot is planted and the left arm is at about the right attitude, the body angle is completely wrong. This bad loop is the result of the actor not having enough room to get a full run captured. He leans into the motion, takes a few steps, and immediately has to begin slowing to a stop, thus straightening his body. When considering a motion capture service provider, take a good look at their available capture space so problems like this won't occur in the data.

Another reason why this particular mocap file is bad because it's only 29 frames long. Not only should the actor have had more distance to run

FIGURE 8.16   Unfortunately, there is no loopable animation here.

in, he should have run for twice the amount of time! When reviewing data to turn into a run, you need enough of the motion repeated to grab a "loopable" segment from the captured motion. This means the data needs to be long enough for you to be able to chop the front and back pieces off, remove any acceleration or deceleration bias, and still have a successful segment.

A Good Run Animation

ON THE CD

Now go to the Chapter8 directory on the CD-ROM that came with this book, and load Goodrun.bip into your Biped. Scrub the Time Slider back and forth to view the animation. Even without pointing to any specific two frames, it's clear that this data is good enough to contain a solid loop. The body remains at relatively the same angle throughout the motion, indicating a *constant* pace (Figure 8.17).

FIGURE 8.17   This data captured from the *middle* of the motion sample is an example of a good run.

The consistent posture means there's no apparent bias towards acceleration or deceleration. This data is also longer than the previous file, and at 45 frames in length, is enough to get almost two full loops of the run.

CREATING A LOOPING RUN

Once you have decided which motion capture file works best, you need to *clip it* so it loops perfectly. The first step in doing that is to determine the length of the loop you need.

Determining the Loop Length

Select all Biped objects (except for the small circular Footsteps object) and go to Frame 0. Make sure you're in the Left viewport. Zoom in and pan your scene so the Biped is to the left of the view. Then go up to Tools | Snapshot (1) and create copies of the selected Biped objects (2) (Figure 8.18).

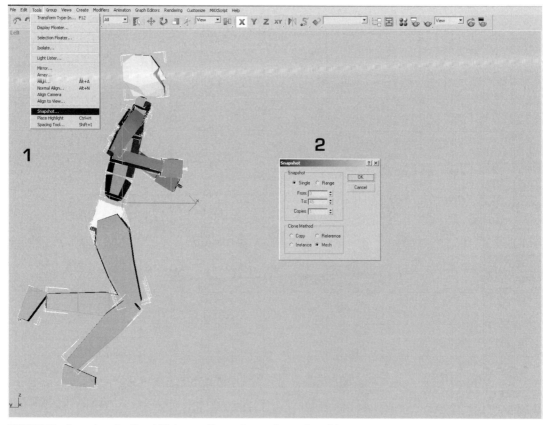

FIGURE 8.18   Snapshot the Biped Objects at Frame 0 to make copies of them.

You made a snapshot of the Biped at Frame 0 because you need some sort of reference pose to determine the length of the loop. Now you need to group those copied objects together to avoid accidentally selecting them. Advance the animation a few frames so the Biped moves away from the snapshot copies. Select those copies, go to the Group pull-down menu (1), and group the selected objects together (2), calling them the default Group01 (you're going to delete the group later) (Figure 8.19).

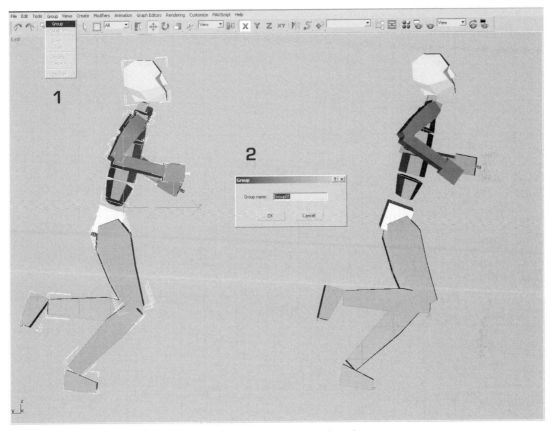

FIGURE 8.19   Group the snapshot copies together to avoid selecting them later.

Now that you have a snapshot of the first frame of the animation and it's been grouped for easy selection, you need to activate In Place mode so you can tell when the loop repeats. Select any part of the original Biped again, and click on the button in the General rollout menu that looks like a bulls-eye so it turns purple (Figure 8.20).

This keeps the Biped "in place" at the center of the world as you work on its motion. It's a great way to view your animations when determining the quality and usability of the mocap data.

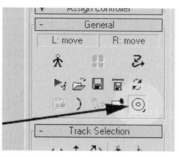

FIGURE 8.20   Put the Biped into In Place mode so it stays in view as you work.

 In Place mode can also be refined to restrict movement to just the X- or Y-axis by choosing one or the other from the fly-out menu (Figure 8.21)

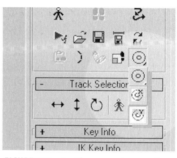

FIGURE 8.21   In Place mode can also be refined to be just the X- or Y-axis.

Next, advance the animation frame by frame, until you come up with the first closest match to the snapshot. The nearest frame at which the snapshot pose is repeated is Frame 26. Since the reference frame is from Frame 0, this means the loop is approximately 27 frames long (Frames 0–26) (Figure 8.22).

Grabbing the Best Loop Segment

Now that you know the duration of the loop, you need to decide *where* in the animation you're going to grab it. While it's always best to try to grab the usable loop from somewhere in the middle of the mocap file, this is only true if the data has a full range of the motion. When using data that you haven't captured or that someone else has altered before you, it's best to just audit the motion using your known loop length as a guide. For example, if Frame 0 to Frame 26 is a complete loop, then it stands to

FIGURE 8.22   The nearest match to the snapshot pose is at Frame 26.

reason that Frame 5 to Frame 31 is a usable loop too. Frame 19 to Frame 45 is the last segment that could be used, as the loop length is consistent throughout the animation.

There are two ways to determine which is the best loop segment: matching up the closest loop start and stop pose, trying different Time Configurations, and playing back the loop candidate. To find the closest matching pose between beginning and end points of the loop, use the Current Frame box down beside your Time Configuration button. Delete the grouped copies of your Biped objects, make sure you're still in the Left viewport, and make sure that the smooth or faceted shading mode is active. Double-click on whatever number or frame is being displayed, type in 36, and hit Enter (Figure 8.23).

Whenever you type a value into the Current Frame box, it remains selected (blue). This makes it convenient to hover your fingers over your keyboard and just type in other frame numbers. To find the best matching loop points, therefore, you can just start typing numbers in that are 26 frames apart and easily compare the poses. With Frame 36 active, type in 10, hit Enter again, and the current frame becomes Frame 10 and the pose changes. See how it works? Now go down through the animation, starting back at 0, and type in sets of numbers that represent potential loop points: 0 and 26, 1 and 27, 2 and 28, and so forth.

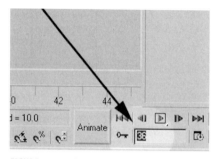

FIGURE 8.23   The Current Frame window displays the current frame, and jumps to a frame when a value is entered.

Using this method it becomes clear that the best matches are Frames 0 and 26 (A), and 11 and 38 (B) (Figure 8.24).

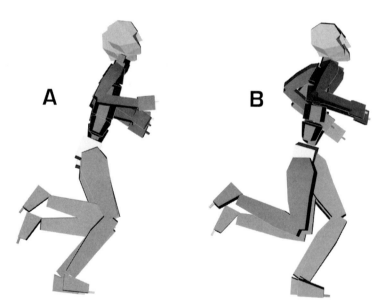

FIGURE 8.24   Frames 0 and 26 or Frames 11 and 38: Both are close matches.

Why Frame 38 and not Frame 37? Well, sometimes the human body doesn't like to conform to a convenient frame count. The actor sometimes doesn't run at a consistent pace, either. While Frame 0 and Frame 26 match up nicely, the actor slowed down a little after Frame 26 as he was running. Even a fractional decrease in speed will add a frame to the loop. Thus, the first two possible loop points are 26 frames apart and the second two are 27 frames apart.

To test the usability of these two sets of loop points, you're going to use Save Segment to isolate the two loop segments. This will make it easier to see which loop is best. Click on the Save Segment button in the General rollout menu of Biped (Figure 8.25).

FIGURE 8.25 Use Save Segment to isolate the potential loops in order to better test them.

Make sure the Start Frame of the segment is 0 and the End Frame is 26; save the segment as Looptest1.bip (Fig. 8.26).

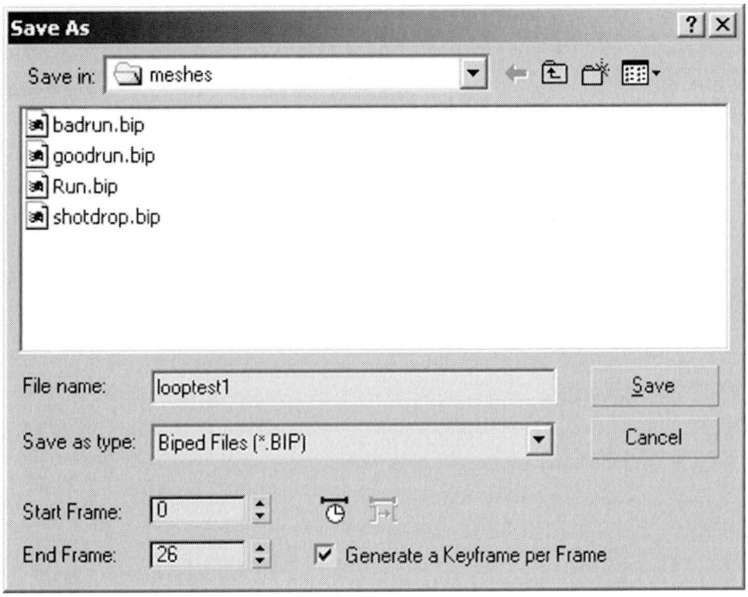

FIGURE 8.26 Save Segment allows you to specify just the part of the animation that you want.

In the Save As dialog menu, notice the option to save a key for every track of every frame of the animation. This is a nice shortcut to adding keys to a longer animation, when necessary.

Now, do the same for the second potential loop: The Start Frame is 11 and the End Frame is 38. Save the second segment as Looptest2.bip. Once you've done that, load Looptest1.bip into your Biped, turn on In Place mode, and study the animation further.

Comparing the Loop Segments

You next need to decide which loop deserves to be chosen and worked on further to become a smooth, *better* animation. Do this by making a few modifications to each loop and comparing their potential. Change your Time Configuration to a Start Time of 0 and an End Time of 25 (note that you don't want to include the last frame, because it is a close match to the first frame). Then, open Track View and change your Filter settings to show only animated tracks. Hit Alt-Ctrl-H to *hold* your scene (just in case), then select and delete all keys at Frames 25 and 26. Next, copy the keys at Frame 0 to Frame 26 (Figure 8.27).

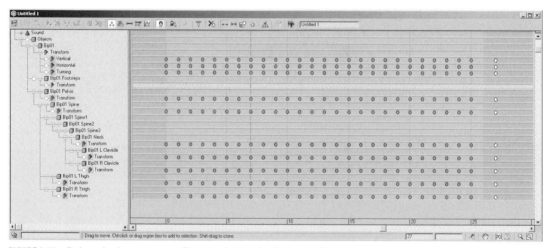

FIGURE 8.27   Delete the last two sets of keys and copy the first set to Frame 26.

Play the animation back to check how it looks. Theoretically, copying the first frame keys to one frame past the end of the loop should produce a smooth loop. However, stepping through the animation, you can see there's definitely a hitch at the end, when transitioning from the last frame of the loop to the first. It seems like the character drops down slightly at the end of the loop, in a limping motion. This indicates that there might not be a sufficient number of frames for the left foot's plant-and-stride motion, which is described in Frames 25, 26, and 1–10. In comparison, the right foot goes through the same range of motions from Frame 11 through 24—that's 13 frames for the left foot to travel versus 14 frames for the right foot to travel. The difference between the duration of motion may be what's causing the hitch. As an experiment (and based on the longer length of the second loop), try making the loop one frame longer.

Hit Alt-Ctrl-F to *fetch* your scene, or simply load Looptest1.bip back into your Biped. Bring up your Track View again, select all keys, and move them one frame forward. Then delete the keys at Frame 1 and Frame 26. Copy the out-of-range keys at Frame 27 to Frame 0 (Figure 8.28).

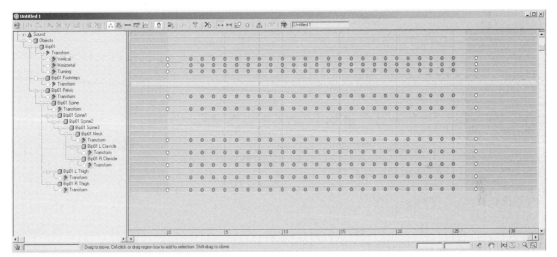

FIGURE 8.28   Try a different approach to making the first segment loop.

Play the animation back and see how it looks. It still has a noticeable hitch at the loop point because of the posture of the torso as it starts to straighten slightly at the end of the segment. It isn't perfect, but it is an improvement over the first loop attempt, and it looks better with the additional frame. Next, try the second segment and see if you can make a better loop out of it. Save the tweaked Looptest1.bip as Looptest1a.bip and load Looptest2.bip into your Biped.

Turn on In Place mode again, change your Time Configuration to a Start Time of 0 and an End Time of 26, and open Track View. Delete the keys at Frame 26 and copy the keys at Frame 0 to Frame 27 (Figure 8.29).

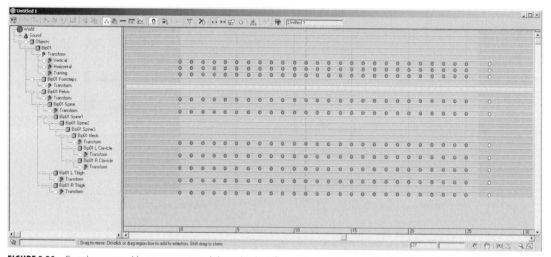

FIGURE 8.29   For the second loop segment, delete the last frame keys and copy the first frame keys to Frame 27.

There's a hitch, but generally, the animation will be easier to work with because the initial work needed to get a decent loop is less than that of the first segment. Save it as Looptest2a.bip and you're ready to refine the loop further.

Doubling the loop

Once you've identified a good segment and roughly adjusted it so it loops, there's one more thing you can do to improve it using the Motion Capture Conversion Parameters menu. Click on the Load Motion Capture File button and load the Biped file you just saved (it will already be entered and highlighted in the field called *File name*). Check the small box beside Loop under Load Frames and enter a value of 1 beside it (Figure 8.30).

Now you've taken the loop you created and tweaked earlier and you've doubled it. The advantages of doing this are that it gives you more frames to work with and it gives you the ability to change the start and end point of the loop to suit the needs of your character. For example, you may want the animation to start on the right foot instead of the left as it does now. Or you may want the animation to start mid-stride. Doubling the loop gives you the option to make those sorts of changes. There's only one minor adjustment you need to make to the new double-loop.

Because the start and end frame of the original loop were the same, there are double keys in the middle of the animation. Open Track View,

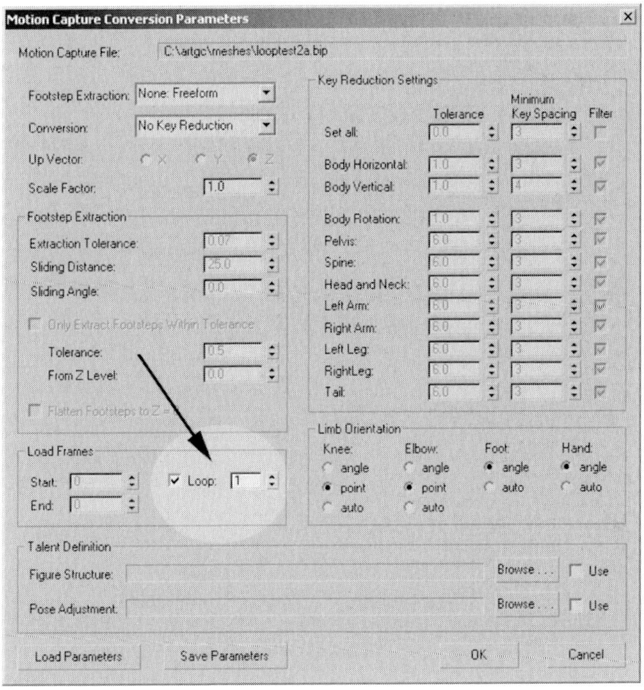

FIGURE 8.30   The Loop option in the Motion Capture Conversion Parameters menu is a handy tool.

select all the keys at Frame 27 (or 28), and delete them. Then select the keys to the right of the deleted column and slide them one frame to the left. Change your Time Configuration to 0 and 54, and play the animation. Even with the keys at Frame 0 and Frame 54 the same, the animations play smoothly (Figure 8.31).

Refining the Loop with Layers

To make the loop run even more smoothly, there are a few more refinements you can make to the animation. First, change the first frame of the loop so that it's more of a *launch* into the run. That way, when the character is stopped and *then* goes into the run, the motion won't be so dependent upon one or the other foot being forward. Do this by making the Start Time 5 and End Time 31 for the Time Configuration settings.

Next, identify the first area that needs adjustment by looking at the *trajectory* of the COM. Click on the In Place mode button to turn it off, and select the Bip01 object. Right-click on it, click on Properties (1), and check the Trajectory box (2) (Figure 8.32).

FIGURE 8.31 Finally, a nicely looping run with only minor areas to fix.

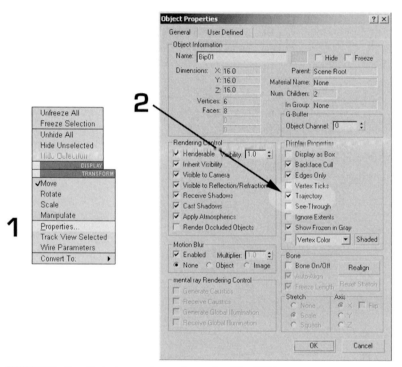

FIGURE 8.32 Turn Trajectory on to see the path of the COM.

Now a red, dotted curve appears that corresponds to the position of the COM as it goes through the animation. Even though the line cuts back to the beginning at Frame 26, you can still see the peaks and valleys of the curve. The difference in their heights relative to one another is a source of one of the problems with the animation (Figure 8.33).

The curve represents the natural up and down motion of the character's COM as he goes through the motion of the run. When you play the animation with In Place mode on, you can sense that towards the end of the motion the character springs a little higher off his right foot than his

FIGURE 8.33   With the Trajectory displayed, the source of one of the problems with the loop is revealed.

left foot. The proof of this is in the height of the second peak of the trajectory compared to the first. Also, the first valley of the trajectory at Frame 0 is lower than the second valley at Frame 13. In order for the animation to be smooth and unobtrusive, the two valleys should be the same height and the two peaks should be the same height.

 You can also see the path of any selected Biped object by turning on the Trajectory button in the Display rollout menu (Figure 8.34).

The easiest way to correct the problem of varying trajectory heights is to use a Layer. With the COM still selected, click on the Create Layer button to add another layer of animation (Figure 8.35).

Before you move the Biped, click the Select and Move icon at the top of your view to make it active. Then hit the Set Key button at Frame 5 and Frame 27 to keep those positions the same.

 Although it's a good habit to have the Animate button on when animating, Set Key works independent of whether the Animate button is on or not.

Next, go to Frame 8 and raise the COM along the Z-axis until it's right on the nearby grid line (A). Advance to Frame 14 and lower the

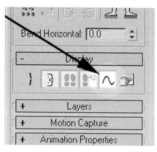

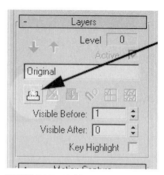

FIGURE 8.34 The Trajectory button shows the trajectory or path of any selected Biped object.

FIGURE 8.35 Adding a Layer is the best way to make major adjustments to the animation.

COM until it's on the grid line below the one you just used for Frame 8 (B). Finally, go to Frame 21 and lower the COM until it's on the grid line used for Frame 14 (C) (Figure 8.36).

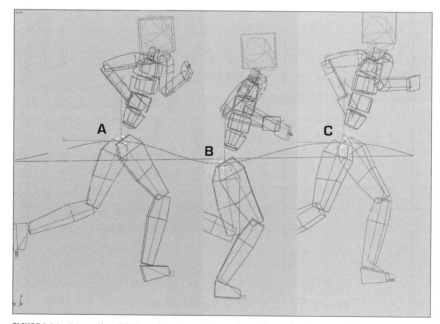

FIGURE 8.36 Move the COM so that the trajectory's peaks and valleys are the same.

Now adjust the feet of the Biped so that they stay firmly on the ground plane. Add another Layer to the animation by clicking on the Create Layer button again.

Adding layers on top of each other when making corrections to an animation is much the same as adding modifiers to the modifier stack. It isn't mandatory, but in case you have to go back and delete or alter one of the changes you've made, it gives you the ability to delete layers if necessary. This gives you an extra level of protection.

Select the right foot and hit the Set Key button for Frame 11 and Frame 18. Then, at Frame 13, rotate it and move it along the Z-axis so that it is perfectly flat on the ground plane. Do the same at Frame 15 (Figure 8.37).

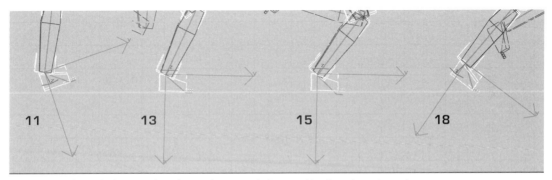

FIGURE 8.37   The right foot needs to be on the ground plane and be flat when planted.

Select the left foot next, and give it the same treatment. Add a Layer, look for where you need to apply Set Key to keep the desired part of the animation, and adjust the rotation and placement. In this case, the only adjustments are minor. Click on Set Key for Frames 24 and 27, and then rotate and move the foot flat at Frames 25 and 26.

The last Layer you need to add resolves an issue with the torso straightening slightly near the end of the animation. Create another Layer, select the first Spine object, and hit Set Keys for Frames 21 and 29. Then go to Frame 25 and rotate the Biped Spine –5 degrees along the Z-axis (Figure 8.38).

Collapse the stack of layers and move to the Front viewport to fix one last problem (Figure 8.39).

In the Front viewport, step through the animation while watching the left foot. From Frame 24 to 26, it needs to be moved and slightly rotated so that its inner edge is along the main grid line at 0, 0, 0. There's no need to use a Layer—just start at Frame 24 and move and rotate the foot accordingly.

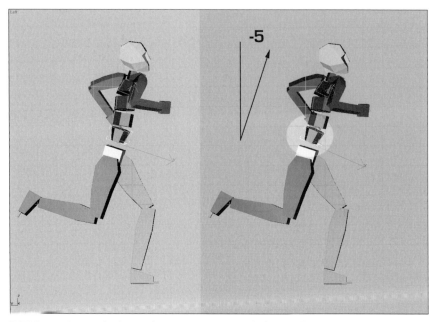

FIGURE 8.38   Rotate the Spine object to overcome a slight straightening at the end of the loop.

FIGURE 8.39   The Collapse Stack button compresses all the animation layers.

When you rotate a Biped object with the Animate button active, you can only do so using the Local axis coordinate system. When you go to move the Biped object after rotating it, the coordinate system will also go to the Local coordinate system. If it does, just change back to the View Coordinate system (Figure 8.40).

Now you can see how your fine-tuning has affected the animation. While it's a great way to view your animations by keeping the Biped in

FIGURE 8.40   Rotation transforms are restricted to the Local coordinate system..

view, *just* using the default In Place mode doesn't give you an accurate playback for the animation if you're viewing it anywhere but from a side view. If you want to more accurately see the animation, put the Biped back in In Place mode, but this time choose In Place Y mode *(Figure* 8.41).

FIGURE 8.41   Hold down the fly-out menu and click on the In Place Y mode.

Now the character will move slightly from side-to-side as it goes through the run animation—an important secondary motion to any run or walk. Change your Time Configuration to an End Time of 32 to get a smooth playback of the animation (Figure 8.42).

The last step to adjusting the animation is to manually move the Biped to the origin point. While In Place mode is a great tool to use during the review and tweaking stage, it's helpful to manually center the Biped as a finishing move on your animations for looping motions like a run or walk. Do this by selecting the COM, turning In Place Y mode off, and going frame by frame to move the Biped back to 0 along the Y-axis using the View coordinate system. Of course, the best way to move it is to

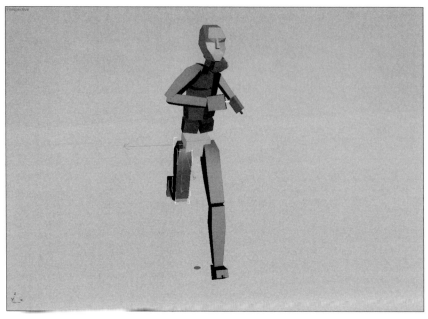

FIGURE 8.42 With the adjustments complete, there's only one more step to finishing the animation.

bring up your Move Transform Type-In menu and enter 0 for the Absolute: World value (Figure 8.43).

FIGURE 8.43 The Transform Type-In menu is always useful.

 While it's true that bringing up Track View and deleting all the Horizontal keys for Bip01 will keep the COM at 0, it deletes both X- and Y-axis translation. Since side-to-side movement in the X-axis is crucial during animations like runs and walks to simulate balance and weight transferal, manually moving the animation to 0 in the Y-axis is a preferable solution.

Once you get the Biped moved to 0 for all the frames of the loop, save the animation using Save Segment. Click on the Active Time Segment button to the right of Start Frame to automatically set the segment to the current animation range. Save the new Biped file as Myrun.bip (Figure 8.44).

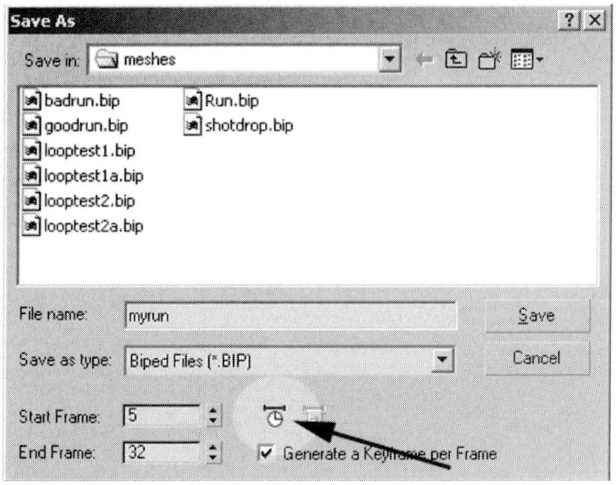

FIGURE 8.44   The Active Time Segment button sets the Start and End frame to match Time Configuration.

As an experiment, try loading Myrun.bip into the Motion Capture Conversion Parameters menu. Don't use Footstep Extraction, and do use Key Reduction. Uncheck the Loop checkbox, because you don't need it, and also uncheck the Body Horizontal, Body Vertical, Body Rotation, Left Leg, and Right Leg tracks under Key Reduction Settings (Figure 8.45).

Play around with the Tolerance and Minimum Key Spacing values, and include the Legs and Body in the reduction pass to see if you can smooth the animation even further.

CREATING A DEATH ANIMATION

Shotdrop.csm is an animation of a character looking down the barrel of a gun to see why it's jammed. The idea was for a sort of blooper series of animations for a game project. The idea was never implemented but the data was still captured. If the first chunk of the data is removed, and the overall orientation changed, shotdrop.csm has strong potential for being a great death animation.

Using the Motion Flow Editor to Rotate the Biped

Create a new Biped or keep the one you've been using for the run animation. Load the Shotdrop.bip file you saved earlier after converting it

Motion Capture Conversion Parameters   ✕

Motion Capture File: C:\artgc\meshes\myrun.bip

Footstep Extraction: None: Freeform ▼

Conversion: Use Key Reduction ▼

Up Vector: ○ X   ○ Y   ◉ Z

Scale Factor: 1.0   ↕

Footstep Extraction

Extraction Tolerance: 0.07   ↕

Sliding Distance: 25.0   ↕

Sliding Angle: 0.0   ↕

☑ Only Extract Footsteps Within Tolerance

   Tolerance: 0.5   ↕

   From Z Level: 0.0   ↕

☐ Flatten Footsteps to Z = 0

Key Reduction Settings

		Tolerance	Minimum Key Spacing	Filter
Set all:		0.0 ↕	3 ↕	☐
Body Horizontal:		1.0 ↕	1 ↕	☐
Body Vertical:		1.0 ↕	1 ↕	☐
Body Rotation:		1.0 ↕	3 ↕	☐
Pelvis:		6.0 ↕	3 ↕	☑
Spine:		6.0 ↕	3 ↕	☑
Head and Neck:		6.0 ↕	3 ↕	☑
Left Arm:		6.0 ↕	3 ↕	☑
Right Arm:		6.0 ↕	3 ↕	☑
Left Leg:		6.0 ↕	3 ↕	☐
RightLeg:		6.0 ↕	3 ↕	☐
Tail:		6.0 ↕	3 ↕	☑

Limb Orientation

Knee:	Elbow:	Foot:	Hand:
○ angle	○ angle	◉ angle	◉ angle
◉ point	◉ point	○ auto	○ auto
○ auto	○ auto		

Load Frames

Start: 0   ↕   ☐ Loop: 1 ↕

End: 0   ↕

Talent Definition

Figure Structure: Browse ... ☐ Use

Pose Adjustment: Browse ... ☐ Use

[Load Parameters]   [Save Parameters]   [OK]   [Cancel]

FIGURE 8.45   Use the Motion Capture Conversion Parameters menu to optimize the upper body during the animation.

ON THE CD

from a CSM file. If for some reason you don't have it, load the original Shotdrop.csm file from the Chapter8 directory on the CD-ROM that came with this book into the Motion Capture Conversion Parameters menu and convert it. After you've loaded the file, go to the Front viewport (Figure 8.46).

There's no rule that says motion capture has to be done in any particular front, back, or side orientation. It can be at an angle, left, right, or facing the opposite direction. This particular data was captured facing the wrong way. One way you can turn him around is to apply a Layer and rotate the COM so that the character faces forward. However, using *Motion Flow mode* offers a better way.

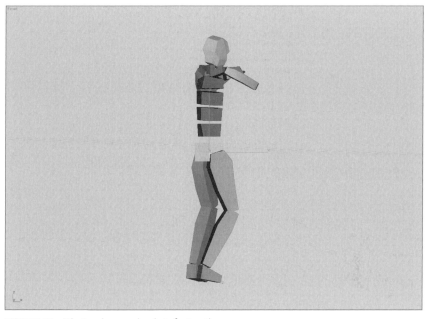

FIGURE 8.46 Obviously somebody is facing the wrong way.

With the Biped selected, go to the General rollout menu for Biped and click on the Motion Flow mode button (the one with the curvy, Z-shaped icon) found to the right of the Footsteps button (Figure 8.47).

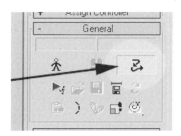

FIGURE 8.47 Using the Motion Flow Editor is a quick way to reorient motion capture data.

Nothing really happens when you click on the Motion Flow Editor button—you have to first input mocap files into the editor using Motion Flow Graph and Motion Flow Script. Think of the Motion Flow Editor as a separate program within character studio. It gives you the ability to combine and alter BIP files to create longer (or just different) animations. To use the Motion Flow Editor, you first have to click on the Show Graph button in the Motion Flow rollout menu (Figure 8.48).

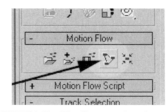

FIGURE 8.48 The first step in using the Motion Flow Editor is clicking the Show Graph button.

This brings up the Motion Flow Graph window. Click the ⬜ Create Clip button active and then click once anywhere in the background space of the window with the funny-looking arrow cursor (Figure 8.49).

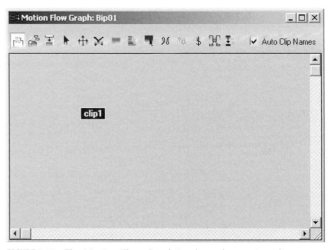

FIGURE 8.49 The Motion Flow Graph is where the motion clips are created.

After you've placed clip1 in the window of the Motion Flow Graph, open the Motion Flow Script rollout menu, and click on the Define Script button (Figure 8.50).

After you click on the Define Script button, character studio waits for you to tell it which clips to enter into the list of clips that are defined by the Motion Flow Script. Click once on the clip1 script you created in the Motion Flow Graph. It turns red to show it's been added to the Motion Flow Script and the script itself now has an entry (Figure 8.51).

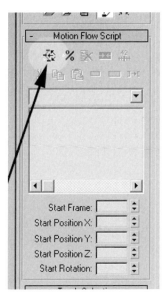

FIGURE 8.50   The Define Script button allows you to establish a connection between motion clips.

FIGURE 8.51   Clicking on clip1 in the Motion Flow Graph enters it into the Motion Flow Script.

Now right-click twice on the red clip1; this will bring up the clip1 dialog so you can load a biped file into it. Notice that the Define Script button goes off. This happens because you've effectively told character studio you're through defining the script (Figure 8.52).

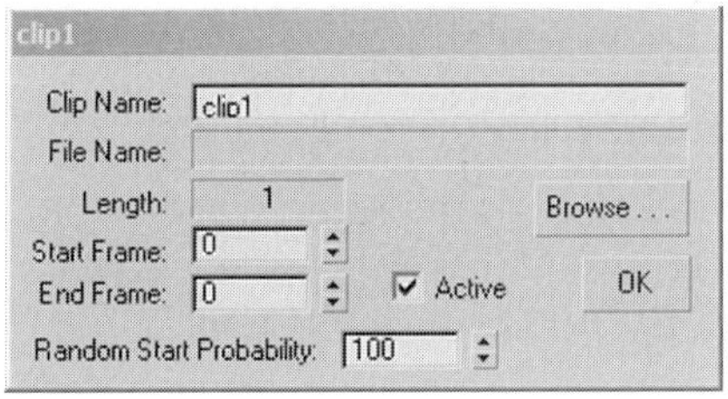

FIGURE 8.52   Right-click on the motion clip icon to load a BIP file into it.

ON THE CD

Click on the Browse . . . button and choose Shotdrop.csm from the Chapter8 directory on this book's CD-ROM. Click OK and close the Motion Flow Graph.

Loading a file into the Motion Flow Editor has no effect whatsoever on the current animation loaded into your Biped. If you turn Motion Flow Editor off, it keeps all

settings and files loaded until you return, even if you save your 3ds max scene and exit the program. The next time you load that file, you'll find that the data in Motion Flow are still there.

Now let's do what you came here to do: rotate the orientation of the data to face forward. Go over to the Motion Flow Script rollout menu and enter 200 in the Start Rotation field (Figure 8.53).

FIGURE 8.53 Entering 200 in the Start Rotation field rotates the character 200 degrees along the Z-axis.

This rotates the orientation along one axis—the Z-axis. The character is now facing front. Scrub the Time Slider to make sure the re-orientation is correct, and then save the altered BIP file by clicking on Save Segment. Click on the Active Time Segment button to change the Start and End frame. Then, since you're only interested in the part of the animation where the character falls down, enter a value of 110 for Start Frame. Call the new animation Deathanim.bip (Figure 8.54).

Quit out of Motion Flow mode by clicking on the Motion Flow mode button again, and load the newly rotated Shotdrop.bip into your Bipcd by clicking on the Load File button in the General rollout menu (Figure 8.55).

There are many more reasons to use the Motion Flow Editor and there is much more functionality to it than illustrated here. It will be covered more fully in the next chapter when you learn how to combine a series of animations to create an animation set. For now, it's enough to know how to use Motion Flow Editor to do a simple rotation re-orientation.

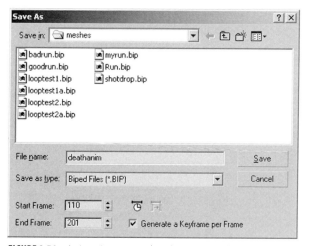

FIGURE 8.54   Animation created in the Motion Flow Editor can only be saved as individual BIP files using Save Segment.

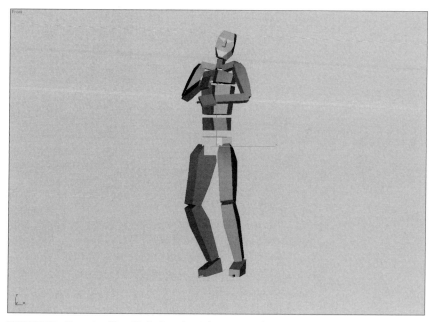

FIGURE 8.55   Now the Biped is facing the right way, ready to die correctly.

Adding Secondary Motion with Layers

When you loaded Deathanim.bip into your Biped, the file reflected the segment that was saved in the Motion Flow Editor. Open Track View and slide all the keyframes over so the animation begins at Frame 0 (Figure 8.56).

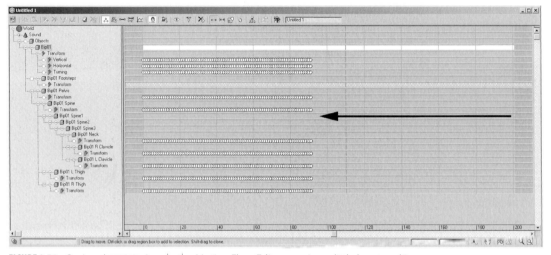

FIGURE 8.56 Saving the animation in the Motion Flow Editor requires a little key-tweaking.

Change your Time Configuration to end at Frame 100, and add a Layer using the Create Layer button in the Layers rollout menu. Turn on the Animate button, select all the Biped Spine objects, and apply Set Key for them at Frames 0, 10, and 54. Since this is a death animation, you need to exaggerate the impact of whatever has inflicted the killing blow. Go to Frame 5 and rotate the selected Spine objects 8 degrees along the Z-axis. This will make the jerking motion of being hit more noticeable (Figure 8.57).

Setting the keyframes at 0 and 10 ensures the animation is still the same at those frames while changing just from Frame 1 to Frame 9. If you scrub back and forth through the animation at the point where the Biped hits the ground, you'll notice the actor's left hand reaches down to break his fall. This sort of performance glitch is why it's important to find great talent when capturing the data. During the mocap session, the director should have noticed the character reaching back and corrected the performance. Still, it's an easy problem to fix. Go to Frame 50 and rotate the Spine objects about –10 degrees along the X-axis, *away* from the fall (Figure 8.58).

Now, select the Head object and apply Set Keys at Frames 0, 10, 30, and 50. Then go to Frame 5, and rotate the Head 50 degrees along the Z-axis so that it rolls forward with the impact of being hit. Then go to Frame 20, and rotate the head forward 40 degrees to make it seem like the

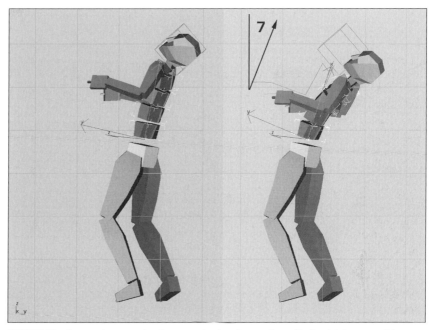

FIGURE 8.57   Rotate the torso back to emphasize the motion of being hit by something.

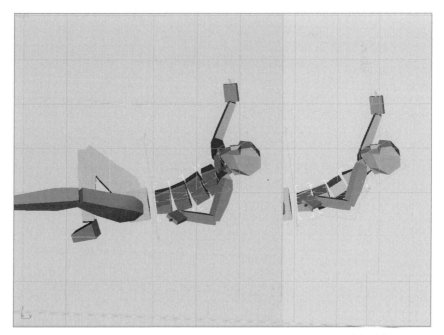

FIGURE 8.58   Twist the Spine objects to begin lessening the anticipation of the fall.

character is facing his attacker with some sort of disbelieving look. Rotate the head about 35 degrees at Frame 45 to give a lull to the head as the character falls back, making the impact with the ground a few frames later even more pronounced (Figure 8.59).

FIGURE 8.59   Extra head motion emphasizes the impact of being hit and hitting the ground.

With the torso and head adjusted, you now need to correct the left arm movement so it doesn't reach back to break the fall. Select Bip01 L UpperArm, and apply Set Keys at Frames 0 and 55. Go next to Frame 45 and rotate the left arm –120 degrees along the Z-axis, and then go to Frame 50 and rotate it –35 degrees along the Z-axis as well (Figure 8.60).

Finally, fix the right leg so it doesn't stay planted during the end of the fall. Otherwise, it makes the fall seem staged. Select Bip01 R Calf, and Set Keys for it at Frames 35 and 65. Go to Frame 50 and rotate the calf and foot until they're pointing out and up, as if the leg had given out sooner during the fall backward (Figure 8.61).

Those minor adjustments make the fall seem more exaggerated and forceful. They remove the deficiencies of the performance and make the fall seem more realistic. Now you need to adjust the velocity of the fall near the ground plane to make the fall seem even more dynamic. Play the animation back to see how it looks. Compare the changes you've made to the original animation by clicking on the Previous Layer button and viewing the unedited version (Figure 8.62).

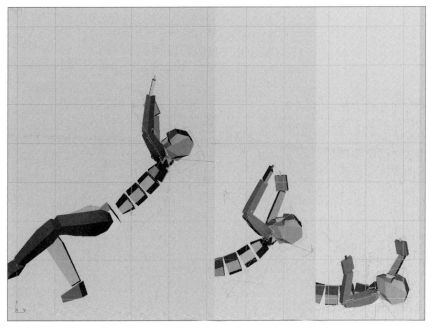

FIGURE 8.60   Rotate the arm to make the fall seem less anticipated.

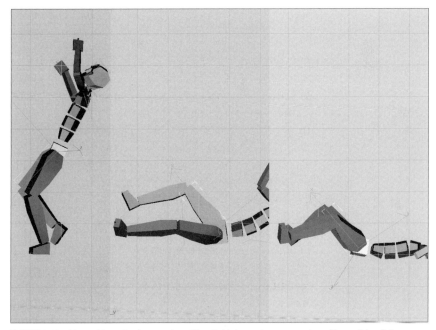

FIGURE 8.61   Untucking the leg and making it kick out improves the effect of the fall.

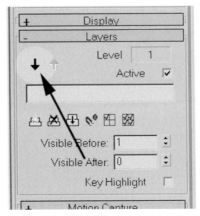

FIGURE 8.62 View the difference the Layer makes by clicking on the Previous Layer button.

Click the Next Layer button (the arrow pointing upward) to return to the animation layer, and collapse it. Save the BIP file as Deathanim2.bip, and move on to the last step in making the mocap into an effective death animation.

Deleting Frames to Increase Impact Effect

So far, the changes you've made to the animation have made it seem less staged and more dramatic. Another trick to give the animation more impact is to delete specific frames, with the purpose of accelerating movements so they seem more abrupt. This technique is particularly effective with motion capture files since there is typically a key set for every frame of every animation track.

Start with the initial impact of the hit the character takes. Open Track View and delete Frames 1, 2, and 4. Then close the gap created by the deleted keyframes by selecting and moving them to the left (Figure 8.63).

Play the animation back to see the effects of removing the keys. Next, you need to give the same treatment to the point at which the character hits the ground. Go to the Track View again, and select and delete the column of keys at Frames 40, 44, 47, 49, and 50 (Figure 8.64).

Before closing the gaps left by these deleted keys, study the spacing between the selected columns. By deleting keys, you've effectively increased the acceleration of the body falling as it hits the ground. Two frames are removed at the point of impact, one frame is removed *two* frames before that, one frame is removed *three* frames before that and finally, one from is removed *four* frames before that. Deleting Frames 49 and 50 adds the perfect "jarring" effect to the motion. The other keys

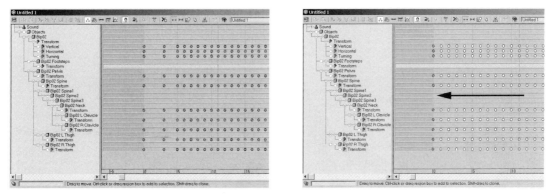

FIGURE 8.63   Deleting the keys and closing the gaps makes the initial impact more abrupt.

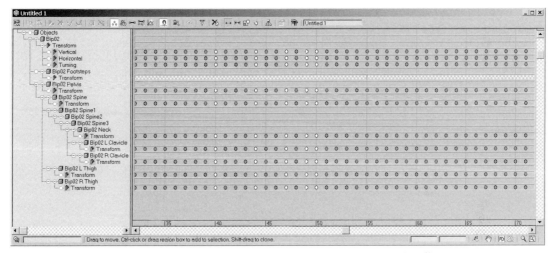

FIGURE 8.64   Select and delete the keys near the impact with the ground to increase the effect.

deleted prior to 49 are to simply incrementally increase the speed of the fall towards the end of the motion.

Close the gaps left by the deletions and play the animation back to see the results (Figure 8.65).

Hopefully this exercise has given you ideas for giving more punch not only to your death animations but also to your jump landings, hits, and any other animations requiring some sort of *impact*.

REPURPOSING A MOCAP FILE

Motion capture data often come in handy for reasons other than those for which they were intended. Combined with keyframe animation, even

FIGURE 8.65   You can almost hear the jarring impact of the character hitting the floor.

the most unlikely data can be turned into something useful and interesting. To illustrate this re-purposing of mocap data, you're going to be giving Betty a special firing animation for her most powerful weapon mode, the railgun. To emphasize to the viewer just how much of a wallop this gun mode packs, Betty needs to exhibit a huge knock-back and recovery when she fires the gun. To get this sort of motion, you're going to use an animation of a character being hit, along with some manual keyframing.

ON THE CD

Start by loading Betty13.max from the Chapter8 directory on the CD-ROM that came with this book (Figure 8.66).

Copying Posture

The pose that Betty's in is created to support a game design element for the weapon type she's firing. Whenever she uses the railgun, she has to wait a few seconds while the weapon charges. Once it's at full power, she fires and goes through the animation you're about to create. So how are you going to transfer the getting-hit animation into the current Betty Biped without losing the current pose? Easy. The fact that it's just a pose makes your job easy. Select the COM (Betty) Biped object, make the ⊕ Select and Move button the active transform button, and right-click on it to bring up the Move Transform Type-in menu (Figure 8.67).

Now make the ↻ Select and Rotate button active, and select *all* Biped objects. Then, go to the Keyframing rollout menu and click on

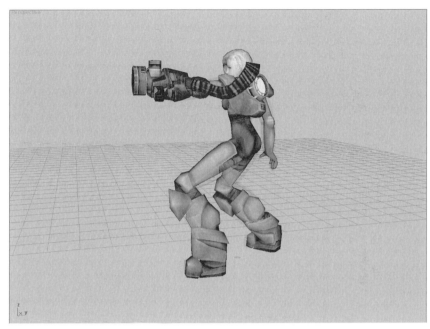

FIGURE 8.66   Betty is back and ready to . . .*shoot* something.

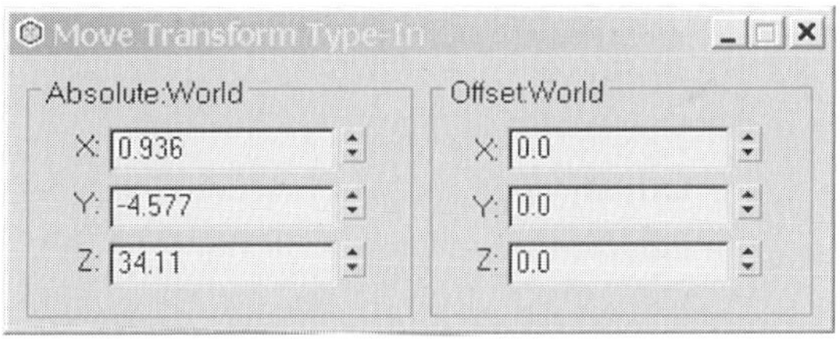

FIGURE 8.67   Keep these numbers handy—you'll need them soon.

the Copy Posture button to temporarily store Betty's current pose in the pose buffer.

When copying postures into the pose buffer, the type of data recorded depends on which transform button is current, and also on which axis of movement is current. When you are copying whole Biped poses and you have to decide between the Body Horizontal, Body Vertical, and Body Rotate animation tracks for the COM, choose Body Rotate. Also, choose Body Rotate before selecting all Biped objects. Otherwise, selecting a track manually will cause all objects to be unselected (Figure 8.68).

FIGURE 8.68   If there has to be just one track for the COM, choose Body Rotate.

Loading the Getting-Hit Animation

ON THE CD

Click on the Load File button in the General rollout menu, go to the Chapter8 directory on the CD-ROM that came with this book, and load Whacked.bip into Betty's Biped. Then, to remove the excess keyframes you won't need for the animation, you need to open Track View, then select and delete all keys from Frame 0 to Frame 69 and from Frame 120 to 135 (Figure 8.69).

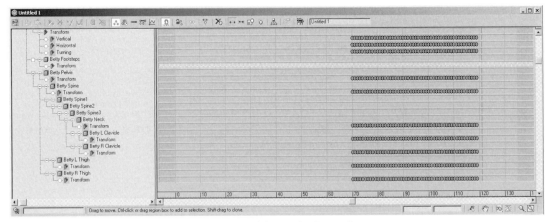

FIGURE 8.69   Trim the getting-hit animation down by deleting the first 69 frames.

Deleting large numbers of keyframes in Track View can sometimes create a huge drain on your computer's processor and bring 3ds max to a crawl. An alternative to deleting keyframes is to save the portion of the animation you want to keep by using Save Segment.

Paste Pose/Posture/Track

Go to Frame 0, turn the Animate button on, make sure all the Biped objects are still selected, and hit the Paste Posture/Pose/Track button. The pose you stored before will now put Betty back into her pre-shoot stance (Figure 8.70).

FIGURE 8.70   Betty resumes her gun-ready stance after you paste in the stored pose.

Select just the COM (Betty). Pasting the stored posture back into Betty unfortunately doesn't move her back to where she was when you copied the pose. Only the rotation animation track for her COM was copied over, so you're going to have to manually move her back into position.

Moving the COM

Bring up the Move Type-In Transform menu, and with the proper axes active, use the X-, Y- and Z-axis coordinates from Figure 8.67 to reposition Betty (Figure 8.71).

When you are positioning a character's COM, but nothing happens when you enter a value into the Move Type-In Transform menu, click either the Body Vertical or the Body Horizontal button and try again.

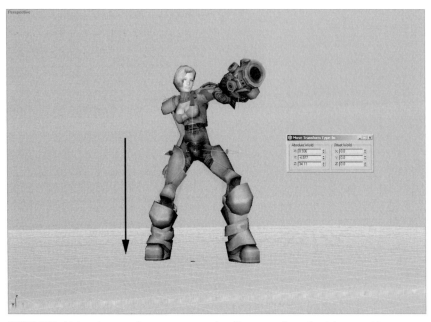

FIGURE 8.71   Using the coordinates you noted earlier, move Betty back into position.

Now, bring up Track View and copy the column of keys at Frame 0 to Frames 1, 9, 10, and 30. This creates the "animation" that will be used for the gun-charging portion of the firing sequence, and it also keeps any Continuity drift out of the motion (Figure 8.72).

FIGURE 8.72   Copy keys to create the "animation" that will be used as the gun charges.

There's no need to *really* animate the character for this "build-up" state, because the duration of it is variable—a pose is all that's required. The keys copied to Frame 30 are for the next step in the firing animation.

Creating the Firing Motion

With the pose copied, you now need to make the actual gun-firing animation. Close Track View, then select and freeze all the Betty mesh objects. Go to a Left viewport, change your Time Configuration to a Start Time of 30, and click the Animate button so it is red and active. You should automatically be at Frame 30 when you change the Start Time; if not, go to that frame. Next, alternately select each foot and lock it down using the Set Planted Key (in the IK Key Info rollout menu). Uncheck the Join to Prev IK Key checkbox as you lock each foot (Figure 8.73).

FIGURE 8.73   Lock down each foot at Frame 30, *unchecking* the Join to Prev IK Key box.

Open Track View again, and copy the column of keys at Frame 30 to Frame 35. Go to Frame 35 and create a pose for Betty that shows her just after the gun *initially* goes off. As you do so, picture yourself holding the gun out like Betty is now and then *BOOM!* It goes off and rocks your entire left side back. The knock-back would drive your hand back, twist your body to the left, and rock your head forward and down. When you pose Betty's left gun arm, try to keep it pointing forward as it goes back, and bring her left hand forward as if she's using it to catch her balance (Figure 8.74).

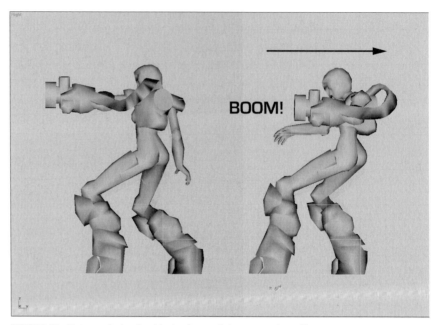

FIGURE 8.74   Betty rocks back with the force of the gun going off.

Moving the Recoil Closer

With the shot having been fired, you can now put to use the animation you loaded into the Biped earlier. However, first you need to select the feet and snapshot them for reference for when you move the recoil animation closer to the firing animation (both in terms of time and in the scene itself). Go to wireframe mode, select the feet, choose Snapshot from the Tools dropdown menu (1), and then hit OK when the Snapshot menu pops up (2) (Figure 8.75).

Change the Time Configuration to an End Time of 110 and open Track View. Select and move all the keys that make up the getting-hit animation to the left so they start at Frame 40. Then select the column of keys at Frame 30 and copy them to Frame 100 (Figure 8.76).

Play the animation back to see how it looks. During the getting-hit animation, the character is off the ground and a little too far to the right. You need to reposition her so everything matches up with the beginning and end pose.

Aligning the Right Foot by Moving the COM

Go to the Layers rollout menu and click the 🖼 Create Layer button to make a new Layer. Switch to the Front viewport, turn the Animate

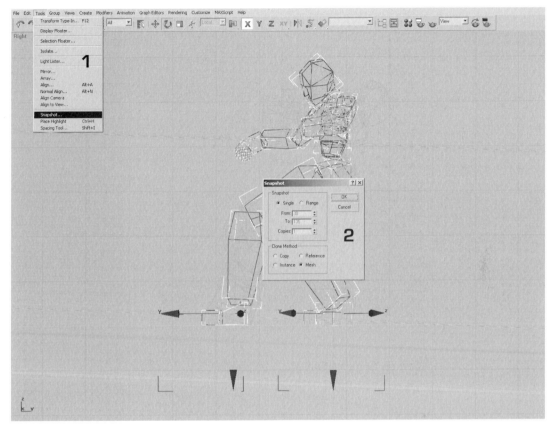

FIGURE 8.75   Snapshot the feet to use as a reference for the recoil positioning.

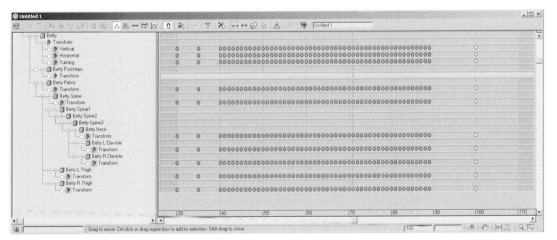

FIGURE 8.76   Move the "recoil" keys closer to the point where Betty fires the gun.

button on, and select COM (Betty). Make sure the Select and Move button is the active transform button, and apply Set Keys for the COM at Frames 35 and 100. You want the motion to remain the same before and after the recoil. Now, go to Frame 40 and move the COM so that the feet line up with the snapshots you took earlier. Concentrate on matching the green right foot instead of the blue left (the weight is on the right foot when the character goes back) (Figure 8.77).

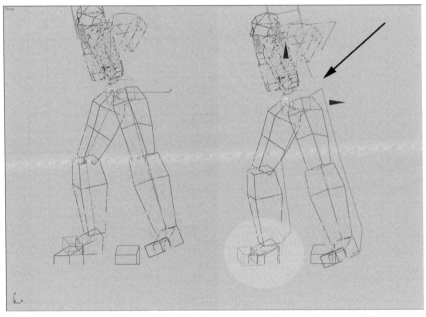

FIGURE 8.77   Move the COM until the right foot becomes aligned with the right foot's snapshot reference.

 There's no way to manually select both Body Horizontal and Body Vertical buttons in the Track Selection rollout menu at the same time. You either click one button or the other. However, if you click on the Restrict to ZX or Restrict to YZ buttons, then Body Horizontal and Body Vertical both *become selected, allowing you to set a key for both animation tracks simultaneously (Figure 8.78).*

If you use the Axis Tripod for your X-, Y-, and Z-axis selection/translation, a key can be set for both tracks; simply move the COM using the corner selection icon as you move it in two axes simultaneously (Figure 8.79).

Next, while still in the Front viewport, go to Frame 90 and again move the COM until Betty's right foot lines up with the right foot's snapshot reference (Figure 8.80).

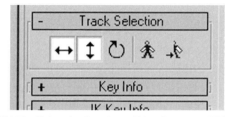

FIGURE 8.78   Using the Restrict to ZX or Restrict to YZ buttons, you can set keys for *both* Body Horizontal and Body Vertical animation tracks for the COM.

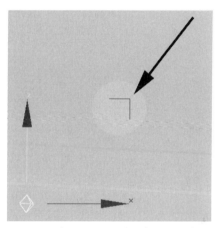

FIGURE 8.79   By using the Axis Tripod and moving the COM via the corner selection icon, you can set keys in both Body Horizontal and Body Vertical tracks.

Now, scrub the animation back and forth between Frames 40 and 60. The character bounces around a little, starting from Frame 45 and ending at Frame 53. Go to Frame 45 and move the COM until the right foot once again lines up with the reference. Then go to Frame 53 and do the same thing. Scrub the animation back and forth, and wherever you see the foot deviate from the reference, move the COM until the foot lines up during the entire animation. Ignore the foot position at Frames 36–39 because you're going to move the *foot* instead of the COM to line it up for those frames. Move the COM at Frame 95 to align the feet, but ignore Frames 91 to 94 and 96 to 99 for the same reason.

Go through the animation in the Right viewport as well, moving the COM at each frame where the foot doesn't line up, taking into

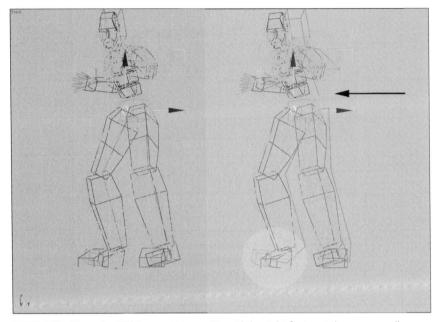

FIGURE 8.80   Move the COM over at Frame 90 until the right foot matches up as well.

consideration the bouncing motion from Frame 45 to 55 (just move the COM along the Y-axis) (Figure 8.81).

Don't worry if the positioning isn't exact. The main point here is that you massage the getting-hit motion via a Layer to get the feet in the right position by *first* moving the COM. Don't worry about the foot going through the floor for now.

 Don't attempt to use Set Planted Key in a Layer—wait until the layers have been collapsed. Try it sometime and you'll quickly see why. The foot and leg will just do weird things.

Adjusting the Upper Body

With the overall position of the character aligned correctly, you need to adjust the torso, arms, and head to better fit the idea of firing a weapon. Currently, the hands come up to the face after being hit, and the torso and head are turned too far to the right. Select the Spine objects, arms, and head and apply Set Keys for them at Frames 35 and 100. Then advance to Frame 40, and pose the upper body so it's facing forward more

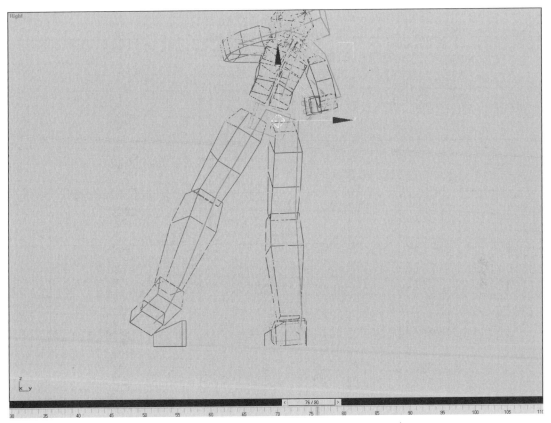

FIGURE 8.81   Move the COM in the Right viewport as well, so the foot lines up properly.

and so it fits the action of having just shot the weapon (instead of having been hit). Rotate all the Spine objects, the arms, and the head. Don't forget to involve the clavicles, too. They're a very important and often overlooked part of the arm that is crucial in imparting the motion of the arm (Figure 8.82).

Then, to complete the feeling that she's immediately looking to get back to her default position to fire the weapon again, go to Frame 0 and rotate the upper body so the body is facing a little bit forward; the spine should also be bent more along the Y-axis as she struggles to get her balance back. Rotate her head so it faces forward and slightly down (Figure 8.83).

Finally, go back to Frame 45 and rotate the head down so it faces forward. The head will always beat the body to recovery like this because the eyes are always looking forward or at the target. Scrub through the

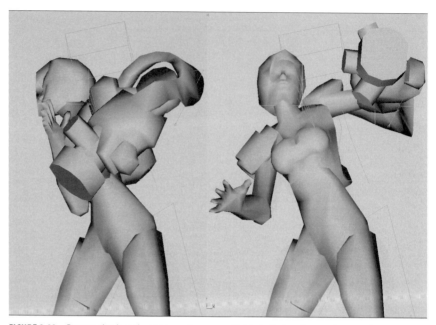

FIGURE 8.82   Rotate the head, spine, and arms so Betty is facing forward more.

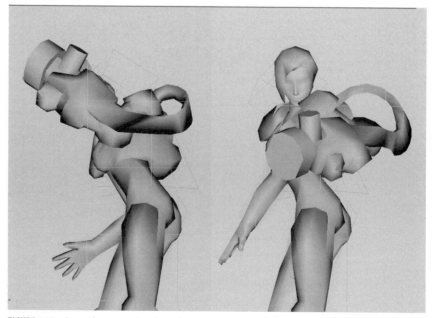

FIGURE 8.83   Pose the upper body so Betty starts to regain her balance for another shot.

animation and adjust the head so that it's always facing somewhat forward (Figure 8.84).

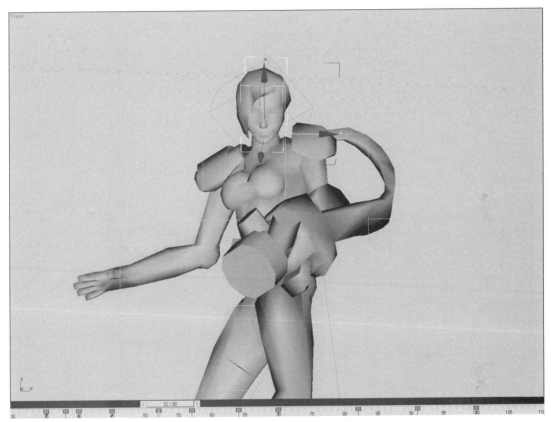

FIGURE 8.84   The head will always try to face forward so the eyes can see the target.

Once the head adjustments are finished, collapse the Layer, and fix the feet where they go through the floor in Frames 35 to 40.

Making Adjustments with the Set Multiple Keys Function

While Layers are one way to make adjustments to a mocap file to bend it to your needs, Set Multiple Keys is another way. Open Track View and select all keys for just the Betty R Thigh track from Frame 40 to 89 (Figure 8.85).

With the keyframes selected, close the Track View, go to a Front viewport, and advance to Frame 59. Zoom in on the right foot and look at the way it's bent along the Z-axis (Figure 8.86).

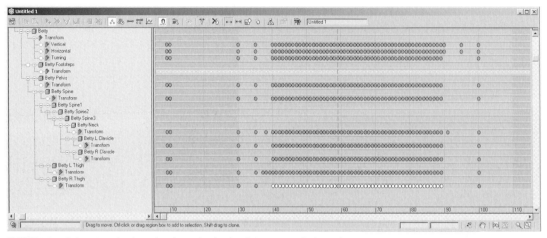

FIGURE 8.85   Select just the keys for the right thigh of the appended got-hit motion.

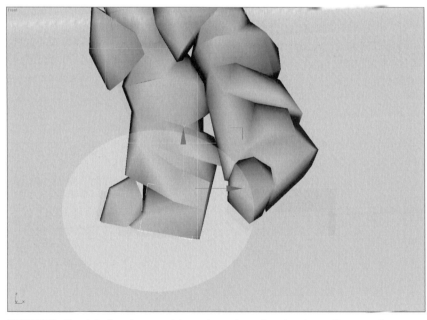

FIGURE 8.86   The right foot is rotated throughout the animation due to floor matting.

If you study the animation, the foot is at an unnatural angle because of the soft floor pad that the motion was performed upon. You can quickly and easily fix this problem using Set Multiple Keys.

Turn the Animate button *off,* and select and rotate the foot along the Z-axis until it's flat on the floor (1). Then, click on the Set Multiple Keys in the Keyframing rollout menu (2), and the Biped Multiple Keys menu will appear. Click on the Apply Increment button (3), and the rotation is applied across all selected keys in the Track View (Figure 8.87).

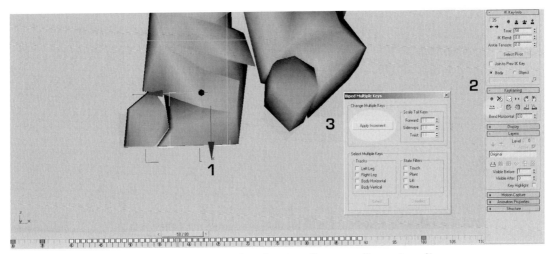

FIGURE 8.87   Use Set Multiple Keys to have a transform function affect a specific number of keys.

Whenever you use Set Multiple Keys and Apply Increments, the immediate results sometimes seem to stretch or deform the geometry. See if the Apply Increments worked by scrubbing your Time Slider back and forth or hitting the period (.) key and comma (,) key a few times. Also, remember you have to rotate or move the selected object along one axis at a time, and hit Set Multiple Keys and Apply Increments before moving on to another axis or transform type. In other words, you can't do a series of moves and rotates, then hit Set Multiple Keys, and expect them all to work.

Play the animation back to see if there are other areas to fine-tune. Experiment with deleting keys for the arms, spine, and head at different places during the animation to make the motions smoother. That wraps up turning Betty getting hit into Betty recoiling from a punch into Betty recovering from a lot of kick from her gun (Figure 8.88).

FIGURE 8.88 Betty's gun has got one heckuva kick.

SUMMARY

There are three types of motion capture files you can use with character studio and 3ds max: CSM, BVH, or BIP. The first two are more for the motion capture professional who needs access to marker data and other calibration elements. As an animator, you mainly just need to know how to convert CSM and BVH files to BIP files in character studio. This is done through the Motion Capture Conversion Parameters menu accessed in the Motion Capture rollout menu. It's in this menu that you can reduce the number of keys that make up a mocap file (keys are set for every frame of every animation track) or generate a loop by simply repeating the data.

When it comes to working with mocap files, it's always best to do a capture for every project for which you need the motions recorded. However, time and money sometimes make it necessary to hunt down or buy stock motion capture data and adjust it to fit your needs. When considering which mocap file to use, study the data and look at the quality of the motion and the usability of it. Will it fit with the character and can it be easily and quickly modified? A good way to illustrate what factors to look for in a mocap file is to compare good and bad run animations. A good run animation has no trace of the initial acceleration into the motion or of the deceleration as the character comes to a stop.

You can add or remove frames in a motion capture file to exaggerate and emphasize physical forces like centrifugal force and impact. Applying Layers in character studio gives you the ability to alter and adjust your mocap data as you see fit.

Motion capture files can be used for many purposes. Don't think inside the box and use the data only as it was intended. Instead, experiment with combinations of motion capture data to come up with something entirely different.

PUTTING IT ALL TOGETHER

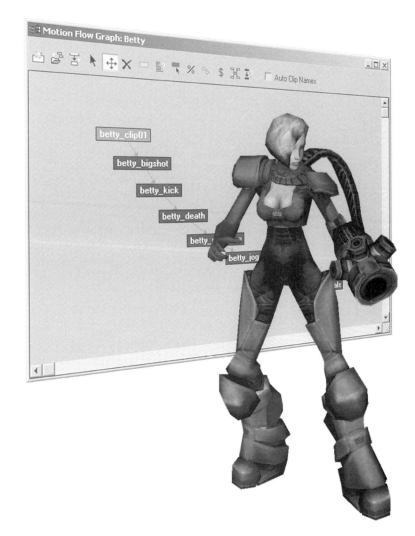

Y ou might have noticed that in Chapter 8 you didn't establish a Frame 0 pose. When working with motion capture, it's best to massage the data into what you need and save it as an individual BIP file. As you go through the process and create a number of files, Motion Flow mode allows you to string the files together, either on top of Frame 0 or by adding them into the grouped motion clips later. Finally, when all your motions have been strung together and your required animation set is complete, you will need to *export* the motions with your character into a format that can be used by the game engine.

MOTION FLOW MODE

Made to create transitions between motions and to reorient motion files as required, the Motion Flow Editor is perfect for linking all the separate animations you create; it completes the animation folder analogy. While there are many useful features in Motion Flow mode, in this chapter you'll be sticking to just the process of stitching your animation set together.

Preparing an Animation for Motion Flow

There are three things you need to look for or correct in a motion clip before bringing it into the Motion Flow Editor. First, the first column of keys needs to start at Frame 0. Even if there isn't any animation from Frame 0 to Frame 50 for some reason, the first column of keys set for all Biped objects as seen in the Track View needs to be at Frame 0. If not, when you bring the clip into Motion Flow, the transitions and segment length of the animation could be wrong. Load Betty15.max from the Chapter9 directory on the CD-ROM that came with this book (Figure 9.1).

ON THE CD

Bring up the Track View and you'll see that the keys are off to the right instead of starting at Frame 0. This sometimes occurs when you save a segment instead of just saving the whole BIP file (especially if in Motion Flow). Select all the keys and slide them over so the first column is on Frame 0 (Figure 9.2).

Second, you need to make sure there are keys at the last frame of the animation, making it a completely *closed* motion clip. As you string the animations together, they therefore don't affect one another. In the case of Betty's kick animation that you've loaded, copy the first set of keyframes to the end (Figure 9.3).

The third and last thing you need to do is add an extra column of keys at the end of the motion clip. When a motion clip is brought into the

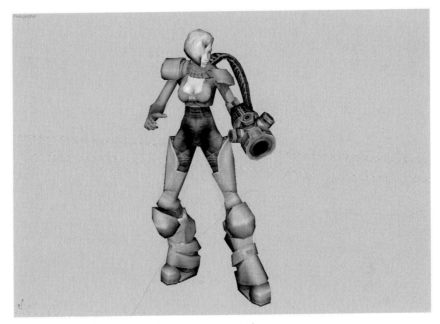

FIGURE 9.1   Betty is ready to get all her moves together.

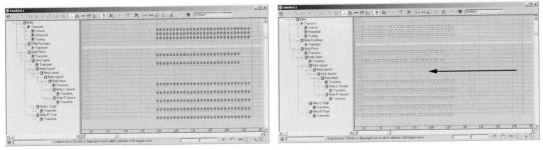

FIGURE 9.2   Slide the keys over so the first column starts at Frame 0.

Motion Flow Editor, its last frame is "eaten" when another motion clip is tacked onto the end of it. This happens even if there's no transition defined. 3ds max and character studio just assume the last frame is either a duplicate of the first (for loops) or is expendable in the transition. Select and drag the last column of keys one frame over to create a "cushion" of keyframes (Figure 9.4).

Note that motion clips don't have to be just one animation. When you keyframed Betty's idle, shooting, and swimming animations earlier in the book, the resulting file was pretty big; it is an excellent choice for being the first motion clip because of the inclusion of Frame 0 in the

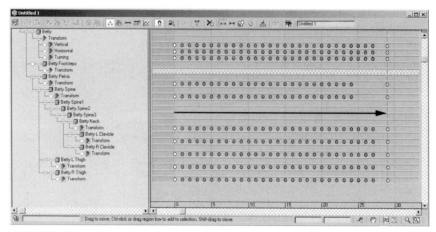

FIGURE 9.3 "Close" the motion clip so it isn't accidentally altered by another motion added to the end of it.

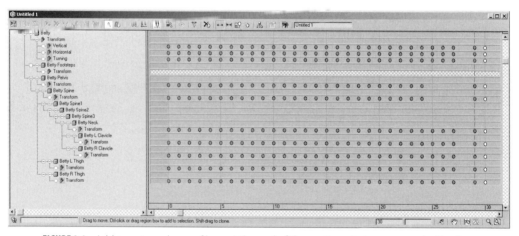

FIGURE 9.4 Add an extra column of keys at the end of the motion clip to serve as a buffer that can get absorbed by the succeeding clip in Motion Flow.

default pose. A motion clip can contain more than one motion, and since you've gone to all the trouble to add time tags to the file, it's an even better reason to make it Clip1.

ON THE CD

Get some practice making sure your clip is ready to be brought into Motion Flow by loading Betty12.max again from the Chapter7 directory on this book's CD-ROM; add a frame to the end of all those keyframes (Figure 9.5).

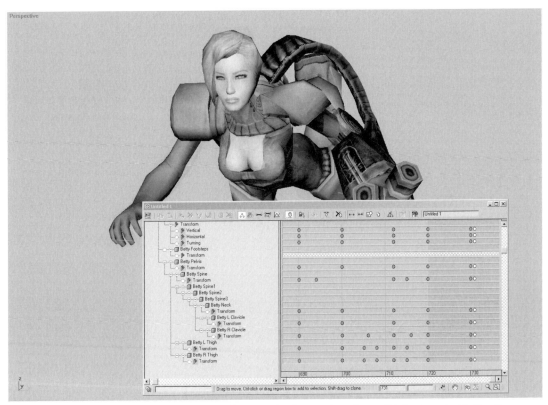

FIGURE 9.5   Make all the animations you created for Betty the first motion clip you'll bring into the Motion Flow Editor.

Once you copy the keys at the end, save the file as betty_clip01.bip. Now that you know how the clips need to be prepared, you can create your animations set using Motion Flow.

Creating the Motion Flow Script

To string all your animations together, you have to create a motion flow script, specifying the order in which the animations are linked and any transitions or re-orientations that need to be done. Creating this script always involves the same process, so, still using Betty12.max as an example, perform the following steps:

1. Select any Biped object.
2. Click the Motion Flow Mode button to make it active (purple) (Figure 9.6).

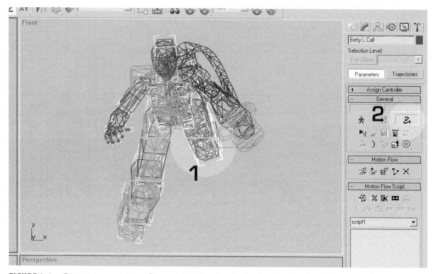

FIGURE 9.6 Creating a motion flow script begins by being in Motion Flow mode.

3. Click the Show Graph button to make it active.
4. Make the Create Clip button active in the window called Motion Flow Graph: Betty.
5. Enter as many clip boxes as you need (enter eight for Betty) (Figure 9.7).

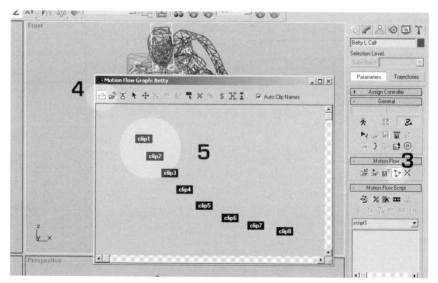

FIGURE 9.7 Create the Motion Flow Graph.

Arrange the motion clips in a way that makes it easy to link them all together. Usually a stair-step configuration is best, but any system you devise will work. To move the clips around, you first have to click the Move Clip button to make it active (Figure 9.8).

FIGURE 9.8   Arrange your motion clips by activating the Move Clip button and positioning the clips.

6. Right-click on the empty motion clip boxes.
7. Browse for the right motion clips.
8. Load the motion file into each clip box. Load the betty_*.bips files from the Chapter9 directory on this book's CD-ROM in the following order (Figure 9.9):

ON THE CD

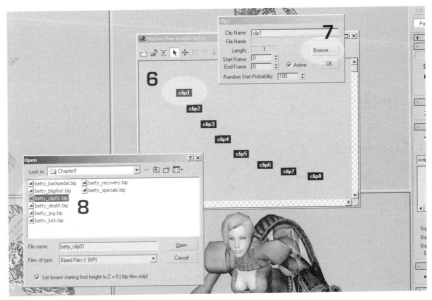

FIGURE 9.9   Load the motion clips into the Motion Flow Graph.

a. betty_clip01
b. betty_bigshot

    c. betty_kick

    d. betty_death

    e. betty_recovery

    f. betty_jog

    g. betty_backpedal

    h. betty_specials

9. Once all the motions are loaded, open the Motion Flow Script rollout menu.

10. Click the Define Script button to make it active.

11. Choose the Create new script box and hit OK (Figure 9.10).

FIGURE 9.10 Create a new Motion Flow Script.

12. Click on each clip box in the order in which you want them strung together. For Betty, click on the motion clips in the following order (Figure 9.11):

    a. betty_clip01

    b. betty_bigshot

    c. betty_kick

    d. betty_death

    e. betty_recovery

    f. betty_jog

    g. betty_backpedal

    h. betty_specials

13. Close the graph window and click on a clip name in the script to the right so that it's highlighted (blue).

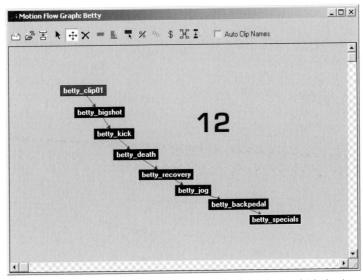

FIGURE 9.11   Click on each clip in order to specify the order in which they're played in the script.

14. Click on the Edit Transition button.
15. Edit the transition parameters (Figure 9.12).

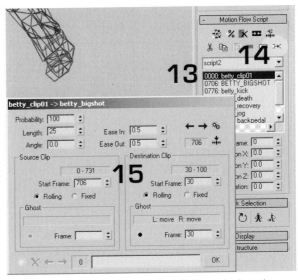

FIGURE 9.12   Define the Motion Flow Script and adjust the transitions between clips.

Adjusting Transition Length between Motion Clips

With your script defined and your motions entered, you now need to get rid of any transitions between motion clips. Close the Motion Flow Graph window and bring up the transition parameters for the first script entry (Steps 13 through 15 in our earlier list). Enter a transition Length of 0 and change the Start Frame value for the next clip to 731 (Figure 9.13).

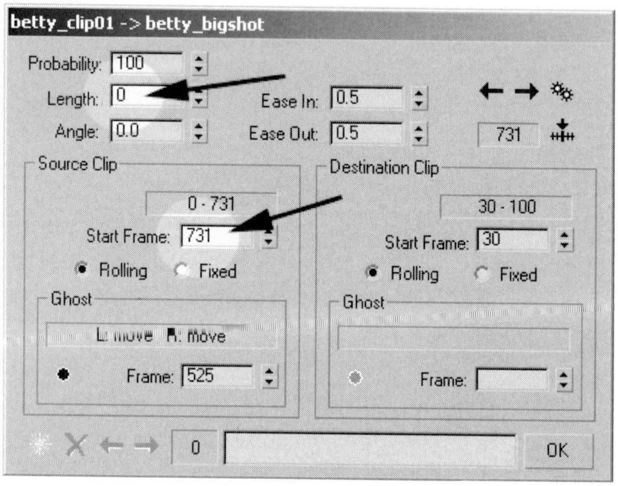

FIGURE 9.13   Adjust the Length and Start Frame values to remove any transition between clips.

The red stick figure you see when opening the transition parameters menu represents the destination motion and is only important when you're creating a transition to the next motion clip. A yellow stick figure, representing the source clip, allows you to scrub the Time Slider back and forth, comparing the relative positions of the character during the transition.

The value you use for the Start Frame is easy to calculate: Enter the number to the far right of the Source Clip (just above the Start Frame box). After you've changed the two values, click on the Next Transition in Script button, advance to the next animation clip, and change Length and Start Frame accordingly (Figure 9.14).

Rotating Motion Clips

Once you've removed any sort of transition that occurs between the motion clips, the next thing to look for is the orientation of the clips. Each successive clip starts at the end of the clip before it, and the rotation of the

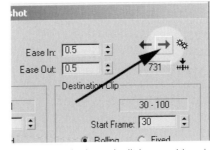

FIGURE 9.14   Cycle through all the transitions in a script by clicking on the Next Transition in Script button.

COM is relative. This means you sometimes need to rotate the animation clip using the same method you used earlier to rotate an entire motion. Go to Frame 731 and look at Betty in the Top and Front viewports (Figure 9.15).

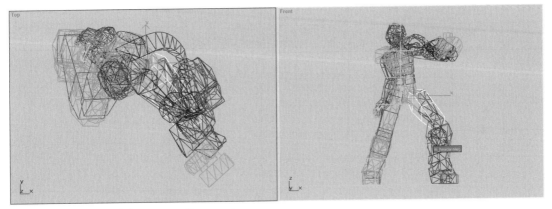

FIGURE 9.15   The second clip is rotated incorrectly.

Go back to the transition parameters menu for the first motion clip entry in the script, and enter 40 in the Angle box (Figure 9.16).

 It usually takes some trial and error to dial in the correct angle when rotating motion clips using the transition menu.

As you enter values in the Angle box, the character rotates accordingly (Figure 9.17).

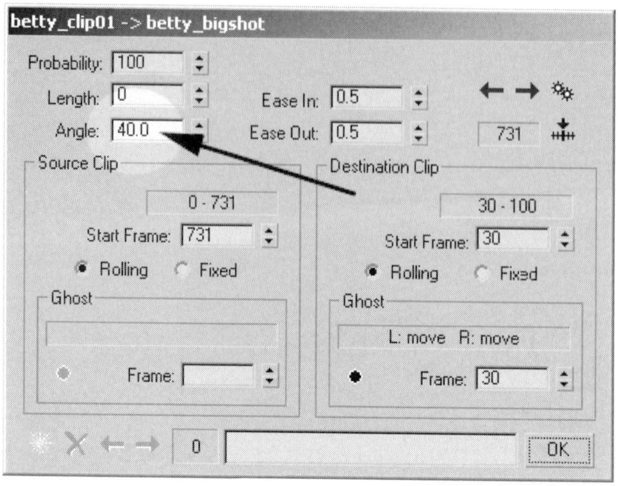

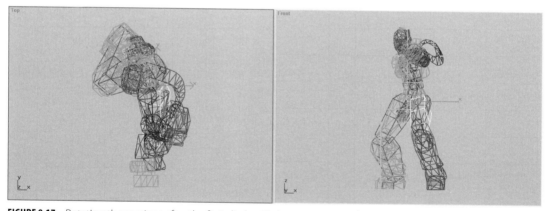

FIGURE 9.16   Entering a value in the Angle box rotates the next animation clip.

FIGURE 9.17   Rotating the motions after the first clip by 40 degrees corrects the second clip.

You'll notice that the transition menu settings affect the *next* motion clip in the script. Keep in mind, however, that *all* the motion clips following the first motion clip in the script are rotated 40 degrees, because the orientation of each clip is relative to the one preceding it.

Now you need to check the other motion clips and make sure they're oriented properly. With the transition parameter menu still open, click the ➡ Next Transition in Script button again to take you to the next motion clip.

You can advance to the first frame of each animation in the script by highlighting a particular motion clip and clicking on the ⊞ *Go To Frame button found in the Motion Flow Script rollout menu.*

The next transition, from betty_bigshot to betty_kick, needs a little bit of rotation so that Betty's head is facing forward instead of at an angle (Figure 9.18).

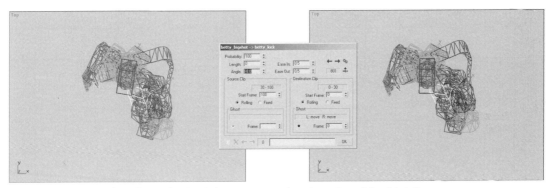

FIGURE 9.18   Enter a value of –8 in the Angle box to correct the orientation of the third clip.

 When entering values in the Angle box to rotate motion clips, a positive number will rotate the character clockwise *and a negative number will rotate it* counterclockwise.

Go to the next transition and scrub the Time Slider to play the death animation. It's more or less oriented correctly because Betty falls relatively straight back, perpendicular to a side view. The next transition needs to be corrected, though. Betty_death to betty_recovery needs an Angle value of –58 degrees added to the transition so that she falls straight back and returns to her feet facing forward (Figure 9.19).

Don't worry about the relative height being off. You can fix it using a Layer once you finish all the transitions, save the BIP, and re-load it into the Biped. Advance to the next transition. Even though it may go unnoticed, Betty's head is rotated a little bit too far, so the entire animation needs to be rotated 5 degrees to make her head face forward (Figure 9.20).

For the next transition, scrub the animation back and forth, watching it in the Front viewport. Even though Betty's head isn't facing forward, her feet and body placement suggest an angle correction of –10 degrees will be enough to line her up properly (Figure 9.21).

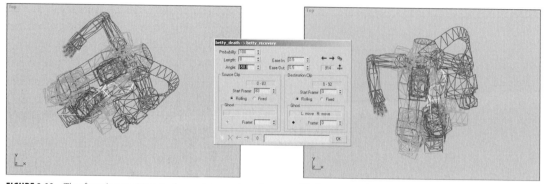

FIGURE 9.19 The fourth transition in the script needs to have a –58 degree angle applied.

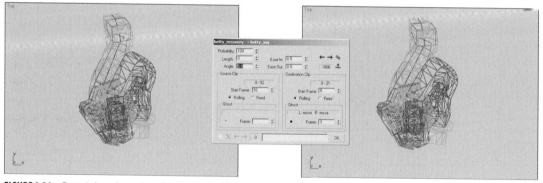

FIGURE 9.20 Betty's head needs to be rotated 5 degrees.

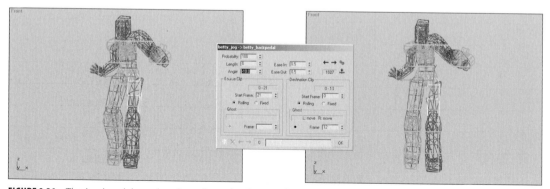

FIGURE 9.21 The backpedal needs to be adjusted so Betty is facing forward more.

The last motion clip is made up of several animations, like betty_clip01. Go to Frame 1082, where the character faces somewhat forward in the Front viewport. You can see that the motion needs to be rotated about another –10 degrees to line the clip up correctly (Figure 9.22).

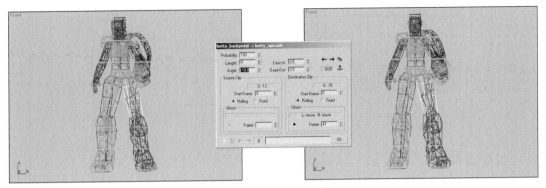

FIGURE 9.22   The last transition needs –10 degrees applied to it as well.

The last motion clip doesn't give you the option of adjusting the transition, precisely because it *is* last and has nothing to transition to. With the transitions tweaked, the animations are ready to be saved and re-loaded into the Biped. Click on the 🔲 Save Segment button in the General rollout menu. Click on the Active Time Segment button to get the correct animation range, and *uncheck* the Generate a Keyframe per Frame box in order to avoid adding needless keyframes. Call the new BIP betty_01 (Figure 9.23).

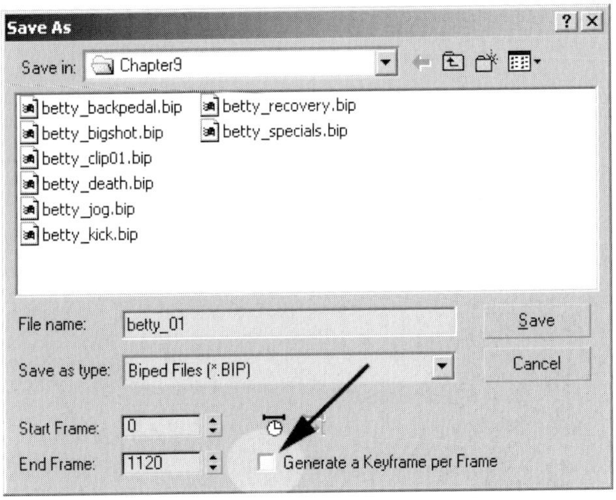

FIGURE 9.23   Make sure to uncheck the Generate a Keyframe per Frame button to avoid adding needless keyframes.

Clicking on the Motion Flow Mode button to turn it off drops you back into normal character studio mode. Hit the Load File button, and the file you just saved will be automatically entered in the file name box. Hit the Open button, and the newly linked animations are now ready to be adjusted even further.

Always view the Motion Flow Editor as a tool to be used to temporarily attach all your animations together. Exporting the animations to a new file and loading them into the Biped gives you the ability to edit them further. Another reason to save and reload the new BIP file is that the Motion Flow Editor loads the animation clips from the directory specified. This makes it difficult when others have to access the same 3ds max scene and/or the animations, because the file will look for the motion clips in the same directory. If it doesn't exist and you don't have the files, the animations can't be loaded. Saving the new BIP file removes the dependency on motion file location.

Some of the adjustments you need to make to the new BIP file include offsetting any motion (like the betty_recovery clip), adding the buffer between animations, and adding time tags. Once the animation set is complete, it's time to move on to the export process.

THE EXPORT PROCESS

Implementing real-time game characters invariably requires some sort of export process. For *Q3A*, the characters were exported to 3ds max's ASCII format (called ASE), and then the programmers would wave their mathematical wands, and the characters would magically appear in the game. A configuration file set the frame rate per animation and defined when the animation started and stopped. Using this kind of batch-file approach works, but is definitely not "artist friendly."

However, not all companies eschew the visual tool approach and force the artist to (shudder) type stuff after a lengthy export. WildTangent's Web Driver technology and Criterion Software's RenderWare™ toolset represent the new breed of graphically oriented exporters that improve the art development path. To illustrate just one instance of the export process, the following section details the use of WildTangent's 3ds max 4 exporter. It requires you to install a series of WildTangent programs onto your machine, so if you'd rather skip it and go to the Final Thoughts section, please do.

Installing the WildTangent 3DS Max 4 Exporters

Before you give the WildTangent exporter a try, read the Known Issues section of the Read Me file in the Demos | WT directory on this book's CD-ROM to make sure your system is supported. If it looks like there won't be any compatibility problems, close all programs, including 3ds max. Go to the Demos | WT directory and run the wtwdinstFull setup file. This installs WildTangent's Web Driver onto your system. Think of it as a miniature operating system that allows you to run content created on their proprietary platform.

Next, run the WildTangentMax4Plugins setup to install the actual 3ds max 4 exporter. As soon as the exporters are installed, run 3ds max 4 again. Go to the Utilities panel, click the More . . . button, select Wild-Tangent Actors from the list of utilities, and click OK (Figure 9.24).

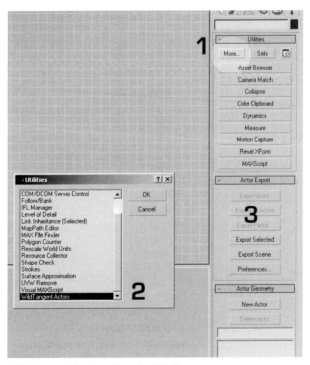

FIGURE 9.24   After installing the WildTangent exporter, you access it through the Utilities panel.

Load Betty16.max from the Chapter9 directory on this book's CD-ROM, and then select just Betty's mesh objects (Figure 9.25).

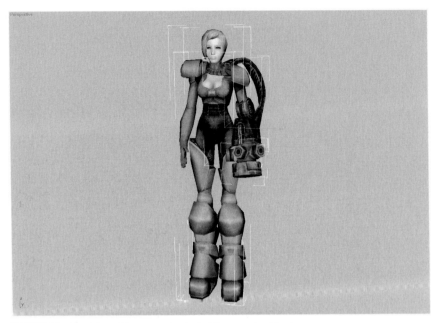

FIGURE 9.25 Load Betty16.max and select all her mesh objects.

Creating and Exporting an Actor

Next, click on the New Actor button in the Actor Geometry rollout menu. By default, it assigns a name to the actor, choosing one of the selected objects. Highlight the name that appears in the box and rename it to Betty (Figure 9.26).

FIGURE 9.26 Change the actor's default assigned name to Betty.

Click anywhere in the viewport to make the name change stick, and hit the Export Actor button under the Actor Export rollout menu. A blue status bar will appear at the bottom of your screen as the program exports the selected actor to a special viewer. When it's done, you'll see a new program indicator flashing at the bottom of your screen on your Windows toolbar. Click on it to bring up the viewer window (Figure 9.27).

FIGURE 9.27   This is the WildTangent actor viewer as seen using Windows Explorer.

Hold down your left mouse button and drag in the viewer window to rotate the camera around the exported Betty. Hold down the right mouse button to pan, and hold down both buttons while moving forward and backward to zoom in and out. Hit the B key to toggle through gray, white, and black backgrounds.

Since the default camera settings cause a clipping issue, Betty looks a little strange from a distance. As you zoom in, however, she looks fine. The default location for the file you just created is stored in a Documents and Settings | [User] | Application Data | WildTangent | Generated Files | Web directory. Close the Viewer window, go back to 3ds max, and click on the Preferences button in the Actor Export rollout menu. Click on the Web-Ready Format tab when the Export Preferences menu pops up, and highlight the directory path under Web-Ready Output. Type in c:\artgc\export (or whatever drive you want instead of c:\) (Figure 9.28).

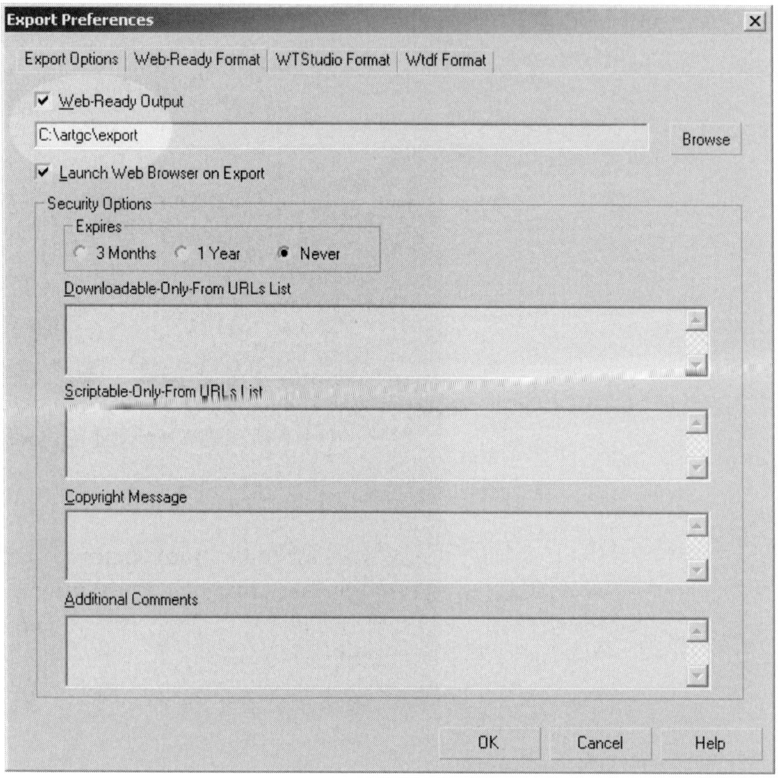

FIGURE 9.28   The Export Preferences menu determines where the exported actors go.

When the prompt to create the directory appears, click OK. Now, whenever you export an actor in this particular 3ds max scene, it will go to this directory.

Exporting an Actor with Animations

Here's where all those time tags come in handy. Click on the Add Time Tag box and note the frames in which the Swim Forward animation takes place (Frame 680 to Frame 720) (Figure 9.29).

250 Jump1 Start
260 Jump1 End
280 Jump Idle
300 Jump Land Start
307 Jump Land End
330 Jump2
360 Jump3
390 Jump4 Start
402 Jump4 End
420 Jump Shoot
450 Jump Shoot Idle
470 Jump Shoot Landing Start
480 Jump Shoot Landing End
525 Swim Idle Start
625 Swim Idle End
680 Swim Forward Start
720 Swim Forward End
750 Bigshot Start
819 Bigshot End
840 Kick Start
868 Kick End
890 Death Start
972 Death End

FIGURE 9.29   Click on the Add Time Tag box
to get a list of the start and stop frames for
the animations.

Open the Actor Motions rollout menu and click on the New Motion
button. Rename it in the name field to Swim Forward. Hit the Tab key or
double-click in the Start Frame box, and enter 680. Enter 720 in the End
Frame box (Figure 9.30).

Hit the Export Actor button once again, and open the Viewer Web
page again (Figure 9.31).

If the clipping issue bothers you and you can edit an HTML page, do the following:
Go to the directory to which the viewer is exported and find the file called Wild-
Tangent.html. Using FrontPage, Notepad, or another HTML editor, open the file
and go to line 339. Change the single line:

```
camera.setClipping( 10000*globalPositionIncrement,
    2*globalPositionIncrement);
```

to the following:

```
camera.setClipping( 10000*globalPositionIncrement, 4.0)
```

This change increases the Z-buffer accuracy, but increasing it too much will start to
clip away the front parts of your model, so you may want to tune it a bit. The

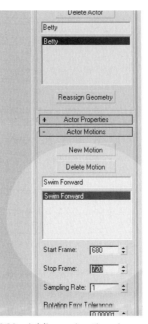

FIGURE 9.30 Adding animations is as easy as naming and specifying an animation range.

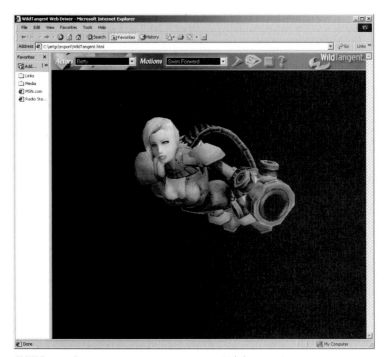

FIGURE 9.31 Betty is now swimming in your Web browser!

exporter tries to set a good default that works with most models, but depending on the size of the model, these numbers can be increased for better Z behavior. Save the file and keep it somewhere handy to overwrite the default WildTangent.html file that's written whenever you export an actor.

To get a character like Betty in the game, all her animations had to be entered in the motion list before she was exported. Additionally, there are other settings you can adjust, such as *promoted bones* and WildTangent materials creation. Feel free to explore the WildTangent exporter, and visit *www.wildtangent.com* for more involved tutorials.

Because it exports to a Web page, the WildTangent exporter gives you a way to create a model or several models, animate them, export them, and share them with anyone capable and willing to download WildTangent's Web Driver.

FINAL THOUGHTS

Character animation is without a doubt the greatest excuse for getting paid that I can think of. As I've gone though this book, giving you tips, tricks, and instructions, I have hoped you'll be able to come away with a newfound confidence that you can make your characters come to life. 3ds max and character studio are excellent tools to work with and they get better with every iteration. That fact, combined with the increasing power of PCs and game consoles, leaves the future of real-time character animation wide open. I have no doubt that within the next five years we'll be seeing 10,000-polygon characters that animate blazingly fast with tons of cool pyrotechnics and other procedural effects.

It will be your duty as a character animator to make use of any technological innovation that comes along and to bend it to your creative will. Character animation will always be one of the most difficult and the most rewarding forms of computer graphics. Getting better at it means spending thousands of hours on practice and experimentation. Most of all, getting better as a character animator requires mastering your tools so that the interface is forgotten and your thoughts are translated to results. Whichever tool you use, whatever project you're on, never be satisfied with what you have done (if time and schedule permits!). Always strive for that cooler pose or that dynamic clean movement. Within all of us is the ability to improve and achieve.

Feel free to contact me with any of your questions or comments by e-mailing me at *st33d@nak3d.com*.

Best of luck!

ABOUT THE CD-ROM

The companion CD-ROM to *Animating Real-Time Game Characters* contains all the files necessary to follow along with the tutorials and exercises in the book. Feel free to use the models and animations as starting points for creating your own characters.

RECOMMENDED SYSTEM REQUIREMENTS

In order to make use of the CD-ROM, you need to have at least the following system requirements:

- Pentium II 400MHz processor
- 128 MB RAM
- CD-ROM drive
- Windows 2000, Windows NT, or Windows XP
- 3ds max 4 with character studio 3.*x*

It's also recommended that you have some sort of 3D graphics card that supports hardware acceleration and some sort of sound capability to fully experience the demos.

CHAPTERS

In addition to tutorial and lesson files, each Chapter directory contains jpeg images that correspond to the illustrations in the book. If for some reason, you can't see a particular detail due to the black and white printed page, refer to these color images.

DEMOS

Under demos you'll find files needed to play the *Betty Bad* demo and several music visualizers and feature real-time characters created by the author. Please consult the README.RTF file before installing them. All demos and programs associated with the demos are property of their respective owners.

MOCAP

The BIP files included are combinations of keyframe and motion capture animations that are samples of real-time game character animation sets. Feel free to use them for your own characters or simply load them into a Biped to review the animations.

INDEX

A

Active Time Segment button, 325

Actors, creating and exporting, 374–376

All Links option of Type-In dialog, 114

Anchor keys, 238–240

Angle, value settings for rotations, 367–369

Animation

animation sets, 175–181

categories of character animation, 180–181

character identity and, 172–175

character implementation, 186–189

death animation sequence, 325–327

details in, 280

drift, correcting, 240–243, 255

dynamic action, 267–268

exporting animations with actors, 376–379

Footstep *vs.* Freeform mode, 192

game environments and, 177

ideology of, 280

idle poses, 176, 236–238, 248–250

jumps, 259–280

keyframe animation, 181–183

layers and, 224–229, 317–325, 331–336

memory and, 177–179

modeling to accommodate, 32

optimizing with key reduction, 299–304

organizing files, 192–193, 202–203

secondary motion, 219–220, 243–246, 265, 266, 271–272, 279–280, 324, 331–336

selection sets, 193–196

shooting weapons, 250–259

smooth loops in, 284–286

snapshots as references, 274–277

special moves, 235

swimming, 281–292

Time Configuration, 200–201

track selection, 197

track view, 197–201

walking, realistic, 187–189

see also Keyframe animation; Loops, animation; Motion capture (mocap) animation; Motion Flow mode

Arms
   Bipeds adjustments, 61–67,
     72–73
   copying limb poses, 283
   gun arm weighting, 128–133
   weighting, 105–113
Artists, inspiration for character
    design, 2–3
Asset Browser of 3ds, 8–9

B
Backface Cull, 26
Battle Chasers, 6–7
Bias, keyframe animation, 210
BioVision Hierarchical (BVH)
    files, 296–299, 300
Bipeds
   arm and leg adjustments,
    61–67, 72–73
   body adjustments, 59–61,
    70–71
   coordinate systems, 60–61
   creating, 55–58
   da Vinci poses and, 81–83
   display options for, 140–141
   dog rigs, 73–74
   dolphin rigs, 74–75
   fitting to mesh, 38–39, 57
   four-legged creatures and,
    68–74
   head adjustments, 59–61,
    70–71
   hierarchy in, 60
   keyframing and, 193–196
   leg attachments, 60
   loading BIP files, 123–125
   loading CSM or BVH files,
    296–299
   meshes for, 53–55
   poses, saving, 67–68

   rotating with Motion Flow
    Editor, 325–331
   Rubber Band mode and
    joints in, 62, 63
   selection sets and, 193–196
   Spring controllers and, 84–88
   steps to set up Biped rig, 52
   structure adjustment, 58–59
   tail adjustments, 70–71
   transparency of, 140
   tri-jointed legs, 75–78
BIP files, loading into Bipeds,
    123–125
Bodies
   Biped adjustments, 59–61,
    70–71
   weighting torsos, 117–120
Body Horizontal and Body Ver-
    tical, simultaneous selec-
    tion of, 346
Booleans, modeling, 16–17, 18
   openings in geometry and, 17
Bracketing, 240–243
Breasts, 84
   weighting of, 143–144,
    158–163
Bulge Sub-Object settings, 95
BVH format files, 296–299, 300

C
Characters
   design of, 2–7
   identity and design attributes,
    173–174
   implementation of, 186–189
   individuality of, 172
   inspiration for, 2–3
   motivation of, 174–175
   preparing for animation,
    172–173

Character Studio Motion (CSM) files, 296–299, 300
Child Overlap settings, 147–150
Clipping, adjustment for actor exports, 377–379
Continuity, keyframe animation, 209–212, 239–240
Converting CSM or BVH files, 297–299
Coordinate systems, in Bipeds, 60–61
Copy Posture button, 338–339
CSM files, 296–299, 300

D
Da Vinci poses, 81–83
Death, animation sequence, 325–337
Deep Paint (Right Hemisphere), 48
Define Script button, 328–329
Demos, 382
Design, character design
   aesthetic considerations, 2–4
   implementation and technical considerations, 4
   inspiration for, 2–3
   references for, 4–7
   technical considerations, 4
   see also Modeling
Dogs, Biped rigs for, 73–74
Dolphins, Biped rigs for, 74–75
Doubling keys, 240–243
Drift, correcting, 240–243
Dummy objects, 55–57, 78–79
   in weapons aiming mechanisms, 257–259

E
Ease From and Ease To settings of TCB Controller, 212–216

Edges
   making visible, 44
   turned, 21–23
Edit Mesh modifier, UVW maps and, 41–44
Elbows
   modeling, 37
   weighting adjustments, 107–113
Emotion, facial rigs and, 83
Envelopes
   applying Physique, steps for, 138–139
   copy and paste for symmetrical limbs, 150–153
   parent / child overlap adjustments, 147–150
   radial scale adjustment, 144–147
   turning off unnecessary, 139–144
Environments and animations, 177
   underwater environments, 281
Export process, 372–379
   WildTangent 3DS Max exporters, 373
Extruding, modeling, 16
Eyebrows, 80–81
Eyelids, 79–81
Eyes, 79–81
   weighting of eyes and eyeballs, 165, 166–168

F
Faces and facial rigs
   animation and facial rigs, 76–81
   eyes and eyelids, 79–81
   for high-res meshes, 83–84

Faces and facial rigs (*cont.*)
  lips and tongues, 80–81
  single-bone "muppet," 78–79
  weighting faces, 163–168
Feet
  animation of walking,
    187–189
  keyframe animation and,
    205–207
  locking with Set Planted,
    238–240
  weighting of, 155
File sharing, Bipeds and, 52
Fingers
  modeling, 37–38
  secondary motion animation,
    243–244
  weighting, 113–116
Footstep mode, 192
Four-legged characters, Bipeds
    for, 68–74
Frame zero, keyframing,
    196–197
Freeform mode, 192

G
Game controls, animations and,
    179–180
Game technology and anima-
    tion, 180–181
Generate a Keyframe per
    Frame button, 371
Genre, animation sets and,
    175–177

H
Hair
  modeling with splines, 20–21
  weighting of, 163, 164
Hands
  keyframe animation and,
    205–207

modeling, 37–38
secondary motion animation,
    243–244
weighting values, 113–116
Heads
  Biped adjustment, 59–61,
    70–71
  jump animations and,
    271–272
  modeling, 33
  secondary motion animation,
    243–246, 271–272
  weighting, 163–168
Hescox, Richard, Web address,
    3
Hierarchy
  in Bipeds, 60
  weights assignment and,
    114–115
High resolution mesh template
    modeling, 17–20
Hips
  envelopes for weighting,
    153–156
  modeling, 35–36
  weighting, 125–128, 153–156
Hips and rear, modeling, 35–36
Holes or openings in geometry,
    Booleans and, 17
Hotkeys
  comma (,), 124
  to fetch scenes, 315
  function keys, 24, 315
  "I" key, 12
  override toggle and, 217–218
  period (.), 124
  slash (/), 86, 124
  vertex deselection, 131

I
Idle animations, 176, 205–209,
    236–238, 248–250, 281, 292

IK Blend, 206
IK Keys, 236–237
  IK Key Info rollout menu,
    205–207
Impacts
  of falls, 336–337
  jump landings, 265–267,
    277–280
Implementation
  animation and, 186–189
  of real-time jumps, 261–262
  technical considerations and,
    4
Initial Skeletal Pose option,
  108–110
In Place mode, 123–125,
  309–310
Inspiration
  for character design, 2–3
  for dynamic animation,
    267–268
Interpolation, animation and,
  189

J
Jaws, 70
Jitter, key reduction to elimi-
  nate, 304
Join to Prev IK Key, 246–248
Joints, 37
  elbows, weighting adjust-
    ment, 107–113
  Rubber Band mode and, 62,
    63
  tri-jointed legs, 75–78
  wrists, 113
Jumps
  jump-split pose, 263–264
  landing impacts, 265–267,
    277–280
  real-time jumps, implement-
    ing, 261–262

running jumps, 260–261
secondary motion in, 265,
    266
shooting while jumping,
    273–274
standing jumps, 260–261
turn-around jump shot,
    268–273
weapon kickback and, 277

K
Keyframe animation, 181–183
  active animation range, 204
  anchor keys, 238–240
  Biped preparation, 193–196
  copying keyframes, 201–202,
    251
  Ease To and Ease From set-
    tings, 212–216
  frame rates, 201, 253
  frame zero, 196–197
  Generate a Keyframe per
    Frame button, 371
  idle poses, 204–209,
    236–238
  IK Key Info rollout menu,
    205–207
  Join to Prev IK Key,
    246–248
  layers and, 224–229
  playback speed, 201
  secondary motion, 219–220
  TCB (Tension, Continuity,
    and Bias) controller,
    209–216, 240–243
  Time Configuration and,
    200–201
  Time Slider bar, 202,
    216–217, 224
  Time Tags, 229–231
  Track View, 251–252
  see also Swimming animation

Key reduction, settings for,
    303–304
Knees, modeling, 37

L

Layers
    animation and, 224–229
    loops refined with, 317–325
    managing, 321
    motion capture data and, 304
    secondary motion added
        with, 331–336
    Set Planted Key and, 348
Legs
    attachments, 36
    Bipeds adjustments, 61–67,
        72–73
    copying limb poses, 283
    four-legged creatures and,
        68–74
    knee joints, 37
    leg attachments, 60
    tri-jointed legs, 75–78
    weighting, 99–105, 120–123,
        153–156
    weighting with envelopes,
        153–156
Level of Detail (LOD), 4
    Multi-Res Mesh modifier and,
        31
Links
    assigning vertices to, 95–99
    copying and pasting link set-
        tings, 150–153
    vertices, removing from,
        105–107, 126, 153
Link Sub-Object settings, 95
Lips, 80–81
    weighting of, 165
Loops, animation
    comparing segments,
        314–316

doubling, 316–317
finding matching poses for,
    311–312
layers used to refine,
    317–325
loop length, 308–310
mocap and, 308–325
smooth loops in keyframe
    animation, 284–286

M

Memory, 177–179
    deleting keyframes and, 340
Menus and menu bars, 95–96
    command panels, 24–26
    IK Key Info rollout menu,
        205–207
    Motion Capture Conversion
        Parameters menu, 316–317
    Move Type-In Transform
        menu, 341–342
    Quad menu, 95–96
    Structure rollout menu, 61–62
    Structure sub-menu, 58–59
    3DS menu bar, 12
Meshes
    for Bipeds, 53–55
    color of, 32
Mitts, 37
Modeling
    animation accommodation
        and, 32
    Asset Browser to import ref-
        erences, 8–9
    Booleans, 16–17, 18
    elbows and knees, 37
    extruding, 16
    fitting the Biped, 38–39
    function and, 31–39
    hands and fingers, 37–38
    hips and rear, 35–36
    legs and groin area, 36

necks and heads, 33
optimization, 29–31
patch modeling, 15, 20–21
polygon modeling, 15
primitives, 15–16
real-time *vs.* rendered charac-
    ters, 15
reference images and, 8–11
shoulders, 34–35
smoothing, 23–29
surface issues, 21–22
Surface tools, 20–21
techniques, 15
3D outlines and, 9–10
tips for, 13–15
turned edges, 21–23
waists, 35
Motion Capture Conversion
    Parameters menu, 316–317
Motion capture (mocap) ani-
    mation, 181–182, 183–186
BVH files, 296–299, 300
creating loops, 308–325
CSM files, 296–299, 300
evaluating files for, 305–307
files on CD-ROM, 382
key reduction, 299–304
Motion Capture Conversion
    Parameters, 298, 301
Motion Flow Editor and,
    325–331
repurposing mocap files,
    337–354
Set Multiple Keys function to
    adjust, 351–354
Motion controllers, 84–88
Motion Flow Editor, 325–331
Motion Flow mode
creating a Motion Flow
    script, 361–365
preparing animation for,
    358–361

rotating motion clips,
    366–372
transitions between clips, 366
Mouse controls, 198, 202
Mouths, 70
weighting of, 165
Move Type-In Transform
    menu, 341–342
Multi-Res Mesh (MRM) modi-
    fier, 31
"Muppet" facial animation,
    78–79
Muzzle flash, 158

N
Names, older naming conven-
    tions, 117
Necks
modeling, 33
weighting, 117–120
Nubs. *See Dummy objects*

O
Objects
dummy objects, 55–57,
    78–79, 257–259
mesh objects, 54
model breakdown and,
    31–32
Object space, 206
Optimization
with key reduction,
    299–304
modeling and, 29–31
Optimizing with key reduction,
    299–304
Organizing files, 192–193,
    202–203

P
Parent Overlap settings,
    147–150

Patch modeling, 15
  Surface tools and, 20–21
Pelvises
  spline links and, 155
  Triangle Pelvis, 127
  weighting of, 144
Physique
  applying and initializing,
    93–95
  Rigid *vs.* Deformable Link
    Assignment, 92–93
  steps to applying, 93
  vertices assignment, 92
Planting limbs, keyframe ani-
    mation, 205–207
Playback
  Biped Playback button, 213
  playback speed, 201
Poly-count, character design
    and, 4
Polygon modeling, 15
Ponytail links, 70
Poses
  copying limb poses, 283
  da Vinci poses, 81–83
  idle poses, 176, 236–238,
    248–250
  Initial Skeletal Pose option,
    108–110
  jump-split pose, 263–264
  matching poses for loops,
    311–312
  saving, 67–68
Primitives, modeling, 15–16

Q
Quad menu, 95–96
Quadrupeds, Bipeds for, 68–74

R
Radial Scale settings, 144–147

Real-time *vs.* rendered charac-
    ters, 15
Recoil animation, 254–255,
    277, 293, 343–351
Red Monika, 6–7
Reference images
  character design and, 4–7
  loose *vs.* tight, 5–7
  modeling and, 8–11
References, Snapshot tool and
    animation references,
    274–277
Remove from Link option, 124
Rotation
  Angle box values, 367–369
  Motion Flow Editor to rotate
    Bipeds, 325–331
  rotating motion clips,
    366–372
Rubber Band mode, 62, 63

S
Scale Transform dialog, 42
Scripts, creating a Motion Flow
    script, 361–365
Secondary motion animation,
    219–220, 243–246,
    271–272
  in jumps, 265, 266, 279–280
  layers to add, 331–336
  side-to-side motion, 324
Selection sets, 193–196
Set Keys, keyframe animation,
    205–207
Set Multiple Keys function,
    351–354
Set Planted Key, 236–237
Shooting, 283
  aiming mechanisms, 257–259
  while jumping, 273–274
Shooting weapons, 250–259

Shoulders
   gun arm shoulder, 130
   modeling, 34–35
   parent / child adjustments for
      envelopes, 147–150
   rigid weighting and, 147
   weighting, 117–120
Side-to-side motion, 324
Size, animations and, 177–179
Skeletal animations
   da Vinci poses and, 81–83
   technical considerations and
      character design, 4
   see also Bipeds
Skinning. See Physique
Smoothing, 23–29
Smooth loops in, 284–286
Smooth modifier, 23
Snapshots as references,
      274–277
Snapshot tool, animation refer-
      ences and, 274–277
Special moves, 235
Spring controllers, 84–88
Structure sub-menu, suggested
      value settings for, 58–59
Sub-object panel, 17–18
Surfaces, surface flaws and
      modeling, 21–22
Swimming animation
   forward movement,
      286–292
   frog-kick motion, 287–290
   treading water, 281–284
System requirements, 381

T
Tails, animating, 70–71,
      220–229
TCB (Tension, Continuity, and
      Bias) controller, 209–212

doubling to avoid drift,
      240–243
Ease To and Ease From set-
      tings, 212–216
Technical considerations and
      character design, 4
Templates, high resolution
      mesh template modeling,
      17–20
Tendon Sub-Object settings, 95
Tension, keyframe animation,
      210
Texture maps
   in modeling process, 53
   quality of, 46–49
   UVW coverage, 39–45
Time codes, motion capture
      and, 186
Time Configuration, 124,
      200–201
Time Slider bar, 202, 216–217,
      224
Time Tags, 229–231
Tongues, 80
Torsos, weighting, 117–120
Track selection, 197
Track View, 197–201, 251–252
   active animation ranges and,
      204
   filtering information in, 198
Track view, 197–201
Trajectories, 317–319
Transitions between clips, 366
Triangle Pelvis, 127
Turned edges, 21–23
Type-In Weights dialog box,
      101, 109, 114

U
UVW coordinates, texture maps
      and, 39–45

V

Vertex deformation, technical considerations and character design, 4
Vertices
  assigning to multiple links, 99–105
  Deformable *vs.* Rigid, 92–93, 95
  deselecting, 131
  link assignment, 95–99
  manually assignment of, 92
  modeling and isolation of, 18
  optimization and modeling, 29–31
  removing from envelopes, 141–143
  removing from links, 105–107, 126, 153
  scaling of, 42–43

W

Waists
  modeling, 35
  weighting, 153–156
Walking, realistic, 187–189
Walking, realistic animation, 187–189
Weapons, 234–235
  aiming mechanisms, 257–259
  firing motion animation, 343–351
  firing pose, 250–253
  muzzle flash, 258
  recoil animation, 254–255, 277, 293, 343–351
Web addresses
  author's contact info, 379

WildTangent, 379
Weighting
  breasts, 143–144, 158–163
  da Vinci poses and, 81–83
  envelopes used for, 138–156
  feet, 155
  gun arm, 128–133
  hands and fingers, 113–116
  hips, 125–128
  legs, 120–123
  neck, shoulders, and torso, 117–120
  pelvis, 144
  removing vertices from links, 153
  saving weighted values, 116–117
  shoulders, 147–150
  type-in weights, 156–168
  Type-In Weights dialog box, 101, 109, 114
  values for, 99–105
  waist, hips and legs with envelopes, 153–156
  zones for, 156
  see also Envelopes
WildTangent
  3DS Max exporters, 373
  web address for, 379
Wrists, 113

Z

Zones for weighting, 156
Zooming
  mouse control of, 198, 202
  with Zoom Extents, 62